Beyond Gender

REFERENCE

The Series in Death, Dying, and Bereavement
Robert Neimeyer, Consulting Editor

Formerly The Series in Death, Education, Aging, and Health Care
Hannelore Wass, Consulting Editor

Leenaars, Wenckstern—Suicide Prevention in Schools
Leng—Psychological Care in Old Age
Leviton—Horrendous Death, Health, and Well-Being
Leviton—Horrendous Death and Health: Toward Action
Lindeman, Corby, Downing, Sanborn—Alzheimer's Day Care: A Basic Guide
Lund—Older Bereaved Spouses: Research With Practical Applications
Neimeyer—Death Anxiety Handbook: Research, Instrumentation, and Application
Papadatou, Papadatos—Children and Death
Prunkl, Berry—Death Week: Exploring the Dying Process
Ricker, Myers—Retirement Counseling: A Practical Guide for Action
Samarel—Caring for Life and Death
Sherron, Lumsden—Introduction to Educational Gerontology, Third Edition
Stillion—Death and Sexes: An Examination of Differential Longevity Attitudes, Behaviors, and Coping Skills
Stillion, McDowell, May—Suicide Across the Life Span—Premature Exits
Vachon—Occupational Stress in the Care of the Critically Ill, the Dying, and the Bereaved
Wass, Corr—Childhood and Death
Wass, Corr—Helping Children Cope With Death: Guidelines and Resource. Second Edition
Wass, Corr, Pacholski, Forfar—Death Education II: An Annotated Resource Guide
Wass, Neimeyer—Dying: Facing the Facts. Third Edition
Weenolsen—Transcendence of Loss Over the Life Span
Werth—Rational Suicide? Implications for Mental Health Professionals

Grieving Beyond Gender

Understanding the Ways Men and Women Mourn

Revised Edition

Kenneth J. Doka ♦ Terry L. Martin

Routledge
Taylor & Francis Group
New York   London

Routledge
Taylor & Francis Group
270 Madison Avenue
New York, NY 10016

Routledge
Taylor & Francis Group
27 Church Road
Hove, East Sussex BN3 2FA

International Standard Book Number: 978-0-415-99571-9 (Hardback) 978-0-415-99572-6 (Paperback)

Library of Congress Cataloging-in-Publication Data

Doka, Kenneth J.
  Grieving beyond gender : understanding the ways men and women mourn / Kenneth J. Doka and Terry L. Martin. -- Rev. ed.
      p. cm.
  Includes bibliographical references and index.
  ISBN 978-0-415-99571-9 (hardback : alk. paper) -- ISBN 978-0-415-99572-6 (pbk. : alk. paper)
    1. Grief. 2. Bereavement--Psychological aspects. 3. Death--Psychological aspects. 4. Grief therapy. I. Martin, Terry L. II. Title.

BF575.G7.D64 2010
155.9'37--dc22
                                                                    2009038061

Visit the Taylor & Francis Web site at
http://www.taylorandfrancis.com

and the Routledge Web site at
http://www.routledgementalhealth.com

To Luz Calzada, my daughter-in-law's mother, both for the wonderful work in raising Angela, and, in her all too brief life, for the great gift she was to my son, grandchildren, and to me.

KJD

To my wife and closest friend, Gail, whose support and gentle questioning has helped me through the most difficult times. Also for my mentor and closest male friend, Dr. Dana Cable. His influence is found throughout this book.

TLM

To the Saturday Night Outlaws—Past and Present

Dana Cable

Neil Heflin-Wells

Jane Nichols

Van Pine

Lu Redmond

Catherine Sanders

Sherry Schachter

KJD and TLM

CONTENTS

SERIES EDITOR FOREWORD

About 15 years ago one of the authors of this book and I participated in a meeting of the *International Work Group on Death, Dying, and Bereavement* (or IWG for short), a sort of invitational "summit conference" for grief and loss scholars and professionals. Intrigued by the then emerging diagnosis of complicated grief, we took advantage of the unique structure of IWG to propose a small work group to discuss the topic and to draw upon the long and deep experience of several of the participants in the meeting to gain a clearer understanding of "the work of mourning," and its personal, systemic and cultural complications. We then met together with eight other senior colleagues in the field for a dozen hours over the next few days, letting the conversation move forward spontaneously toward the "growing edge" of our own understanding, rather than the usual sort of "conference talk" in which one expert after another holds forth about something he or she seems to have all figured out, while others are cast in the passive role of listeners.

It was in this context of animated conversation among peers of various disciplines—sociology, psychology, social work, medicine—that several men in the group began to explore factors that complicated grieving from a variety of vantage points, from the struggle to rework centrally important life meanings in the wake of loss, through processes of disenfranchised or unacknowledged grief, to competing social and historical discourses that framed the role of male and female grievers differently. Curiously, the typically outspoken women in the group sat silently through much of this conceptual romp, until one of our elder members, who had been knitting increasingly furiously during the exchange, finally threw down her needles and afghan in exasperation and blurted out, "But where's the *feeling* in all this intellectualization?!" Appropriately called up short, we males in the group looked blankly at one another for a moment before general laughter rippled through the group, and we realized as one that we had in fact just exemplified the gendered styles of engaging grief that we had been trying to examine! We therefore began again, moving toward a sharper understanding of the complications that could arise from the dominant styles of mourning in men and women, including a penchant for a cognitive approach to loss for the former, and for a more emotionally resonant engagement with grief for the latter.

In many ways Doka and Martin's *Grieving Beyond Gender* represents an extended answer to our work group's passionate question. More importantly, perhaps, it represents a thoughtful, clinically useful response to the questions raised by grief counselors about how to understand the quite different modes of mourning displayed by different clients—whether the tearful wife trying to share with her spouse her feelings about the traumatic death of their child, or the taciturn husband at a loss as to how to help his wife move beyond her painful emotion. Equally, Doka and Martin tackle questions that can arise for the deceased themselves, as when their mode of expressing their grief emotionally, cognitively, or actively fails to square with the expectations of others in the broader culture, in the family, or even in their own minds.

At the heart of Doka and Martin's thesis is their resistance against a "one size fits all" approach to mourning. Instead, they erect a clarifying distinction between *intuitive* grievers, who naturally gravitate toward the exploration and expression of the turbulent emotions that can follow a cardinal loss, and instrumental grievers, who seek cognitive and practical mastery of the challenges it poses. Such stances, as the authors note, may be reinforced by socialization practices regarding the proper roles of women and men, respectively, but they are not simply reducible to gender, as a host of other factors ranging from basic inborn temperament to preferences for emotion regulation equally influence grieving styles and the adaptive strategies to which they give rise. Helpfully, the authors are careful to ground each pattern of adaptation or conceptual distinction in concrete clinical vignettes of adults and children struggling with a range of losses, so that the distance between theory and practice is consistently bridged in a way that promotes real-world applications.

What sorts of questions can the reader expect to be answered in the pages that follow? Although these are too numerous to summarize, a sample would include, "How do the coping styles of intuitive and instrumental grievers differ, whatever their gender?" "Are there blended styles that combine aspects of both, and what are the pros and cons of this more integrated stance?" "How can the misunderstandings that arise within families about very different patterns of grieving be overcome?" "How can we understand the apparent capacity of some grievers to master their emotions, and does this represent a pathological or resourceful stance?" "What does a bereaved person need, when he or she feels stuck in a grieving pattern that is dissonant with his or her own sense of identity, as with an emotional male who experiences pressure to maintain a sense of 'manly' self control?" "How do grieving styles evolve across the adult lifespan?" "How does one's tendency toward high or low levels of self-monitoring or chameleon-like adjustment to different social settings interact with one's grieving style?" "What light do models of cognitive-evaluative processes in emotional expression or studies of repressive coping shed on private and public adaptation to loss?" "How do various Jungian personality types grieve differently?" "What is the role of culture in shaping universal and specific dimensions of the grieving experience?" Engaging such questions and proffering possible answers provides generous leads both for researchers looking to investigate novel issues on the leading edge of grief theory, and for clinicians in the trenches seeking fresh approaches to working with bereaved clients. The latter in particular are likely to benefit from the broad synopsis of helping strategies that Doka and Martin discuss, including various bibliotherapeutic, narrative, self-help, expressive arts and ritualistic approaches. Throughout their extensive review of these models and methods, the authors are consistent in embracing two implicit principles: choose techniques that respect both instrumental and intuitive grieving styles, and build on the griever's strengths, rather than concentrate only on deficits.

In summary, Doka and Martin have once again pushed forward the boundary of our understanding individual differences in responses to bereavement, in a compact book that fulfills its promise to elucidate *Grieving Beyond Gender*. I am pleased that the *Routledge Series in Death, Dying, and Bereavement* provides a vehicle for making it available as a welcome resource to a broader professional community.

Robert A. Neimeyer, PhD
Series Editor

FOREWORD

I have found myself doing it more and more in the past several decades. Sometimes it is quite cumbersome, and I wish that I didn't have to make special note of it. But I always do; whether speaking directly to one bereaved person or to a large anonymous audience, whether writing for those who grieve or those who want to help them. What is this that I have to add no matter who is the target or what is the medium? I must always qualify discussion of someone's grief or suggestions for intervention with some phrase such as "depending upon their personal style" or "as is personally suitable to you." And what is the old adage that I also inevitably find myself expressing at some point in such discussions? "One man's meat is another man's poison." These statements go in tandem for those of us who work with the bereaved: Not only must we recognize what the mourner's needs are, we must be aware that not meeting them not only doesn't help, but actually hurts.

We have not always grasped this. In earlier days in thanatology, focusing as we did on understanding general and common reactions to loss, we paid relatively scant attention to the uniquenesses and idiosyncrasies of one's grief, except insofar as its expression departed from "the" norm. Such norm was all too often predicated upon the Western mental health bias that affective expression was necessary for healthy grief. To be sure, at times, there would be some attention paid by careful observers to cultural influences and the demands brought about by diverse types of death. In general, however, the tendency was to assume that when one's responses failed to match expectations for intensely experienced feelings and external expressions of them it signaled some kind of aberration. This left those with differing grief styles—or differing grief experiences either because of those styles or because of where their particular loss circumstances left them (such as the sudden death, traumatized mourner who is emotionally numb for a while)—being misunderstood, secondarily victimized, and/or pathologized by both professionals and lay persons.

We have evolved as a field now to be clear that each person's grief and mourning is influenced, shaped, and determined by a constellation of 43 psychological, social, and physical factors which combine to make one's bereavement experience and responses as individual and distinct as their fingerprint (Rando, in press). Four important corollaries flow from this: (1) No two mourners will have the same experience even if the same person has been lost, (2) there is no one correct way to mourn, (3) what is appropriate in one bereavement situation is not necessarily so in another, and (4) appropriateness can only be determined by viewing one's responses in context.

To this important discussion, Terry Martin and Ken Doka have contributed significantly through the years. From their earlier publications and presentations up through this text, *Grieving Beyond Gender: Understanding the Ways Men and Women Mourn*, the topic of patterns of grief has been carefully elucidated. The spotlight they have shone on adaptive grief styles—anchored on a continuum that runs from those who are instrumental in their grief on one end to those who are intuitive in theirs on the other end (although most of us are blendings of the two)—has resonated intensely with those who study and work with the bereaved. Indeed, in the years I have taught from their first book, I am consistently told by audience members and supervisees that these specific conceptualizations are among the most informative and useful in understanding and working with those impacted by loss.

With rich, clear, and meaningful examples, Martin and Doka carefully describe each of these grief patterns, which they note are related to gender albeit not determined by it. Most readers will be familiar with the *intuitive* style, in which feelings are intensely experienced and expressed. The norm against which bereaved responses have traditionally been measured, this has been the goal for which many well-intended but poorly informed clinicians strive. Unfortunately, in the process, they have inadvertently caused significant problems for those bereaved who are not so inclined to grieve in this fashion. Here the authors are masterful at capturing the experiences, functioning, needs, and coping of those who are *instrumental* in their grieving—where thinking is predominant to feeling, there is a general reluctance to talk about emotions, and mastery of oneself and the environment is sought, often accomplished through problem solving and directed activity. Martin and Doka go further than merely describing grief patterns and pinpointing the impacts of personality, gender, and culture in shaping them. They not only discuss the experience of grief that is associated with each pattern, they reveal how the pattern influences the actual expression of the mourner's grief and what types of adaptive strategies tend to be utilized to cope with that grief. Thus, we come to understand not only what each pattern is like, but the underlying dynamics and forces that influence both its manifestations and the mourner's ultimate adjustment to loss. The authors perform a superb service by explicating so clearly each pattern. This is so well done that those of us who are primarily either intuitive or instrumental (as opposed to being more blended) can now have a strong sense of how others with different grief patterns than ourselves truly experience their grief and tend to cope with and manifest it. We are given the gift of being enabled to see their loss through their own eyes in ways we may never have been able to before.

Further, Martin and Doka not only provide a comprehensive understanding of why we observe the differences we do among bereaved persons, but give specific intervention guidance to enable us to promote what for each person is healthy grieving within themselves and, where possible, among the couples, families, or systems within which they exist. Through their specification of treatment strategies and discussion of interventions that support the strengths of each individual mourner and supplement his or her relative weaknesses, these authors confront "conventional wisdom" and straighten it out with healthy doses of reality, both empirical and clinical. They effectively flesh out cognitive responses to loss, which for too long have been overshadowed in favor of affective ones, and make it explicitly clear why clinicians who try to promote adaptive strategies in mourners that are incongruent with their inner experience do a significant disservice to them. And, importantly, they convincingly argue in no uncertain terms that differences in patterns of grieving are just that, differences not necessarily deficiencies.

After providing rich descriptions and compelling examples of intuitive, instrumental, and dissonant grief, and outlining how each may have been created in the biography of the mourner, nitty-gritty therapeutic suggestions fill the treatment chapters and give counselors the tools to reach the mourner with any pattern of grief. There are critically important practical and clinically-oriented discussions about assessment; rationale; interventive intentionality; use of language; and the particular advantages and disadvantages of cognitive, affective, behavioral, and spiritual adaptive strategies. As well, they offer guidelines for minimizing dissonance in grievers; cautions about a call for androgeny; three critical rules for counselors; pragmatics for implementing a variety of vehicles for intervention; and special considerations found in dealing with male instrumental grievers, couples and families, and workplace grief. Their message is consistent: It is not the style of grieving that is the problem—ait is only a problem when counselors fail to recognize and adapt their approaches to that style or to offer a range of appropriate services suitable to diverse groups of individuals experiencing grief.

In *Grieving Beyond Gender: Understanding the Ways Men and Women Mourn,* we are presented with the information and tools to know how and why grievers are so different from each other; to help them identify what they must do to mourn in ways that are consistent with who they are and what they need; and to find personally effective strategies to cope with their loss(es), their mourning of it, and with the other bereaved persons in their world. Those working with the bereaved can no longer espouse a notion of individuality of grief without comprehending the patterns of grief explicated in this book and then following its guidelines for ways to promote healthy accommodation of loss in each mourner *depending upon their personal style.* From now on in our field, we need to give at least as much attention to the mourner as we do to the death and to the grief and mourning it precipitates.

Therese A. Rando, Ph.D., BCETS, BCBT
The Institute for the Study and Treatment of Loss
Warwick, Rhode Island, USA
December 7, 2009

☐ References

Rando, T. A. (Forthcoming in 2010). Coping With the Sudden Death of Your Loved One: Developing a Self-help Plan After Traumatic Bereavement.

ACKNOWLEDGMENTS

We would be amiss if we failed to recognize all those who, in one fashion or another, left their mark on these pages. Both of us wish to acknowledge our colleagues in the Association for Death Education and Counseling (ADEC) and the International Work Group on Death, Dying, and Bereavement. Many have contributed ideas at these conferences that it is difficult to list all the names. Nonetheless, some names do stand out for special acknowledgment. Without slight to all who helped, we want to acknowledge and thank Dana Cable, Charles Corr, Donna Corr, Neil Heflin-Wells, Gene Knott, Robert Neimeyer, Jane Nichols, Lu Redmond, Sherry Schachter, Judy Stillion, Ron Wilder, and J. William Worden. We give a special thanks to Therese A. Rando—not only for her insights and contributions to our thinking and the field, but also for her generous Foreword.

Both of us want to acknowledge all those in our colleges who offered support and encouragement. Terry wishes to thank all his colleagues at Hood College, especially the college administration who affirmed all of his professional activities in thanatology, including lending its organizational and financial support to the Hood College Summer Institute in Thanatology. He wishes to thank his psychology department colleagues for their support and encouragement, including Bob Boyle, Dana Cable, Wanda Ruffin, and Linda Scott. In particular, Linda Scott was characteristically unselfish with her time and talents and provided invaluable suggestions to several sections of the book. Terry also wants to thank all of his friends at ADEC. Finally, he wishes to thank all of his students who over the years have taught him as much as he has taught them.

Ken wishes to thank those at the College of New Rochelle from whom he has received a high level of organizational support and collegial encouragement. He wishes to give special thanks to President Stephen Sweeney, Vice President Dorothy Escribano, Dean Marie Ribarich as well as Wendi Vescio Vera Mezzacuella, and Diane Lewis offered ongoing support.

Ken also wishes to acknowledge the constant support and stimulation he receives from the Hospice Foundation of America. President Amy Tucci and past President David Abrams as well as the staff provide continuing opportunities to develop and to present new ideas. Its annual teleconference, as well as its publication of books, and the newsletter *Journeys* provide avenues for the dissemination and evaluation of innovative concepts. In addition, the publication of *She Came to Live Out Loud* by late founder Jack Gordon's wife, Myra MacPherson, provided a study of a family's journey through illness and loss, which further afforded opportunities to discuss the implications and insights of grief counseling.

Both of us also wish to recognize the support we received from family and friends. Ken wants to thank his son, Michael; his daughter-in-law, Angela, and his grandchildren, Kenny and Lucy; his godchildren, James Rainbolt, Scott Carlson, Christine Romano, and Keith Whitehead, and their families; his nephew, Dylan Rieger, and especially Kathy for all their love and companionship. In addition, Ken would like to thank his brother, Frank, his sister, Dorothy, and both of their families. They, and numerous friends and neighbors, make every project a labor of love.

Terry wants to first thank his wife, Gail. Her loving support has made this project possible. He also wishes to acknowledge the support of his family who has been faithful in its support of his efforts, especially his "step" children and grandchildren who have added a dimension to his life he never thought possible. Terry wishes also to recognize the contributions of his canine companions—both past and present—who were always ready with unconditional positive regard when he felt overwhelmed (especially at feeding time). Finally, this book would never have happened without Dana Cable—his friend and mentor—whose wisdom and integrity was invaluable, and whose friendship sustained him.

Finally, we want to thank the editors at Routledge, especially Dana Bliss, for their patience and support. The ideas of our editor grace these pages. Finally, we wish to thank all those at Routledge—known and unknown to us—who labored over this book.

Definition and Overview

If you have ever wondered why you grieve differently from others you know, or why someone you love is not reacting to the same loss in the same way as you, you are not alone. Perhaps you are curious about why the majority of your clients show deep feelings about their losses, yet others seem scarcely affected. Or, maybe you are concerned about those hospice bereavement cases that do not respond to any of your offers of support, even though, given the nature of the death, your team may have "coded" them as being "at risk." This book addresses these and other issues concerning grief and loss. But first, we establish the foundation for our efforts and define terms.

Chapter 1 introduces the thesis for the rest of the book—that individuals grieve differently and that two basic patterns can be drawn from the literature and from case reports. Furthermore, neither of these two patterns is necessarily desirable over or superior to the other. The book traces the history and development of the thesis and briefly describes the instrumental and intuitive patterns of grief. The chapter concludes with an outline of the book.

Chapter 2 revisits the many definitions and various aspects of grief, grieving, mourning, loss, and bereavement. After a review of existing models, a new way of understanding grief is introduced that is based on the creation and distribution of energy. The chapter goes on to explain how and why this energy manifests differently from person to person.

Chapter 3 reintroduces the instrumental and intuitive patterns of grief and differentiates between the two patterns by the experience of grief, the expression of grief, and primary and secondary adaptive strategies. This chapter further explores the more commonly recognized intuitive pattern.

The fourth chapter explores in some depth the instrumental pattern, particularly emphasizing distinct aspects and variations within that pattern. The chapter concludes with a brief discussion of a blended pattern of grief that combines, to a greater or lesser degree, elements of both the instrumental and intuitive patterns.

The final chapter in the section, Chapter 5, explores disordered variants of the patterns. It begins by differentiating maladaptive or "dissonant" patterns from initial responses to a loss and introduces several types of dissonant patterns. This chapter also ties certain male dissonant patterns to the notion of gender role strain. The section ends by considering the relationship of dissonant patterns to complicated mourning.

Is the zeitgeist or spirit of the times right for such an understanding of grief, as well as for the general premise of the patterns of grief? For example, it is quite possible that the enthusiastic responses to concepts such as "death as taboo" or "disenfranchised grief" would have been substantially muted during less favorable historical times. Likewise, there have been periods where a more rigid concept of grief may have prevailed. Many may find our ideas questionable, yet there is a tremendous heuristic value in proffering these novel and (some would say) risky hypotheses. You, the reader, must be the judge.

Introduction and Plan of the Book

When Brad's infant son died, he was surprised and troubled at the extent of his wife's grief. Every night she disconsolately cried herself to sleep. He was also perplexed at his own lack of tears. "Why am I not grieving?" he constantly asked himself. Yet as he asked this question, he would be alone in his workshop sculpting a memorial stone for his child. "What is wrong with me? Why can't I feel grief?" he reflected, as he pounded his hammer on a chisel.

Friends often wondered about Alicia. When her husband John died, she used the insurance to finance her graduate education. She thinks of John frequently, taking comfort that her new job has allowed her to continue to support their family. But friends keep questioning her, wondering, as one put it, "if she is doing too well."

Bob, too, wondered about his grief. When their son, a training pilot, was lost at sea, his wife availed herself of all the counseling the airline provided. All Bob wanted to do was to take his own plane up every afternoon to search for signs of wreckage.

☐ Understanding Patterns of Grief: Beyond Gender

All of these individuals are grieving a significant loss. And all are troubled by what they believe to be inappropriate responses to loss. In fact, each has effective ways to experience and adapt to his or her losses, yet they each reflect a societal understanding that the keys to experiencing grief lie in overtly expressing emotion and consciously seeking support.

Grieving Beyond Gender: Understanding the Ways Men and Women Mourn challenges that presumption. Its basic thesis is that there are many different ways in which individuals experience, express, and adapt to grief. Affectively oriented strategies are one way, but other strategies, building upon activity or cognition, can be equally effective.

This book describes two patterns of grieving. One is an *intuitive* pattern where individuals experience and express grief in an affective way. In this pattern, grieving individuals will find adaptive strategies that are oriented toward the expression of affect. But there is another pattern as well, one that we label *instrumental*. Here, grief is experienced physically, such as in a restlessness or cognition. Here the adaptive strategies individuals use tend to be, as the vignettes indicate, cognitive and active as well. These two patterns are seen as end points on a continuum. Many individuals may exhibit more *blended* patterns that draw from both intuitive and instrumental reactions and responses in the ways that individuals experience, express, and adapt to loss. Other individuals may show inconsistencies between the ways that grief is experienced and expressed. We label such inconsistent patterns as *dissonant*. Both dissonant and blended patterns are also discussed within the book.

This instrumental pattern is typical of the way many men grieve, due to contemporary patterns of male socialization. Yet as the book emphasizes, while there is a clear relation between gender and grieving patterns, this is not seen as deterministic. Women also may exhibit an instrumental style. And many women and men represent grievers who demonstrate more intuitive patterns. Clearly, patterns are *influenced* by gender but not *determined* by it.

This book is written primarily for grief counselors, psychologists, social workers, mental health counselors, pastoral counselors, and other therapists—especially those who work with men and adolescent boys. Although strongly affirming that these grief patterns are influenced but not determined by gender, the book offers a corrective, building on some of the most current research on the psychology of men, to the bias toward affective expression described in the next section. That corrective also may offer a value for academicians in thanatology or areas related to death studies and certainly would provide validation to bereaved individuals who are trying to understand not only their own reactions to loss, but the responses and strategies of others within their intimate networks.

☐ The Bias Toward Affective Expression

Although instrumental and intuitive patterns exist, are equally effective, and have complementary sets of advantages and disadvantages, instrumental styles are often viewed negatively within counseling, self-help, and grieving literature.

This reflects a general Western bias in counseling that tends to value affective expressiveness as inherently more therapeutic than cognitive or behavioral responses. Sue and Sue (2008), in the groundbreaking work *Counseling the Culturally Diverse*, criticize the counseling paradigm for overemphasizing affect:

> Emotional expressiveness is also valued, as we like individuals to be in touch with their feelings and to be able to realize their emotional reactions. (p. 142)

This bias, Sue and Sue note, can inhibit counseling with other cultural groups that do not place significance on affective disclosure.

This bias is also evident in what has been termed the *grief work* hypothesis (see Stroebe, 1997; Wortman & Silver, 1989). This hypothesis, or operating set of assumptions within the field of grief counseling, has emphasized that unless one expresses one's feelings openly, grieving cannot be successfully accomplished. For example, Vail (1982) expressed the sentiment often found in self-help literature about grief:

> Of course, those who allow themselves to experience the gamut of emotions are probably the least likely to actually go crazy. It is those of us who attempt to suppress, deny, and displace grief who eventually have real problems coping with the loss. (p. 55)

In fact, there is danger in identifying grief with any affective expression. The danger is that the absence of affect is taken to be an absence of attachment. As Weiss (1998) notes,

There may indeed be people who were attached to someone whom they lost to death, who fully acknowledge that loss, and yet do not grieve. Their absence of grief is not defensive; they simply do not grieve. I cannot, myself, understand how a relationship of attachment is consistent with an absence of separation distress or interruption of that relationship, and absence of grief or loss of the relationship, but perhaps it is. There may, perhaps, be people so fully autonomous that they can experience attachments, and on loss of those attachments, experience brief distress, after which they go on as before; or there may be some other emotional constellation that permits attachment without giving loss to grief. (p. 347)

But perhaps there is an answer to Weiss's honest query, one that accepts both the attachment and acknowledges the grief. The answer here would be to look beyond affective distress to other expressions of grief.

This affective bias finds its boldest expression in literature about men and grief. It is unsurprising, given the bias toward affective expressiveness, that many clinicians have seen aspects of the male role placing men at a disadvantage in grieving when compared to women. Women are seen as more ready to accept help and express emotion, both of which are viewed as essential to the process of grieving. Since men are perceived as less likely to show emotion or accept help, they are seen as having more difficulty in responding to loss. Recently at a lecture, one counselor suggested that when grieving men use the word *fine* in answer to how they are doing, it should be viewed as an acronym for "feelings inside, never expressed." LaGrand (1986), for example, states: "This does not mean men are not grieving; it does indicate that they may not accomplish the task as successfully as women" (p. 31).

The underlying assumption is that there are limited ways that one can effectively cope with loss. Staudacher (1991) expresses this succinctly:

> Simply put, there is only one way to grieve. That way is to go through the core of grief. Only by experiencing the necessary emotional effects of your loved one's death is it possible for you to eventually resolve the loss. (p. 3)

While later chapters explore the relationship of gender and grieving patterns, that assumption can be questioned. On the surface, if survivors were to grieve in identical ways, one would also expect analogous expressions of affect, duplicate behavior patterns, and feelings that would be indistinguishable from one another. In fact, there are many ways to cope with loss. To assert that only one pattern is acceptable is empirically ungrounded, at variance with current theory, and clinically unhelpful—points that will be further explored in later chapters.

☐ Beyond Gender: A Journey From Male and Masculine Grief

When this work began, we clearly had an interest in men and grief. It quickly moved beyond that. At the first description of what we called "male grieving patterns," a female colleague remarked that it had validated her own way of grieving—her pattern of adapting to loss. In fact, she had responded to her own early perinatal losses in two distinct ways. She began to do some of the basic work and research on how to best support survivors of perinatal loss. Then, once that research base was established, she became a pioneering advocate who both challenged and changed the ways hospitals dealt with such losses. Her comments were taken seriously, changing the terminology for this book to *masculine grief* (see Martin & Doka, 1996).

There was much to recommend the use of the term *masculine grief*. First, it allowed us to build a clear bridge to Jung on ideas of *animus–anima* (1920). Like Jung, we saw masculinity–femininity as a continuum that exists within a person as well as between individuals. Even our concept of grieving patterns is that they fall along a continuum. The use of these terms draws from that theoretical base.

Second, we believe that this pattern of adapting to loss is related to gender, at least in North America and many Western cultures, even if it is not determined by it. The use of the term *masculine* then reaffirms that gender relationship. It seemed foolish to pretend that gender does not play a role, since it influences so many other aspects of life.

Third, we wished to directly challenge the notion, so prevalent in the popular literature, that many men are ineffectual grievers. We asserted that "masculine" patterns of coping with grief are different, but not less effective than, more "conventional" or "feminine" ways of dealing with loss. Thus, there is a practical rationale for the use of the term. Since most popular literature does offer a view of the male as an ineffectual griever, we believed that only by using a gender-related term might our work be available to clinicians interested in or dealing with male or masculine grievers.

Finally, the use of masculine and feminine has great heuristic value that will, we hope, encourage continued discussion and further research.

However, we ultimately decided to eschew gender-related terms for a variety of reasons. First, they caused confusion. Although we identified a pattern of grief that we believe many males use, we also sought to recognize and to validate female grievers who exhibit such a pattern.

But for many the term *masculine* grief had unfortunate baggage. This was most poignantly illustrated by a conversation with such a griever after a presentation. This woman was a pioneering female rabbi, one of the first to be recognized. "All my life," she said, "I have tried to be perceived as not just one of the guys. You described my grieving pattern. Please, use a language to describe it that does not make me 'one of the guys' again."

It was confusing for other reasons as well. The distinction between *masculine* and *male* was often lost on readers who kept identifying one with another. And it made us apologize about using male examples, diverting us from a critical aspect of our work that instrumental styles are, in fact, utilized by a majority of male grievers.

Moreover, the use of gender-related terms created discomfort. To assert that "masculine" modes of coping with loss are cognitive and active seems to perpetuate stereotypes, only partly true, that view such responses as typical of male response to loss, and it implies that "feminine" responses to loss are more emotive.

In addition, the use of gender-related terms creates its own difficulties. If one end of the continuum is labeled masculine, what is the other end, the alternate pattern, called? The use of the term *feminine* has merit since it seems like the logical complement and is faithful to the theoretical base. On the other hand, the term *conventional* has merit since it reflects current conventions on grief that have tended to view seeking support and emotional responses as both desirable and normative. In addition, it avoids further stereotyping of emotional responses as feminine. But the use of the term *conventional* also runs the risk of appearing to place negative value on the term *feminine*. In short, either term has merit and complementary disadvantages.

And that raised clinical concerns. Some men who do seek support and are comfortable with emotive responses may feel threatened to hear their mode of response described as "feminine." And women who tend toward solitary, active, and cognitive responses may resent the label of "masculine."

In the end, use of the terms *instrumental* and *intuitive* seemed to carry far less baggage. Although these patterns will be more fully developed in subsequent chapters, it may be helpful to offer a brief description now.

First, the very experience of grief is different. For reasons that will be described later, instrumental grievers tend to have tempered affect to a loss. While intuitive grievers are more likely to experience their grief as waves of affect, instrumental grievers are more likely to describe it in physical or cognitive terms. Whereas intuitive grievers often need to express their feelings and seek the support of others, instrumental grievers are more likely to cognitively process or immerse themselves in activity.

> Sam and Jenny shared their disappointment with each other several months after the sudden death of their 17-year-old son. Responding to Jenny's accusations that he failed to validate their grief, Sam stated, "I couldn't allow myself to miss (him) until I figured out what this meant to our family."

This suggests that at least some instrumental grievers attempt to evaluate their experiences cognitively rather than experience them emotionally.

When instrumental grievers do respond behaviorally to a loss, it usually involves immersion in some form of activity. Sometimes this is work, but at other times it may be intimately related to the loss. They may wish to take legal or physical action in response to the loss. For example, one male client whose young daughter died of cancer found it helpful to develop a scholarship fund in her name. Others may take active roles in the funeral. Ryan (1989), while noting concern at his wife's affective response to loss, expressed his own grief by carving his son's memorial stone. Instrumental grievers may also focus on the problems caused by the loss, actively trying to find appropriate solutions or engaging in activities related to the loss.

> When Jack's 20-year-old daughter was killed after losing control of the car, he spent several weeks rebuilding a neighbor's fence damaged in the accident. He later described this activity as crucial to "getting me through those first two months."

In short, this section draws attention to the fact that grievers may experience, express, and adapt to grief differently. Cognition and activity remain two key adaptive strategies often utilized by instrumental grievers. And these strategies, like any set of adaptive strategies, may be either effective or ineffective, depending upon the particular strategy and circumstances. Subsequent chapters will explore this further.

Corr, Nabe, and Corr (2009), in reviewing the relationship between gender and grief, note three distinct perspectives that parallel the authors' journeys. The first position, the *feminization of grief*, stressed that expressing emotion and seeking social support and help from others is critical in effectively coping with loss. This partiality toward affective expression reflected counselor bias toward emotional disclosure (Sue & Sue, 2008). In addition, much of the early work on grief was based on widows—hence, their modes of dealing with loss were oft perceived as a normative standard.

A second perspective proposed that men had their own distinct patterns of grief. These patterns emphasized cognitive and active, problem-solving approaches to grief. In this perspective, men might show more limited and muted emotional responses to loss such as anger or guilt. Men often valued self-reliance and solitude in coping with loss. In this perspective, men had a distinct experience of grief that was different but no less effective in coping with loss. Counseling interventions, then, should not challenge men's way of coping but rather find ways to deal with loss congruent with masculine inclinations. This perspective of men's grief as different and distinct often drew from anthropological sources that ritualized gender differences in grief as well as literature that often emphasized biological differences between the genders (Golden, 1996; Lund, 1999).

Our early work (Martin & Doka, 1996, 1998) already began to offer a transition into a perspective less connected to gender. We began, as mentioned earlier, to describe both a masculine and feminine pattern of grief. In the masculine pattern, individuals often exhibit more cognitive and active responses toward grief while in the feminine pattern the experience and expression of grief was more emotive. In describing masculine and feminine patterns, we were already moving away from the notion that grief responses were inevitably distinct by gender.

Later work (Martin & Doka, 2000) completed the evolution to a third perspective that continued to place less emphasis on gender as a critical determinant of how individuals grieve. Here we proposed that there was a continuum of grieving styles from intuitive to instrumental. In doing so we affirmed there were a number of influences that affected the grieving style of individuals including culture, gender, socialization experiences, birth order, temperament, and other factors. The critical point is that gender influences but does not determine grieving styles. In this model, there is a distinct move away from applying gender-based terminology to describe the different ways individuals grieve. This latter perspective fits in well with current perspectives of grief that move from trying to find universal reactions to a more nuanced understanding of the individuals' pathways of grief.

Since the publication of an earlier book, *Men Don't Cry, Women Do: Transcending Gender Stereotypes of Grief*, in 2000, much has happened to merit a significant revision. There has been some work that has sought to test our model, as well as additional studies on gender and grief. It has been gratifying to see the positive reception of these ideas. Humphrey (2009), in a book published for the American Counseling Association, "highly recommended" the approach (p. 37). Similarly Doughty (2009), in a Delphi study, found widespread acceptance of the model among experts polled.

Moreover, there has been considerable scholarship in the psychology of men that questions some of our earlier assumptions, illuminates dissonant patterns of grieving, and suggests additional therapeutic approaches (see, for example, Englar-Carlson & Stevens, 2006, and Pollack & Levant, 1998). All these advances suggest a need for a review and, in some cases, an expansion of our work.

☐ Plan of the Book

This book is organized into three major parts. The first defines terms; provides an overview of our thesis, rooting it in contemporary theories of grief; and delineates grieving patterns. The second part speculates on factors that may influence individuals' patterns of coping with loss. A final part considers implications, including a self-help section and noting therapeutic interventions likely to be effective with different types of grievers.

As stated earlier, this book arises amid a growing challenge as to what is termed the *grief work* hypothesis (see Stroebe, 1997; Bonanno, 1997; Wortman & Silver, 1989) or the belief that unless one expresses affect, grief is not likely to be successfully resolved. And it builds upon the work of those who have begun to describe a "male" style of relating to loss (e.g., Golden, 1994a, 1994b, 1994c, 1996; Moss, Resch, & Moss, 1997; Moss, Rubinstein, & Moss, 1997). In Golden's early work (1994a, 1994b, 1994c), he emphasized physical as well as cultural difficulties to account for gender differences in grief. In his later work, Golden (1996) deemphasizes gender differences by placing more emphasis on masculine modes of healing that can be utilized by either gender. This book also builds on our own earlier work on masculine grief (Doka, 1994; Doka & Martin, 1998; Martin & Doka, 1996, 1998).

Throughout this book runs a common thread: There are many different styles of coping with loss. Each has distinct strengths and limitations. There are advantages in expressing affect and seeking support. But there are also complementary strengths in stoically continuing in the face of loss and in seeking amelioration of pain in cognitive and active approaches. In short, people who draw from a broad range of adaptive strategies are, in fact, likely to do better. People with the widest range of responses, who effectively integrate all aspects of self, seem best able to respond to crisis. One can learn from both types of responses because, after all, different modes of adaptation are just that—differences, not deficiencies.

CHAPTER 2

Definitions
Understanding Grief

"Everyone seems to think I should be crying since my daughter Laura died. She had a heart attack working in her garden. *But I never cried*—not for Laura, or for my mom, or my dad when they died. The day after Laura's funeral, I finished up her work in the garden. I still sometimes drive over and work there. Everyone said it isn't important anymore. I think it is." —Tom, 62 years old

The question that brought Tom into counseling was why he was not grieving. Yet, as Tom talked about the varied strategies he used after his daughter's death—working in the garden, helping Laura's husband raise their three children, sharing stories of their mom with her kids—it was clear that Tom, in fact, *was* grieving. And his ways of dealing with his daughter's loss did seem to ameliorate his pain.

Tom's question really focused on his definition of grief. He, like many, defined grief as an affective reaction to loss. In the absence of overt affect, Tom simply could not see that he was grieving in his own characteristic way. Tom's limited definition of grief reflects a bias evident not only in the field, but in the counseling profession at large—a bias that places great value on affective expressiveness (Sue & Sue, 2008). Yet the literature on grief has always emphasized that grief reactions may be manifested in a wide range of strategies.

This chapter begins by exploring grief and grieving. It then further develops the thesis that there are a variety of ways in which people adapt to grief. Each of these strategies offers distinct strengths as well as limitations as individuals cope with loss.

☐ Basic Definitions: Loss, Grief, Grieving, and Mourning

Loss

Traditionally, loss and grief are associated with death. In fact, loss is a much broader concept. At its broadest, loss refers to being deprived of or ceasing to have something that one formerly possessed or to which one was attached.

There are different types of losses. In general, loss can be understood as either developmental or situational. Developmental losses are those incurred by most people and are related to maturation and continued development. These losses usually bring about gain as well as loss. For example, the original loss for every living human was birth. Each of us lost the perfect physical environment—our mother's womb. In turn, we gain personhood. Another maturational loss involves the arrival of secondary sex characteristics. Lost is some of the innocence of childhood. What is gained is the ability (for most people) to conceive and have a child.

Other types of developmental losses include getting married (loss of independence, gain of intimacy), having a child (loss of freedom, gain of parenthood), and retirement (loss of some identity and perhaps income with a regaining of some freedom and independence). These losses are often anticipated with pleasure.

Situational losses are less often seen as beneficial and are usually anticipated (if at all) with anxiety. For example, *physical loss* refers to the loss of something tangible that is no longer present. Death involves a physical loss, as would a robbery or the destruction of an object. *Relational loss* refers to losing a relationship with someone to whom one has an attachment. Again, death causes the loss of a relationship, as does divorce, interpersonal breakups, or other losses such as the loss of a job or moving, where ties between individuals are consequently severed. *Symbolic loss* is intangible, involving the loss of a psychological or spiritual attachment such as the loss of one's dreams, hopes, or faith. The death of someone can also create significant symbolic loss (see Rando, 1993).

Such distinctions also help in understanding the phenomenon of anticipatory grief (Rando, 1986; Corr & Corr, 2000) or, as Rando (2000) now prefers, anticipatory mourning. As Rando (2000) notes, *anticipatory mourning* refers to the mourning experienced by the patient, family, and others in a life-threatening illness, over all the losses—physical, relational, and symbolic—experienced throughout the course of illness.

This discussion is also a reminder of the importance of understanding *secondary loss*, or the losses that follow as a consequence of a primary loss. For example, the loss of a job may also entail a series of resultant losses—the loss of self-esteem, income, friends, or dreams. Similarly, the death of a person may engender a wide range of losses in its wake, such as the loss of other, dependent relationships (e.g., in-laws, friends), and losses of income, hopes, and even perhaps of faith. Rando (1993) notes the importance of such secondary losses, reminding counselors that each of these losses will need to be identified and mourned.

In addition, Rando (1993) states that loss is a constant throughout human life for every change involves at least an element of loss. For example, each transition through the life cycle, whether a pleasant milestone (e.g., a wedding, graduation), a loss of abilities (such as in the aging process), or relationship (including changes in relationships that occur in development, for example, the change in relationship that parents might experience as a child becomes an adolescent), brings with it the experience of losses. These losses will vary in intensity and scope as well as in the social support they engender. For example, one can expect severe reactions to the death of someone significant. However, although one may expect *some* reaction to another loss, perhaps not deemed significant, one expects that reaction to be brief and controlled. For example, it is normal to understand someone's momentary upset when his or her favorite team loses, but we also assume that such a response will be limited in scope and intensity.

This raises a critical point: social support also varies for given losses. Whereas the loss of a family member such as a parent, child, or spouse is acknowledged by many to be significant, others may not perceive the loss of other persons such as friends or lover as a significant loss. Similarly, although most physical losses are acknowledged, relational or symbolic losses may have less recognition and support. In such cases, the loss and resultant grief may be disenfranchised. *Disenfranchised grief* refers to a situation where a loss is not openly acknowledged, socially sanctioned, or publicly shared (Doka, 1989a, 2002). In his work, Doka (1989, 2000) emphasized types of losses (e.g., divorce, prenatal deaths, pet loss, etc.), relationships (e.g., lovers, friends, ex-spouses, etc.), grievers (e.g., the very old, very young, persons with developmental disabilities, etc.), or circumstances of death (e.g., AIDS, suicide, etc.) that might disenfranchise grief. In summary, loss encompasses far more than death. It is interesting to remember that Freud (1917/1957), in his seminal essay "Mourning and Melancholia," used as his illustrative example of loss a bride abandoned at the altar. Identifying loss and thereby grief solely with death-related loss then, can obscure the many losses we do experience and grieve. And it can limit the ability of grievers or counselors to draw insights from experiences of earlier adaptations to loss.

These earlier experiences can be powerful indicators of an individual's pattern of grief. Ways of adapting to previous losses, such as a relational breakup, are evidence of an individual's basic pattern.

> From an early age, John, in a wide variety of losses, showed a more instrumental approach. As a teenager experiencing a romantic breakup, he reacted by intensifying his involvement in sports and other activities. This pattern persisted. When his mother died he found solace in planning the funeral and in thoughtfully clearing away her clothing and possessions. Even in his own premature death from cancer in his 30s, he rarely ventilated his inner feelings. Instead he concentrated on making arrangements for the care of his young son.

For that reason, case illustrations used are of individuals experiencing a range of losses. However, most of these illustrations are death-related losses. There are three reasons for this: First, it reflects the base of our experiences. Second, most death-related losses involve physical as well as relational and symbolic losses (secondary losses also tend to be most intense in a death-related loss). Finally, death is a universal experience, whereas other losses, such as divorce, are not.

Bereavement

Another term used to denote a state of loss is *bereavement*. As Rando (1993) states, bereavement shares a root with the word *rob*. Both refer to a state in which something has been violently taken away. Within the field of thanatology, bereavement tends to be used to refer to the basic fact or objective reality of loss, while grief refers to the person's response and reactions to the loss (see Doka, 1989a). Remember, one can experience bereavement without an intense grief reaction. For example, a survivor may have little attachment or connection to the deceased, as in the following case.

Mark was a 15-year-old boy who had lived with his mother, Sue, and stepfather, Tom. Mark's biological father had separated from his mother 2 weeks prior to his birth. For much of his life, and all that he could remember, he lived with his stepfather, with whom he enjoyed a close relationship. His biological father, Jack, played a very limited role in his life, intermittently sending cards and gifts and visiting on rare occasions. When Jack died after a sudden heart attack, Sue called her son in to tell him his father had died. Mark's eyes welled with tears. "Tom's dead?" he said. When his mother told him it was his "real" father, Mark was visually relieved. "Wow," he stated, "for a minute, I thought you meant Tom." His mother reported that he took little interest in details or in sending the flowers that bore his name. "It was much more important to me," she said. But she continued to worry that "one day the loss would hit." Almost 20 years later, she asked Mark as he openly wept at Tom's funeral, if he thought much about his biological dad. He seemed surprised. "He never meant much to me."

Not every such case might yield that reaction. In some cases, it is the very absence of the relationship, or the fact that any future relationship is precluded, that engenders grief. But this case does illustrate the conceptual distinction between grief and bereavement, and reinforces the fact that the meaning of loss both differs among people and is a central component in understanding the grief reaction.

Grief and Grieving

Grief or grieving[1] arises as a reaction to loss. Specifically, grief can be defined as the psychic energy that results from tension created by an individual's strong desire to

1. Maintain his or her assumptive world as it was before the loss

2. Accommodate to a newly emerging reality resulting from his or her loss

3. Incorporate this new reality into an emerging assumptive world

For example, a person whose spouse dies wishes to hold onto that relationship, yet knows it is not possible and is unclear on what the future may be. It is that conflict between the world that was, what it cannot be, and how it may become that creates the tensions that engender grief. This grief energy is converted into the various domains of human experience, including the physical, affective, cognitive, and spiritual. These internal experiences are often expressed outwardly in varied grief-related behaviors.

Such a definition of grief, while building upon classical perspectives (Bowlby, 1980; Freud, 1917/1957), offers certain advantages. First, classic definitions focused on withdrawing the attachment from the deceased or lost object and reinvesting elsewhere. Current treatments of grief emphasize that many individuals maintain a connection with the lost object; however, the nature of this connection is now changed (e.g., Klass, Silverman, & Nickman, 1996; Worden, 2009). The clearest example may be found in divorce. Individuals will grieve a divorce, yet the divorce does not so much end a relationship as change it. Even in death, bereaved survivors may still find a sense of connection in such things as memories, legacies, and their spiritual beliefs.

Moreover, this definition of grief was the possibility of bridging some of the differences between psychological and sociological perspectives of grief. Psychological theories of grief (see Bowlby, 1980) have stressed that the biological/psychological roots of grief lie in attachment. In this regard, mourning and grief, it is noted, seem to be exhibited by primates and other social animals. For Bowlby, adaptation to loss is achieved by "extinction" of behaviors associated with attachment—the reinforcement that comes with physically attaching or reattaching to another. Death represents the ultimate form of extinction since whatever efforts are expended, there can be no physical reinforcement.

Sociological explanations tend to eschew language such as "drives" or "instincts," while emphasizing the symbolic constructions or meanings that are disrupted by the loss (see Nadeau, 1998; Neimeyer, 1997a, 1997b). This definition acknowledges that there is a primal aspect to grief, but notes that the nature of that primal tension is very much affected by the meaning of the loss, the social expectations that frame appropriate manifestations of grief, and the support accorded to people experiencing loss.

Second, this definition of grief uses the term *psychic energy* to connote a dynamic force created by the emotional arousal and tension resulting from the loss. This energy needs to be expended; however, the manifestation of this energy varies in different individuals. And indeed, the theory and research on grief have stressed that grief can be exhibited physically, affectively, cognitively, and spiritually, as well as expressed in a wide range of behaviors (see Doka, 1989a, 1989b; Lindemann, 1944; Rando, 1984; Worden, 2009).

Third, such a definition of grief is congruent with current theories on cognitive appraisal, stress, emotion, and emotion regulation (these will be explored further in Chapter 5). In addition, *emotion* is a word with different meanings. On one hand, particularly in the field of thanatology, emotion generally has been identified with affect or feeling (Elias, 1991). However, that is a narrow definition. A wider use of the term *emotion*, evident in psychological literature, defines emotion as biologically based adaptive reactions that involve changes in physical, affective, cognitive, spiritual, and behavioral systems in response to perceived environmental events of significance to the individuals.

Grief, then, can be perceived in this broader sense as an emotion, an attempt to make internal and external adjustments to the undesired change in one's world brought upon by the loss. Grief triggers changes in various adaptational systems—affective, physical, spiritual, and cognitive—that constitute the individual's response tendency.

Response tendencies are predispositions that operate subconsciously, allowing quick and efficient reaction to environmental challenges, threats, and opportunities. These predispositions are shaped by powerful forces, namely, cultural influences and personality styles. Individual response tendencies veer toward either an affective or intuitive grief response or a cognitive, behavioral, or instrumental response. Whether one's grief is intuitive or instrumental depends on whether the individual is more sensitive or tuned in to their thoughts (cognitions) or their feelings. As noted earlier, instrumental grief is largely a function of the individual's emphasis on cognitions.

These response tendencies have been noted throughout the literature of grief that documents a wide range of physical, affective, cognitive, and spiritual reactions that manifest themselves in varied behaviors. This literature (see Lindemann, 1944; Rando, 1984; Raphael, 1983; Worden, 2009) has documented and described these reactions, and they are discussed in the following.

Physical Reactions

Physical reactions can include a wide range of somatic complaints and distress, including

- Headaches

- Muscular aches

- Nausea

- Tiredness and exhaustion

- Menstrual irregularities

- Loss of appetite

- Pain

- Insomnia

- Tenseness

- Sensitivity to noise

Here the energy generated by the grief may be converted to physical symptomatology as in the following case.

> Bob was overwhelmed when his wife died, leaving him to balance his job with the demands of raising four young children. While he claimed he responded to the loss reasonably well, he complained of incessant neck and back pain. His physician could not find any evidence of physical injury, but the doctor reminded Bob of the language he had been using in describing life after Jen's death. "Everything now is on my back," he often would state.

Many individuals will experience a host of grief reactions that will include physical ones, but some, like Bob, may experience grief *primarily* as a physical reaction.

Moreover, physical complaints may allow an individual to elicit care in ways that do not seem threatening to autonomy. Interventions that use physical behavior as a way to expend energy resulting from grief are also helpful (or commonly used) in assisting individuals to deal with other forms of stress. For example, exercise often is suggested to mediate stress levels. This can be seen in the following case.

> Susan, a middle school counselor, was attempting to assist students after the death of a classmate, an adolescent girl with whom most of them had had an ambivalent relationship. She was seen as sexually and behaviorally precocious. In fact, she had died in a car crash with a college student who had been under the influence of alcohol. While many girls sought out Susan the day following the death, few boys did. Susan questioned a consultant who suggested that the boys have some extra gym time and play dodgeball. She later reported that it was an intensely competitive game with many references to the driver and the crash. At the end of the game, she noted, the boys seemed much less tense.

Affective Reactions

The energy of grief is commonly manifested in affect. Individuals can experience a wide range of affective responses, including (but not limited to) the following:

- Sadness

- Anger

- Guilt

- Jealousy

- Anxiety and fear

- Shame

- Feelings of powerlessness or hopelessness

- Relief

- Feelings of emancipation

These emotional responses bear further comment, as bereaved individuals may be upset at the wide range of feelings they experience in response to a loss. In fact, virtually any feeling can manifest itself following a loss. And it is not unusual that bereaved persons experience a host of affective responses, even contradictory ones, simultaneously.

Some of these feelings may even be positive. For example, Elison and McGonigle (2003) affirm that feelings of relief are common responses to loss. Sometimes the relief is based on an altruistic idea that the deceased's suffering is now over. Other times it may be more a relief to the bereaved that a difficult caregiving experience or a troubled relationship has now been terminated. Naturally, relief can include both senses of relief for the other and for the self—a dual focus.

Even beyond the ambivalent reaction of relief, other affective responses also may be positive. Margaret, for example, felt a deep sense of satisfaction that she had kept her promise to her husband, as he died of ALS (amyotrophic lateral sclerosis), that she would care for him at home. Others may experience a sense of appreciation or gratitude for the relationship, the presence of the other in their life.

In short, since grief is a reaction to a loss, a wide range of feelings may be evident. Although this wide range of affective responses may follow a loss, it is critical to reiterate a central point. Affective responses are but one way grief may be manifested.

Cognitive Reactions

Cognitive reactions can include

- Obsessive thinking

- Inability to concentrate

- Fantasizing

- Apathy

- Dreams

- Disorientation and confusion

- Continued thought about the loss, rehearsing and reviewing the circumstances of the loss

- In cases of death, people may experience a sense of the deceased's presence

- Attempts to rationalize or cognitively understand the loss

Given the effect of loss upon cognitive processes, it is not unusual that work at home, school, or in the office can be adversely affected. It is also critical to remember that cognitive responses are not necessarily attempts to deny or suppress affect. They are simply another way that grief is manifested.

Spiritual Reactions

Grief affects us spiritually as well. These reactions can include

- Searching for meaning in loss

- Changes in spiritual behaviors, feelings, or beliefs

Spirituality, broadly defined, is used here to connote the ways that people seek to understand the meaning and purpose of life. These transcendental systems of belief may center on religious tenets or other philosophical frameworks. Although some losses may fit easily into one's underlying beliefs, other losses may proudly challenge those beliefs. Such was the following case:

When Rita's mother died, she grieved the loss deeply. But her mother's long and happy life, as well as peaceful death at 91 years of age, reaffirmed her beliefs about the way that life should be. She found great comfort in her religious beliefs and rituals. Yet, when her younger brother was brutally tortured and murdered, she had a faith crisis. She could not understand why God would take her brother so young, leaving a wife and children in dire straits. Nor could she find explanation in her faith for the terror and pain he must have experienced.

In such cases, the reconstruction of meaning in the face of loss may become one of the most critical aspects of the grieving experience (Doka & Morgan, 1993; Neimeyer, 1997a, 1997b). For here, grieving individuals must, in the face of loss, reconstruct such issues as their own identity and the identity of the deceased, as well as their assumptions about the world. Loss, then, can create an intense spiritual crisis that challenges all of an individual's core beliefs, necessitating reevaluation, if not a reformation.

Behavioral Experiences

The different reactions that people experience in each of these four response tendencies (physical, affective, cognitive, and spiritual) may be outwardly expressed as behaviors. Among observable behaviors of grief are

- Crying

- Illness-related behaviors (observable symptoms, expressions of illness, etc.)

- Outward expression of emotion (e.g., anger, euphoria, etc.)

- Observable changes in religious/spiritual behaviors and expressions

- Searching behaviors

- Avoiding or seeking reminders of the loss

- Obsessive activity

- Activities that provide some sense of continued connection to the loss (e.g., visiting the cemetery, etc.)

- Physical activities (e.g., exercise, sports, gardening, etc.)

- Social withdrawal

- Absentmindedness

- Accidents

- Changes from preloss behaviors

- Social withdrawal

- Increases in the use of alcohol, smoking, and other chemical use

Although behaviors are external expressions of internal reactions, care should be taken when inferring from the external to the internal. Behaviors such as crying or withdrawal could be outward expressions of a variety of internal states such as anger, sadness, or embarrassment. The connection between the external expression and internal reactions is a clinical question.

This also reinforces that many different behaviors, such as physical activities or activities that provide a connection to the deceased, may be manifestations of grief even if that connection does not seem obvious.

> When her younger sister died, Maria, a high school student, continued to coach her sister's soccer team. Her parents wondered how she could do that and were concerned that she was denying her grief. In fact, continuing to coach made her feel close to her sister and provided opportunities to reminisce with her sister's teammates and their parents.

Over time, many of these behaviors may diminish among bereaved individuals. As with other responses, there can be negative and positive aspects of different behaviors. For example, withdrawal can both isolate one from sources of support or give people space to effectively grieve. Crying may elicit help and restore emotional homeostasis, perhaps even correcting stress-related chemical imbalances (Worden, 2009). But crying can also generate feelings of guilt and shame, and exacerbate withdrawal.

In summation, grief involves multifaceted responses to loss. The energy of grief, generated by the tension between wishes to retain the past and the reality of the present, is felt at many levels—physical, emotional, cognitive, and spiritual—and expressed in a wide range of observable behaviors. In many cases these responses will be varied or blended, even in individuals who tend to have different styles of grief. This is particularly true early in the loss when the amount of energy generated tends to be high. Thus, it is not that the instrumental griever has no affect or exhibits no affectively oriented behavior; rather, it is that his or her response tendencies likely emphasize cognition.

The Individual Experience of Grief

Not only does the *way* individuals express grief differ, the very *experi-ence* of grief is different as well. Some individuals will show few intru-sive manifestations of grief, quickly resuming their regular activities. Bonanno, Wortman, and Nesse (2004), for example, found that 45.9% of their sample of widows fit that pattern, a pattern they labeled *resilient.*

Many factors have been identified in the literature that frames these individual reactions. For example, Worden (2009), Rando (1984), and Sanders (1993) have noted such variables as

- Type of loss

- Relationship and attachment to the lost object (e.g., in cases of death, the relationship to the deceased, issues of ambivalence, dependency, etc.)

- Circumstances surrounding the loss (e.g., was it sudden or long term, preventability, timing, presence or absence of additional stressors, etc.)

- Extent of and responses to prior losses

- Personality of the bereaved and effectiveness in coping with loss

- Social variables (e.g., age and gender, cultural beliefs and practices, social class, presence and strength of spiritual systems, external and internal support systems, etc.)

- Personal variables (e.g., health, lifestyle management, etc.)

Recent research has been inconsistent in assessing the actual degree to which these factors do affect bereavement outcomes. Lund, Caserta, and Diamond (1993) found religion, gender, health status, and marital happiness relatively important predictors of adjustment in a sample of older widows and widowers. Social support was a moderate predictor. As Lund et al. note, social networks often have both positive and negative aspects (e.g., offering encouragement, placing unrealistic expectations, etc.). The most predictive factors were positive self-esteem and personal competencies in managing the tasks of daily living.

In a study of younger German widows and widowers, Stroebe and Stroebe (1993) indicated that in sudden loss, a sustained belief in one's internal control seemed to buffer the stress of loss. They reasoned that people who experience an unexpected catastrophic loss need a strong belief that they can still retain control of their life to recover from depression. On the other hand, people with little belief in internal control may find that the loss reinforces a sense that they have little control over life, exacerbating feelings of depression and hopelessness. Other risk factors did not seem as important in Stroebe and Stroebe's study, though it is critical to remember Sanders's (1993) caution, in her review of research on factors affecting adjustment, that it is difficult to analyze the individual effects of interacting factors.

These factors emphasize that the "very meaning of loss" varies both in different circumstances and among individuals. All of these variables emphasize that a given loss means different things to different people. For example, the meaning of the loss of a child or a spouse will be very different depending on the role attributed to that person by the survivor. If one primarily lives life in the private sphere of home and family, the meaning or role of spouse or parent is likely to be more central than one who has significant roles in the public sphere of work and the larger community. This may be one reason why Schwab (1996) found that mothers and fathers not only varied in the intensity of grief but in their perception of the events. The critical point is that grief is a very individual experience. This will be further discussed in Chapter 5 in the exploration of the appraisal process.

Beyond the psychological and social variables, other factors too can frame the meaning of a loss. Certainly, for example, loss may be perceived differently in other cultures, historical periods, or social and economic circumstances. Take, for example, the interview of a 90-year-old woman a number of years ago. She had been born prior to the turn of the 20th century in Spain. Reflecting on the death of a 4-year-old son in a typhus epidemic, she remarked: "I was very lucky. I had six children, five survived to be adults." Few modern Western parents would have such an interpretation of a similar death. Yet her meaning reflects a time when there was an expectation that not all of one's children would survive to adulthood. Kastenbaum (1971) suggests that in cultures with high childhood and infant mortality, social norms and structures actually serve to limit such attachments.

Thus, to summarize, one both experiences and expresses grief differently. It is that simple statement that underlies much of this book.

Mourning and Grief Work

While grief is defined as the psychic energy generated by the loss, grief work may be defined as a process, both short and long term, of adapting to the loss.[2] It includes the shorter term process of *acute grief* where the griever deals with the immediate aftermath of the loss. Building on Rando (1993), immediate reactions in this period may include such things as

1. Feelings about the loss (e.g., guilt, anger, sorrow, etc.)

2. Reactions to the effects of the loss (e.g., shock, physical symptoms, cognitive confusion and disorganization, spiritual intensity or alienation, etc.)

3. Behaviors resultant from or adaptive to the loss (e.g., acting out, crying, withdrawal)

All of these grieving reactions represent initial, albeit fragmentary, attempts to adapt to the immediate aftermath of loss.

In short, this acute period is characterized by both shock and numbing, and after they recede, by a series of intense reactions and adaptations to the newly experienced loss. Because of the intensity of this period, it should be noted that reactions and adaptations observed may not be typical of those observed later. For here, in this early period, the energy released may overwhelm the person's typical adaptive strategies leading to uncharacteristic responses. The following case illustrates this:

> When Dan's dog, a companion for a decade, had to be euthanized, Dan held him and stroked him as he died. When he went to his car, he uncharacteristically cried for about 10 minutes. After that, his reactions took on more typical forms. He buried the dog, etched a memorial, stored or disposed of the dog's artifacts, and went through a variety of photographs of the animal. After that, he often thought of the dog, but he never again cried.

The role of initial responses and its relationship to patterns of grief is explored further in ensuing chapters.

But beyond this period of adaptation to acute grief, which itself can last for many months or longer, there is a longer term process that involves living the rest of one's life in light of that loss. This process is often referred to as mourning. The term *mourning* has had mixed usage within thanatology. It has been used to refer to the social customs and outward behaviors that manifest grief. Doka (1989b), for example, in the *Encyclopedia of Death* defined mourning as "the culturally patterned expressions or rituals that accompany loss and allow others to recognize that one has become bereaved" (p. 127). For example, attending funerals or wearing black clothes or armbands may be seen as mourning behaviors. In some ways, that is a useful distinction since it reminds us that one may grieve and not mourn, or mourn without grief. Illustrations of the former include many cases of disenfranchised grief (e.g., divorce) that are devoid of rituals or other outward manifestations of loss. On the other side, many attend funerals in support of others but experience little direct grief over that particular loss. Nonetheless, by attending they are mourning.

However useful that definition of mourning has been, Rando's (1993) work on mourning has been increasingly accepted within the field. Rando has built upon Freud's (1917/1957) definition of mourning as a psychological process that occurs as individuals experiencing loss reorient their relationship to the deceased, their own sense of self, and their external world. As Rando's work describes it, this involves three distinct operations. The first involves reorienting one's relationship to the deceased and stimulates the period of acute grief as one acknowledges that current ties can no longer be maintained. A second operation involves redefining oneself and one's own identity after the loss. A third operation involves any modifications that occur as survivors seek to redefine their world and adjust to the many changes necessitated by the loss. In this definition, mourning is a long-term process that involves living the rest of one's life in the face of the loss. Persons who are unable to effectively mourn their loss may experience deterioration in physical or mental well-being or even death (Rando, 1993; Sanders, 1989).

Building on this work, Rando (1993) then offers a model of mourning that identifies three phases of grieving with six "R" mourning processes:

Avoidance Phase

1. **R**ecognizing the loss (e.g., acknowledging and understanding the death)

Confrontation Phase

2. **R**eacting to the separation (which includes experiencing the pain, expressing the psychological reactions to the loss, and identifying and mourning secondary losses)

3. Recollecting and reexperiencing the deceased and the relationship (which includes cognitive and affective dimensions)

4. Relinquishing the old attachments to the deceased and the old assumptive world

Accommodation Phase

5. Readjusting to move adaptively into the new world without forgetting the old

6. Reinvesting in new relationships

Another model is the dual–process model offered by Stroebe and Schut (1995), who posit two sets of interrelated and dynamic processes that individuals utilize in adapting to loss. One set of processes is loss-oriented, where individuals cope with things as the new reality of loss or separation. Restoration-oriented processes refer to the processes that individuals employ as they readjust to the new demands of life now in the face of this loss. This is a critical point. "Restoration" does not mean a return to the old reality, for that no longer exists. Rather it emphasizes that individuals are challenged to develop new patterns of behavior and assumptions as they respond to loss. To Stroebe and Schut, individuals vacillate between these two complementary demands of grieving, "oscillating" as they cope with each in turn.

Worden (2009) offers another popular model of the grief work process. Instead of processes, Worden refers to four tasks that one has to accomplish as one does grief work. These tasks are

1. To accept the reality of the loss

2. To process the pain of grief

3. To adjust to a world without the deceased

4. To find an enduring connection to the deceased in the midst of embarking on a new life

Since these tasks represent cognitive, affective, and behavioral adjustments to the loss, Doka (1993) has suggested the addition of a spiritual task:

5. To reconstruct faith or philosophical systems challenged by loss.

The second valued aspect of this definition is the understanding that these strategies are employed in "disequilibriating" or transitional events that challenge an individual's ability to manage. These strategies then enable the person to manage a transition and adapt to a new reality created by the loss.

Silverman's definition of adaptive strategies is similar to much of the present language that is used to describe coping (see Lazarus & Folkman, 1984; Moos & Schaefer, 1986). But it avoids some of the problems associated with the use of that term. First, for example, the term *coping* has been criticized for failing to make clear distinctions between reactions (such as anger or physical pain) and adaptive strategies utilized to manage that reaction (e.g., ventilating, anger, acting out, seeking information, etc.; see Ellis, 1997). As Weisman (1979), who does use the term *coping*, notes, a clear distinction has to be made between a show of distress and behavior that copes with distress. Guilt, for example, is a form of distress. But writing a letter to the deceased or punishing oneself to expunge guilt are reactions to that distress. This critical distinction is often lost in discussion as coping. Second, coping has been used to describe responses to both extraordinary and everyday problems (e.g., Lazarus & Folkman, 1984; Weisman, 1979, 1984). For example, although most who use the term (see Corr & Doka, 2001) refer to extraordinary events such as dying or experiencing a significant loss, everyday usage can be clouded; people can be said to cope with crises like death or annoyances like taxes. Furthermore, the term coping has other difficulties. It has a negative connotation often perceived as merely managing, while adaptation or adaptive strategies carries no such onus. Adaptation or adaptive strategies carries a different connotation. Adaptation is a process common to humans and, for that matter, other animals, as they continually have to adjust to changes within their environment. Finally, coping suggests a time-bound process, whereas adapting seems more ongoing. Coping has been used in confusing ways. It has been defined as strictly behavioral responses or as a range of varied responses. For those reasons, we prefer Silverman's adaptive strategies. Clinicians, however, are wise to recognize that for each individual, words have different meanings and adaptations can suggest conforming or acceptance. Clinicians, then, should always listen and reflect the words their clients use whether grieving, mourning, coping, dealing, struggling, or whatever terms describe their experiences.

A further point should be made about varied adaptive strategies. Although these strategies represent attempts to manage the crisis, they may be more or less effective in any given situation. Any strategy may, in and of itself, complicate or facilitate one's response to the crisis. For example, venting one's feelings can both allow a release of tension and can simultaneously, depending on the situation or the perception of others, drive away or generate support. Some strategies of avoidance may allow one to function at work, but abusing alcohol to avoid grief can create other difficulties such as health or relational problems, thereby complicating grieving. Individuals who can utilize multiple adaptive strategies and skills may have distinct advantages both in responding to and surmounting crises. Often, exploring an individual's adaptive strategies allows people to assess the strengths and limits of their styles as well as to learn and practice alternate adaptive strategies. Chapter 4 will revisit this issue as it deals with dissonant grieving.

☐ Conclusion: Rethinking Grief Work

One approach to understanding the grieving process has been framed by an often-implicit grief work hypothesis. This hypothesis emphasizes that only by experiencing strong affect such as distress or depression and "working through" such feelings can a bereaved person ever expect to reach a sense of resolution about the loss.

As stated in Chapter 1, the hypothesis has been challenged (see Bonanno, 1997; Wortman & Silver, 1989). In fact, there is little research to support such a hypothesis (Wortman & Silver, 1989), and there is evidence that disassociation from negative emotion and use of alternate approaches such as positive reframing can facilitate grief adjustment (Bonanno, 1997, 2004; Nolan-Hoeksema, 2001; Pennebaker, Zech, & Rimé, 2001).

Ultimately, the problem with the grief work hypothesis is that it identifies grief solely as an affective response to loss and posits one adaptive strategy as the only effective response. Such an approach ignores both the multifaceted manifestations of grief and the multiplicity of adaptive strategies bereaved individuals use as they grieve. It denies that individuals experience, express, and adapt to loss in highly individual ways.

The danger of such an approach is that in the final analysis, it disenfranchises grievers who use such cognitive and behavioral strategies. But as Corr (1998) points out, disenfranchised grief is a far more inclusive concept. Much can be disenfranchised in grief. Corr notes that when grief is identified purely as affect and one insists on a single set of responses as appropriate reaction, considerable risk is incurred:

What is central is the recognition that human beings may and indeed are likely to respond to important losses in their lives with their whole selves, not just with some narrowly defined aspect of their humanity. Failure to describe grief in a holistic way dismisses and devalues its richness and breadth. (p. 13)

The challenge to the grief work hypothesis is part of a larger rethinking of the paradigms of grief. This has included such tenets as a move away from stages (Corr, 1992), an extension of the concept of grief in nondeath circumstances (Doka, 1989a), a recognition of the role of continuing connections with the deceased (Klass et al., 1996), a greater appreciation of the elements of grieving beyond the affective (Attig, 1996; Doka & Martin, 1998; Neimeyer, 1997a, 1997b), the application of new models (Rando, 1993), and the recognition of growth even in the midst of loss (Prend, 1997). This work draws from and hopefully adds to that paradigmatic revision by positing two patterns or adaptive strategies by which individuals respond to loss—instrumental and intuitive.

☐ Notes

1. Whereas the term *grieving* has had wide, varied, and inconsistent usage in the literature (see, for example, Corr, Nabe, & Corr, 2009, or Rando, 1993, for discussion), *grieving*, in particular, has been defined, at times, as the process of adapting to loss. In this book, grief and grieving are used synonymously, referring to internal experiences and external behavior that results as a response to loss. Thus, to say an individual experienced grief, was grieving, or grieved all express the similar idea that in some way that individual was reacting to or presumed to be reacting to the loss. Grief work is used to refer to the process of adapting to loss.

2. In short, adaptation involves the process of continually adjusting to circumstances that have changed or are changing. Adaptation is an ongoing process. People have to adapt daily to minor, sometimes major environmental challenges. Significant loss creates major changes (both long term and short term) to the environment, challenging one to employ all resources (both internal and external) as one tries to adapt to those changes in the world. Grief work is simply a specific instance of an ongoing and multifaceted process. What is, perhaps, most surprising is that individuals continue to form close bonds with others, thus risking future loss and efforts to adapt. In his chapter on grief, Richard Kalish (1985) writes, "Anything that you have you can lose; anything you are attached to, you can be separated from; anything you love can be taken away from you. Yet, if you really have nothing to lose, you have nothing" (p. 181).

CHAPTER

Patterns of Grief and Intuitive Grief

☐ Theoretical Basis for Patterns of Grief

This chapter begins with a discussion of the theoretical basis for the patterns. Then, initial differences between the instrumental and intuitive styles or patterns of grief are discussed. Also examined are less differentiated or blended patterns. Stipulations regarding the patterns are stated, and then the chapter examines the intuitive pattern of grief in detail.

In this section a theoretical basis is constructed that accounts for many of the differences between instrumental and intuitive grief. The chapter begins by revisiting grief as a concept and identifying a model of emotion. Then, a comprehensive model of grief is constructed and the chapter goes on to elaborate on the function and development of the structures and mechanisms responsible for differences among grievers. Finally, the agents that shape the development and influence the individual's unique pattern of responding to loss are introduced.

Grief as Emotional Energy

In Chapter 2, grief was defined as a multifaceted and individual response to loss. In short, grief is energy—an emotional reaction to loss. In order to lay a theoretical foundation for patterns of grief, it becomes necessary to revisit and expand on the definition.

Although the word "emotion" is often used as a synonym for the word "feelings," the modern definition of the term "emotion" is far more comprehensive, with "feelings" being just one component of emotion. For this book's purposes, emotions are defined as biologically based, adaptive reactions involving changes in the physical, affective, cognitive, spiritual, and behavioral systems in response to perceived environmental events of significance to the individual.

Grief, then, is emotion, an instinctual attempt to make internal and external adjustments to an unwanted change in one's world—the death of someone significant to the griever. Grief involves both inner experience and outward expression. Building the foundation begins by looking more closely at emotion and adopting the general model of emotions proposed by Gross and Munoz (1995).

The model in Figure 3.1 incorporates both a component as well as a process view of emotions. The component perspective of emotion includes a biologically based adaptation program for survival and a conglomeration of response programs (spanning all of the adaptive systems or modalities) referred to as response tendencies. These various programs represent learned predispositions, which usually operate at a subconscious level and enhance the chances of an individual's survival by being readily available and quickly activated.

Whereas the adaptational program is genetically and biologically determined, response tendencies result from previous and ongoing

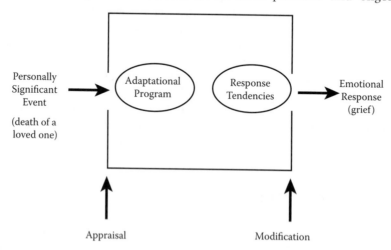

FIGURE 3.1 General model of emotion (Gross & Munoz, 1995).

interactions with the environment. From birth, the person's response tendencies are molded by powerful, often imperceptible influences. As will be shown, two of the most influential forces are the individual's culture (both societal and familial and their influence on gender-role development) and personality.

Two processes are active in emotions. Appraisal is the cognitive-based, semiconscious process, which activates the adaptational program and continues to shape the eventual response. The second process is modification, a conscious effort on the part of the individual to determine the final emotional outcome.

Whether one is more intuitive than instrumental in his or her grief depends on a variety of factors related to emotion. Thus far, as seen in Figure 3.1, emotion has been reduced to its fundamentals—two components and two processes. How do these various components interact to produce either the instrumental or intuitive style of grief? Using the aforementioned model as a starting point, a comprehensive model of grief will be offered.

Figure 3.2 presents a comprehensive model for understanding instrumental and intuitive grief. In the first phase of the model, an individual appraises an event involving a loss as negative.[1] The appraisal process is essentially the way the individual gives meaning to an event, in this case,

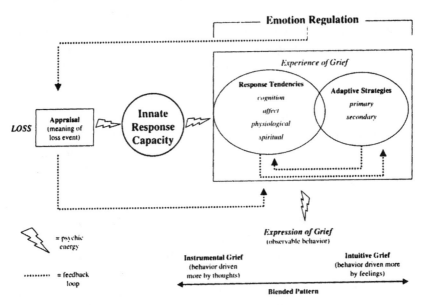

FIGURE 3.2 Comprehensive model of grief.

a loss. This initiates a preprogrammed biological response—the arousal of psychic energy—that varies in capacity from person to person.

This instinctual arousal of energy triggers changes in various adaptive systems—affective, cognitive, physical, and spiritual—that constitute the individual's response tendency. Response tendencies are predispositions, operating subconsciously and allowing people to quickly and efficiently react to environmental threats, challenges, and opportunities. These predispositions are shaped by the powerful forces of culture and personality and are mediated by the process of emotion regulation.

Emotion regulation mediates the griever's adaptive strategies as well as response tendencies. Adaptive strategies represent the conscious, effortful aspect of emotion regulation and are the griever's attempt to manage both his internal experience of grief and the outer expression of that grief. Whether one is more cognitive or affective in his or her response tendencies and his adaptive strategies determine whether his or her is more instrumental or intuitive in nature.

The proposed comprehensive model is not closed. In other words, actions that happen later in the process can produce a change in the appraisal process, resulting in different arousal levels of psychic energy, different response tendencies, different adaptive strategies, different expressions of grief, and so on. In particular, the griever's choice of adaptive strategies produces changes in behavior that may influence the griever's immediate internal or external environment, thus generating a new appraisal of an altered situation. In fact, it is the constant alteration of the griever's perception of his or her plight that continually generates energy, eventually resulting in an accommodation to the loss. Additionally, previous adaptive strategies modify response tendencies that in turn, influence the selection of current and future adaptive strategies.

Gross and Munoz (see above) identified modification as a process involving a conscious effort on the part of the individual to shape his final emotional response. While this is useful, we have chosen the term "emotion regulation." Emotion regulation is emerging as an important concept in the general study of human behavior and has both automatic (subconscious) and conscious properties. Furthermore, it plays a pivotal role in mediating between shaping agents and response tendencies.

Thus, patterns of grief are a function of two variables: the individual's innate response capacity and emotion regulation, with emotion regulation governing response tendencies and adaptive strategies and, through feedback generated by the chosen adaptive strategy, indirectly influencing the appraisal process.

☐ The Appraisal Process

The appraisal process is the starting point since it involves cognition, and cognition is crucial to differentiating instrumental from intuitive grief. What is cognition? What roles does cognition play in how people live and what people do?

Definition of Cognition

"Cognition," as used here, refers to conscious and subconscious mental activities that involve thinking, remembering, evaluating, and planning.

Cognitive activity is vital to the instrumental griever; it connects his or her feelings and motivations and serves to differentiate the instrumental style of grieving from the intuitive grief pattern. Understanding the dominant role played by cognition in grief is tantamount to understanding the instrumental grief response. Searching to further clarify the relationship of cognition to emotions and thus grief (instrumental grief in particular) leads directly to the field of stress research and the role of cognitive appraisals in emotions.

Cognitive-Appraisal Stress Theory

Relating stress to grief is not a revolutionary idea; grief is the response to the stress of bereavement. One theory that has dominated the field of stress research since the 1980s is the cognitive-appraisal stress theory.

In the cognitive-appraisal theory, stress is seen as a threat to the individual's well-being and as a source of undesired emotions (Lazarus, 1966, 1991; Lazarus, Averill, & Opton, 1970; Lazarus & Folkman, 1984). The quality and intensity of emotion result from ongoing attempts to understand and make judgments regarding what the individual's senses are reporting about what is happening between that person and the environment. Negative emotions arise when the individual perceives a phenomenon as a danger or a threat to his or her sense of well-being or, in some cases, to his or her very survival!

The person then considers options for responding to these dangers or threats and eventually chooses a course of action. This chain of cognitive events is cognitive appraisal. The stress inherent in the death of a significant other triggers the cognitive appraisal process, which is fundamental to the instrumental grief response. Cognitive appraisal processes determine how, and how well, the individual copes.

Just as cognition is both necessary and sufficient for emotions, emotions affect cognition (Lazarus, 1991). After the initial appraisal is made and emotion arises, secondary and subsequent appraisals can engender thoughts that are emotional. In a "kindling" sense, once aroused, emotions produce feedback that affects subsequent thoughts, which produce additional emotions, which produce new feedback, and so on. Apparently, the personal meaning one gives to an event (and its attendant responses) is a function of both thinking and feeling. Whether one is more tuned in to his or her thoughts or his or her feelings determines whether he is an instrumental or conventional griever. Now return to the model of grief and explore the nature and development of response tendencies.

Response Tendencies

As noted in Figure 3.2, the individual's response tendency is initiated by a chain of events beginning with the appraisal of an event as a loss, which, in turn, triggers the arousal of psychic energy (adaptational program). This energy is channeled into the various inner modalities constituting the response system—cognitive, physiological, affective, and spiritual. Chapter 2 explored how these modalities found expression in various reactions to loss. One should not infer that there is a one-to-one correspondence between the inner experience of these modalities and their final expression seen in observable behavior. As will be shown, much of the outward expression of grief depends on the griever's chosen adaptive strategies.

While response tendencies represent habitual responses to loss, they remain somewhat plastic, that is, modifiable. How do response tendencies develop? Can individuals actively shape their response tendencies by modifying and modulating their experience as well as their expression of grief? Is there any one process, beyond the appraisal process, that is responsible for both the experience as well as the final expressions of grief? These questions are best answered by examining the concept of "emotion regulation" (Izard, 1991; Thompson, 1994; Gross & Munoz, 1995).

Emotion Regulation

Even the earliest studies of the link between thoughts and feelings demonstrated that some people could modulate their emotions at will. In one instance, prior to seeing a movie of people suffering personal injury while working with machine tools, subjects were instructed to either be more involved with events on the screen or to detach themselves from the emotional impact of the scenes (Koriat, Melkman, Averill, & Lazarus, 1977). The results indicated that participants could either, by using cognitive strategies, become more emotionally enmeshed in an event or achieve emotional detachment. Stated differently, these subjects managed their emotions by regulating them.

Additional researchers concluded that infants (Rothbart, 1991) and children (Saarni, 1989) developed strategies and skills for managing their emotional experiences and expressions. This process of modifying emotions is called emotion regulation. Thompson (1994, p. 27) formally defined emotional regulation as, "the extrinsic and intrinsic processes responsible for monitoring, evaluating, and modifying emotional reactions, especially their intensive and temporal features, to accomplish one's goals." What is not clear is exactly what is being regulated.[2] Is emotion regulation primarily concerned with the management of expressions of emotion or the underlying arousal processes leading to those expressions—or both?

The answer to this question lies at the heart of understanding grief as well as implementing effective interventions with grievers.[3] At present, researchers do not know whether emotion regulation is primarily the management of expressions of emotion or the underlying arousal processes leading to those expressions.

☐ Functional Aspects of Emotion Regulation: Adaptive Strategies

It is important to understand that emotion regulation is a process that helps people achieve their goals (Campos, Campos, & Barrett, 1989; Fox, 1989). Emotion regulation is not just a way of suppressing emotions, but a vehicle for expressing them as well. The reader should distinguish between emotion control, which implies restraint of emotions, and emotion regulation, which refers to the attunement of emotional experience to everyday events and the achievement of goals (Davis, 1983). Emotion regulation has been defined in terms of how one uses emotions to achieve one's goals. Other writers have added that it is the individual's goals that determine the nature, type of, and persistence of emotion regulation (Walden & Smith, 1997).

Thus, emotion regulation involves both subconscious and conscious processes that govern the experience and expression of grief. Emotion regulation reflects the individual's inherent arousal capacities and influences the development of his or her response tendency. Along with the appraisal process, emotion regulation also modifies the griever's ongoing experience and expression of emotional (or psychic) energy. Ultimately, how the individual adapts to loss is largely a function of how he or she distributes emotional (or psychic) energy. He or she does so by selecting adaptive strategies.

The term "adaptive strategies" describes the conscious regulatory efforts of the individual. How the griever regulates the psychic energy created by his or her loss reflects what objectives are important to him or her at the time. This has important implications for counselors and therapists working with the bereaved, since the efficacy of the regulatory efforts must be evaluated with respect to the griever's individual pursuits. Furthermore, the professional should keep in mind that these pursuits may change as a function of place, person, or time. These regulatory efforts will be revealed in the adaptive strategies the individual chooses.

Hence, a griever modifies or adjusts the final expression of his or her grief through choosing adaptive strategies. This process acts in concert with the individual's response tendencies to produce the grief response. Response tendencies represent the subconscious, automatic responses to bereavement and are mediated by the appraisal process and subconscious aspects of emotion regulation. Adaptive strategies are the conscious, effortful acts on the part of the griever to manage his or her experience as well as how he expresses his or her grief. Yet the reader should remember that adaptive strategies, once learned, influence response tendencies (see Figure 3.2).

Figure 3.3 shows how the processes of emotion regulation, both subconscious and conscious, govern the experience and expression of psychic or grief energy. Emotion regulation operates subconsciously in shaping and modifying response tendencies, while it represents a conscious process in influencing the griever's choice of adaptive strategies, which in turn influence future subconscious processes.

Primary adaptive strategies are those that represent the griever's dominant mode of regulating emotional energy, while secondary adaptive strategies may be employed to supplement or temporarily replace primary strategies. Primary adaptive strategies provide important clues to differentiating instrumental from intuitive grievers.

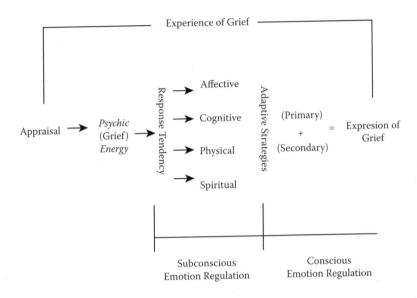

FIGURE 3.3 Emotion regulation of grief.

☐ Adaptive Strategies and Patterns of Grieving

The basic style of the griever is reflected in his or her choice of primary adaptive strategies. Intuitive grievers usually choose primary adaptive strategies that permit an unfettered, uninhibited experience of the affective component of grief. These strategies represent a means to an end. They may also choose secondary strategies that allow them to manage the other modalities of emotional experience—cognitive, physical, and spiritual.

On the other hand, instrumental grievers select primary adaptive strategies that help them distribute cognitive psychic energy into planned activity. They often choose secondary adaptive strategies to manage the intensity and duration of their feelings, cope with physical responses, and deal with spiritual issues such as facing the challenges to their belief systems posed by the death of a loved one.

Thus, individuals play a decisive role in selecting how they experience and express their emotions. Grievers may begin to regulate their responses either before (proactively) or after (reactively)[4] the response begins. A proactive regulatory effort might involve the adaptive strategy of avoiding situations that have led to unpleasant emotions in the past or choosing an environment incompatible with the unpleasant emotion.

The sought after environment could be physical (choosing to be with friends in order to distract oneself from feelings of loneliness) or mental (engaging in thought control, meditation, positive imagery). Grievers often choose "dosing" methods of mental control. Proactive regulation itself can give rise to new appraisals, different levels of arousal, different response tendencies, and so on. The following case illustrates proactive emotion regulation.

Matt had just turned 27 when his fiancée, Susan, died suddenly after experiencing a lethal allergic reaction to a snake-bite. He sought counseling after receiving an invitation from Susan's parents to spend her birthday with them. Although Matt had always enjoyed a good relationship with Susan's parents, he felt anxious and ambivalent about the invitation. From previous experience, Matt had discovered that being with Susan's family stirred up painful memories. After a recent visit (at her parents' request), Matt was overwhelmed with feelings of despair and hopelessness. By contrast, "hanging with my single friends" had proven both relaxing and fun for him. After an intense discussion with his minister about his conflicted feelings, he decided to write a letter to his fiancée's parents, explaining his feelings and asking them to forgive him if he avoided contacting them for the foreseeable future. Susan's parents responded immediately to Matt's letter with one of their own. Their letter lay unopened for several days, until Matt chose to risk the feelings he knew that reading the letter would ignite. To his relief, Susan's parents expressed their own ambivalence about being around Matt and encouraged him to "get on with" his life.

Whereas anticipation of a negative event or response stimulates proactive attempts to avoid painful emotions, reactive emotion regulation begins late in the cycle of emotion response. Reactive regulation means modulating or modifying already existing thoughts and feelings so that the outcome response is altered. Hiding one's true feelings or maintaining strict control over impulses or behaviors is an example of reactive regulation. The following case illustrates a reactive emotion regulation.

After surviving several years beyond his life expectancy, Margi's younger brother, Michael, died from complications arising from cystic fibrosis. He was 41 years old. Michael and Margi had been extremely close growing up. After their parents died and following Margi's divorce, they grew even closer and made sure they spoke with each other almost every day. Margi shared her brother's last days with him, temporarily closing her busy law practice to remain at his bedside. She was overwhelmed with intense feelings at Michael's funeral and, as she described it, "I spent about four days in a haze." Despite her intense grief, Margi knew she needed to return to her legal practice if she wanted to remain competitive in the local economy, which had a surfeit of attorneys. "I knew I needed a plan to get my feelings under control if I was to be able to concentrate at all, so I set up a schedule for grieving: I could only think about Michael for an hour every evening. Believe you me, I spent that hour being miserable!" (Question: "How did you keep your mind away from thoughts of your brother?") "Oh, I've always been able to distract myself from thinking things I didn't want to. Remember, I had lots of practice during his fight with CF. I just know how to turn my thoughts on and off."

Of course, as will be discussed in Chapter 5, grievers can choose adaptive strategies that do not lead, ultimately, to a healthy resolution of their loss. Hence, adaptive strategies can subdue (or enhance) the intensity of feelings, strengthen (or defeat) action plans, and retard (or speed) recovery.

In summary, instrumental grief is a response tendency that is driven primarily by thoughts rather than by feelings, while the response tendency of an intuitive griever reflects the preponderance of psychic energy that is experienced as feelings. Both patterns of grief response can be modified or modulated according to environmental demands and individual needs by choosing adaptive strategies and employing them either proactively or reactively. Emotion regulation is at the heart of grieving. The next section will look briefly at the development of emotion regulation and introduce the change agents shaping this development.

☐ Development of Emotion Regulation

How do emotions develop? How does emotion regulation emerge in the developing child? What role does biology play? What is the role of personality in shaping emotion regulation? Is the family a purveyor of emotion regulation? How important are gender differences in emotion regulation?

In exploring the object of emotion regulation, Thompson (1994) concluded that emotion regulation targets the various neurological processes governing emotional arousal. Congenital differences in central nervous system reactivity may represent differences in how and to what infants attend. As the infant develops, his or her attention processes become more complex than the earlier, simple strategies, such as shifting vision from an undesirable stimulus to one more desirable in order to avoid negative feeling states.

Older children use more internal strategies for emotion regulation. For example, a child might discover that thinking about the coming summer vacation becomes an antidote to worrying about tomorrow's exam. Children also regulate, to an extent, their access to support systems, when they become aroused by a noxious event. They choose whether to seek support and from whom they will seek it. Of course, the way in which parents or others respond to cries for help from the child who experiences unpleasant, painful feelings either reinforces or fails to reward future help-seeking behaviors. As emotion regulation becomes more complex and sophisticated, it is shaped more by environmental factors. Gender role socialization, the family, and cultural influences assume a larger role in determining the development of emotion regulation as they interact with individual biological predispositions and the child's emerging personality (see Sidebar 3.1).

Sidebar 3.1. Instrumental grief as a mature pattern

Among the many questions that arise about the patterns is, "Isn't instrumental grief simply the same pattern displayed by young children, that is, isn't this pattern an example of the griever who hasn't matured enough or become strong enough to handle difficult feelings for extended periods of time?" The question is a good one, since it is widely accepted that children have a "short sadness span" (Wolfenstein, 1966) and often grieve intermittently.

The answer is "no." In this case, the questioner may be confusing the experience of grief with the expression of grief. Instrumental grief is a pattern, marked by tempered affect and heightened cognitive activity, not a series of discrete experiences ("now I'll have feelings, now I won't, now I will..."), although most grievers sometimes choose to modulate and dose their feelings. Efforts of this sort are mature, sophisticated strategies for dealing with uncomfortable levels of affect and are used by intuitive and blended grievers as well as instrumental grievers.

Actually, this concern about immature responses calls into question interpretations of children's reactions to loss. Children often act out their internal experiences symbolically through play. Since traditional views of grief tend to overemphasize the importance of affect, these behaviors have been seen as the child's way to avoid or minimize painful feelings. It is equally likely that these responses are ways that children express physical, cognitive, and even spiritual energy created by their losses. Also, doing things like watching television or random play are interpreted as the child's attempts to escape uncomfortable feelings. While this may be so, could not a child experience grief without expressing it? And how are we to know if one bereaved child's minimal responses represent an attempt to avoid feelings or are indicative of that particular child's smaller capacity for feelings of any type, or of his or her inclination to process the world cognitively rather than affectively? Could this child's behaviors be part of an overall emerging pattern of responding to loss—an instrumental pattern?

☐ Summary

1. Grief is an emotion. Feelings are just one of the adaptational aspects of emotions. The other modalities of adaptation are the cognitive, the spiritual, and the physical.

2. A comprehensive model of grief and patterns of grieving includes an initial appraisal, which creates psychic energy. This energy is distributed among various adaptational systems according to the griever's response tendencies. Response tendencies are subconscious predispositions that are mediated by the process of emotion regulation and shaped by culture and personality.

3. The appraisal process initiates the grief response by attaching meaning to the event as a significant personal loss. This is accomplished through cognitive activity. Appraisal is also strongly influenced by the process of emotion regulation.

4 The mechanism primarily responsible for shaping and modifying both internal and external aspects of response tendencies is emotion regulation. Emotion regulation also plays a conscious role in determining

which adaptive strategies are chosen by the griever and how these strategies are implemented.

Patterns of Grief

This section begins by illustrating the various patterns of grief using the following case example.

It was Friday morning. After briefly discussing an upcoming fishing trip with his youngest son, making dinner plans with his wife, and teasing his teenage daughter about her date that evening, David left for the post office where he planned to mail a check to cover his younger son's fraternity dues. He never got there. A massive heart attack killed him as he waited at a traffic light. He had just turned 46.

David's family was shocked by his death, yet they each responded to the crisis in different ways. His eldest son, Josh, showed no emotion until his voice quivered and failed him as he eulogized his father at the funeral on Monday. On Tuesday, he returned to work. He remained impassive, avoiding any discussion of his father and refusing any offers of help and comfort from his girlfriend. Yet, when he was alone, powerful feelings threatened to overwhelm him. Josh dealt with this threatened loss of control by drinking himself to sleep every night. Two weeks later, he received his first DWI. Finally, after an angry outburst at his supervisor, he reluctantly agreed to see a counselor. He never kept his first appointment. Within a year of his father's death, Josh had withdrawn from everyone, including his girlfriend. He had also developed ulcerative colitis and was well on the road to alcoholism.

David's 15-year-old daughter, Sarah, was inconsolable. She returned to school several days after the funeral but found it impossible to concentrate. She had trouble sleeping and cried for hours every day. Sarah eventually found comfort in attending a bereavement support group sponsored by a local funeral home. Sarah's mother urged her to also get professional counseling, following an episode of acute anxiety. After 8 months, she reported feeling much better, although she still experienced painful feelings whenever she thought about her father.

As soon as he heard of his father's death, Vincent stopped preparing for his final exams and immediately returned home. Although he felt overwhelmed with feelings, he managed to limit his crying to the times he shared with his sister and his mother. Two days after the funeral, Vincent returned to school and successfully completed his exams. He later told a frat brother that he was able to do well on his exams only because he knew his father would have wanted him to "get on with living." In the months that followed, Vincent was often overwhelmed with painful memories of his father, yet he found he could remain focused on his classes if he shared difficult feelings with his closest friends.

Janice, David's wife, threw herself into making the necessary arrangements for his funeral. She wept at the funeral on Monday, but by Wednesday she was immersed in settling her late husband's estate. Although Janice made several inquiries about support services for her daughter and accompanied her to the first bereavement support group meeting, she chose not to return. She found the raw emotionality of the group uncomfortable and unhelpful. She felt restless and channeled her excess energy into her garden, enjoying the time alone to reflect on her years with David. When her friends called to offer their support and companionship, Janice politely declined, stating that she preferred to be alone with her thoughts.

Although Janice felt sad and diminished by David's untimely death, she was never overwhelmed by the intensity of her feelings. Much of her grieving involved thinking about the issues and the challenges created by David's death as well as discovering the skills she needed to confront those challenges. Janice confronted (and conquered) everything from an unruly lawnmower to an overzealous insurance agent. The following fall, Janice enrolled at a local college, and 2 years later she was well on the way to completing dual degrees in secondary education and nutrition.

Each of these family members grieved, but their grieving took very different forms. The daughter's grief, although intense and persistent, eventually subsided. She found comfort in sharing her plight with other grievers who had similar losses. She also benefited from professional counseling. Her response to her father's death represents the pattern generally thought to be *intuitive* grief. In many respects, the wife's response is the most interesting, since it defies classification. She experienced her grief as more rooted in thinking than in feeling, and she focused her energies on solving problems presented by her husband's death. She preferred reflection and chose not to talk with others about her feelings, finding these self-disclosures uncomfortable and unhelpful. She discovered outlets for her grief that were apparently healthy. In this case, the wife's grief could be seen as *instrumental* grief.

Although there were clearly observable differences between the wife's and daughter's responses, both had similar outcomes. Conversely, the sons' public reactions appeared similar, while the outcomes were very different. Josh's response was seemingly impassive, but it eventually resulted in damage to his relationships, job, and health. His outward stoicism belied his inner anguish and turmoil. This might be seen as the typical "male" response to bereavement. In fact, this son's reactions represent a maladaptive or dissonant response. (Dissonant responses are explored further in Chapter 5.)

Vincent, too, appeared outwardly unaffected by the death, yet found effective ways to express his grief through sharing feelings with just a select few and channeling his energy into his academic work. Unlike Josh, Vincent chose strategies that did not damage his health or relationships. His reactions represent a more blended pattern of grief.

☐ Patterns of Grief and Adaptive Strategies

Identified so far are two distinct major patterns of grief—intuitive and instrumental. These patterns vary in two general ways: by the griever's internal experience of his loss and the individual's outward expressions of that experience. In other words, patterns (or styles) of grief differ according to the direction taken by converted, grief-generated psychic energy, as well as by the external manifestation of that energy. The modalities of internal experience that are most useful in discriminating between the patterns are the cognitive and the affective. The intuitive griever converts more of his or her energy into the affective domain and invests less into the cognitive. For the intuitive griever, grief consists primarily of profoundly painful feelings. These grievers tend to spontaneously express their painful feelings through crying and want to share their inner experiences with others. The instrumental griever, on the other hand, converts most of the instinctual energy generated by bereavement into the cognitive domain rather than the affective. Painful feelings are tempered; for the instrumental griever, grief is more of an intellectual experience. Consequently, instrumental grievers may channel energy into activity. They may also prefer to discuss problems rather than feelings.

Thus, it is the relative degree to which the griever's thoughts and feelings are affected that accounts for the differences between the patterns. However, what a griever is experiencing can never be directly observed; it only can be inferred by observing how the individual expresses his or her experience. In particular, the griever's desire for social support, the need to discuss feelings, and the intensity and scope of activities are varying ways of expressing grief and are often important in distinguishing between patterns. These expressions of grief usually (but not always) reflect choices, both past and present, that the griever has made or is making to adapt to losses. These choices are the griever's adaptive strategies.

Intuitive and instrumental grievers usually choose different primary adaptive strategies. Primary adaptive strategies are the principal ways grievers express their grief and assimilate and adapt to their losses over long periods. These strategies tend to differ according to the pattern of grief. Grievers use additional or secondary adaptive strategies at various times and under specific circumstances. Secondary adaptive strategies are those strategies that grievers employ to facilitate the expression of the subordinate modalities of experience. For example, intuitive grievers choose additional strategies that aid them in accomplishing tasks requiring planning, organization, and activity—all expressions more common to their instrumental counterparts. Conversely, instrumental grievers need to find ways to express their feelings about their losses, and whereas intuitive grievers are quite familiar with strong feelings, instrumental grievers are less so. These secondary adaptive strategies are not as familiar or accessible as primary adaptive strategies, nor are they as critical to the individual's overall adjustment to the loss.

Now that the two patterns have been described, a most important caveat must be stated: Few people display the "ideal" intuitive or instrumental response. Most grievers are a blend of both styles. This can best be seen as an example of patterns fitting the "normal curve" or "normal frequency distribution." If one were to measure every person's pattern, assigning a score representing the strength of that particular pattern, those scores would be hypothetically distributed in the shape of the normal curve. This is particularly true if one is measuring either psychological (in this case patterns of grief) or physical characteristics (height and weight). Figure 3.4 illustrates this effect.

As can be seen, the patterns of grief are arranged along a continuum, with the majority of people clustered toward the center and a very

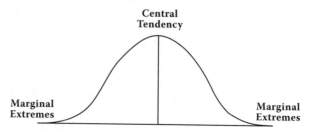

FIGURE 3.4 Normal distribution.

few at either extreme. While theoretically there exist those whose pattern is a perfect 50–50 blend of intuitive and instrumental styles, in reality most people lean toward one pole or the other. Therefore it would be correct to state he/she is more intuitive than instrumental and vice versa. This further highlights the contention that there is no one "right" way to grieve. The blended styles or patterns of grief are less likely to be identified with a clearly defined specific primary or secondary adaptive strategy. Blended grievers choose strategies that are more evenly balanced, reflecting the greater symmetry between the cognitive and affective responses of the individual. The overall responses of blended grievers are more likely to correlate with what have been identified as the various phases (Parkes, 1987) or stages (Kavanaugh, 1972) of grief. For instance, early on, the griever may need to subjugate feelings in order to plan and implement funeral or other arrangements. Later, he or she may give full vent to feelings, seeking help and support in sharing. Later still, cognitive-driven action may overshadow the individual's feelings as the griever finds it necessary to return to work, assume parenting roles, and so forth. This is particularly true of those grievers who have a near perfect blending of both the instrumental or intuitive patterns.

Now that it is understood that most people are either more instrumental or intuitive, we can say that, in reality, there are three primary patterns: intuitive, instrumental, and blended. Figure 3.5 highlights the distribution of styles in terms of "standard deviations" from the center of central tendency. To further discussion of the three styles or patterns of grieving, we will arbitrarily designate that anyone within one standard deviation of the mean (the 50th percentile) can be understood as blended. Those who fall beyond one standard deviation from the mean are either primarily intuitive or primarily instrumental. (Although the graph shows deviations as either positive [+] or negative [–], this is not to be seen as a value judgment of either pattern.) Whether the pattern is primarily instrumental, intuitive, or blended, the griever with the greatest number of available and useful

FIGURE 3.5 Normal distribution with standard deviations.

strategies has a distinct advantage over the griever limited to just a few. This may become a special burden for those instrumental or intuitive grievers at the more extreme ends of the continuum. However, blended grievers, whose experience of grief may be more diffuse than either intuitive or instrumental grievers, may also be burdened by their style since the blended style may necessitate a greater repertoire of adaptive strategies.

In Section II of the book, the origins of the patterns of grief are explored. For now, remember the following caveats:

1. Patterns of grief exist along a continuum; that is, it is extremely rare to observe either a "pure" intuitive or a "pure" instrumental pattern of grief. Although there are key elements that are useful in discriminating between the two, these represent differences in degree, not kind. The vast majority of individual grievers experience and express their grief in ways common to both patterns but toward either end of the continuum. Whether grievers are intuitive or instrumental or blended depends on whether their internal experiences are more affective than cognitive or a fairly equal portion of both. It also depends on their willingness to talk about their feelings rather than their issues, and whether they are more focused on difficulties related to their internal experiences or to solving external problems created by the loss. Since it is rare to find grievers at either extreme, the safest description for almost all would be blended. But this denies us the usefulness of understanding that patterns are, indeed, different. Likewise, it would be foolish to arbitrarily select a point on the continuum and declare that "beyond this point blended becomes instrumental or intuitive." Perhaps the wisest course is to understand that

most grievers are more instrumental than intuitive or more intuitive than instrumental, rather than as either instrumental or intuitive or blended.

2. A few grievers may respond to different losses with a different pattern of grieving, and to refer to a person as an instrumental griever or an intuitive griever or a blended griever can be misleading. However, most individuals are relatively consistent in their pattern of grief, whether it is primarily instrumental, intuitive, or blended, although their position on the instrumental–intuitive continuum may change through life. This may be particularly true of the griever's choice of primary and secondary adaptive strategies. In other words, a griever may be more instrumental in his grieving earlier in life and become less instrumental in grieving over time. The same holds for those whose primary pattern of grieving is intuitive. This is consistent with the theorizing of Carl Jung (1920), who believed that those aspects of ourselves that are not dominant during the first half of life tend to find more expression as we age. Jung embraced the concept of balance, believing that we achieve balance between all the different aspects of ourselves over the course of a lifetime (see Chapter 6, Sidebar 6.3).

3. For the sake of clarity and brevity, those who consistently display elements inherent to the instrumental pattern will be referred to as instrumental grievers, those who follow the intuitive pattern as intuitive grievers, and those whose experiences and expressions are a balanced combination as blended grievers. The reader should continue to view the patterns along a continuum.

4. Whether a griever skillfully negotiates the challenges presented by being bereaved and moves on with living, or flounders and stagnates, remaining forever compromised by his or her experience, depends on whether he or she chooses and successfully implements effective adaptive strategies. Both instrumental and intuitive grievers may choose ways of adapting to loss that are more or less complementary to their natural style of grieving, and result in a more positive than negative outcome. Unfortunately, the griever who chooses and maintains a primary adaptive strategy that is incongruent with his or her inner experience does so at peril. Also, both intuitive and instrumental grievers must find additional ways to express themselves that may be unfamiliar. For instrumental grievers, this means they must find outlets that allow them to vent whatever internal levels of affect they experience. On the other hand, intuitive grievers need to discover ways to facilitate the expression of their cognitions as well as

their feelings. Thus, effective adaptive strategies must accomplish two goals:

a. They must facilitate the expression of the griever's dominant inner modality of experience (affect for the intuitive griever, cognition for the instrumental style).

b. They should also expedite expression of the subordinate modality of experience. This means expressing feelings for the instrumental griever and cognitive-based activity for the intuitive pattern.

5. Although the blended pattern equally combines the elements of the intuitive and instrumental patterns, it should not be seen as a goal or ideal form of grief. No pattern is superior or inferior to the other. It is the individual griever's choice and implementation of effective adaptive strategies that determine how well he or she adjusts to a loss.

Now that the basic patterns have been identified, along with certain stipulations, the balance of this chapter will examine, in detail, the intuitive pattern of grief. In-depth discussion of the instrumental pattern follows in the next chapter.

☐ Intuitive Grief

Intuitive grievers experience their losses deeply. Feelings are varied and intense and loosely follow the descriptions of acute grief that have been cited so frequently in the literature (see, for example, Lindemann, 1944). Emotions vary, ranging from shock and disbelief to overwhelming sorrow and a sense of loss of self-control. The intuitive griever may experience grief as a series or waves of acutely painful feelings. Intuitive grievers often find themselves without energy and motivation. Their expressions of grief truly mirror their inner experiences. Anguish and tears are almost constant companions.

Intuitive grievers gain strength and solace from openly sharing their inner experiences with others—especially other grievers. Some intuitive grievers are very selective about their confidantes and, consequently, may not seek help from a larger group. Others seek out larger groups, especially those with similar types of losses. For intuitive grievers, a grief expressed is a grief experienced (or a burden shared is half a burden). Because openly expressing and sharing feelings is traditionally identified as a female trait, intuitive grieving is usually associated with women. Of course, this is not always the case; male intuitive grievers grieve in ways similar to female intuitive grievers.

Some intuitive grievers may seek professional counseling to have the intensity of their feelings and responses validated as being part of a normal grief process. This is especially true of the male intuitive griever, whose experiences and expressions run counter to gender role expectations. Other intuitive grievers, both male and female, look to counseling to provide new, effective adaptive strategies or to augment current strategies.

☐ Characteristics of Intuitive Grieving

The following are summaries of the features of grief and grieving that differentiate the intuitive from the instrumental griever. Intuitive grievers differ from their instrumental counterparts in three ways. First, their experience of grief is different. This may represent the most significant difference between the two styles. Second, the intuitive griever expresses his or her grief differently. This expression usually reflects a third difference between patterns: choice of primary adaptive strategies. Before proceeding, it should be remembered that these elements are not separate entities. Rather, these features are part of a system of functioning and interact with one another to produce the emotional response that is grief.

The Experience of Grief: Intensity of Affect Over Cognitions

Intuitive grievers experience grief, above all, as feelings. As illustrated in the following, their descriptions of these feelings reveal vivid brief glimpses of intense inner pain, helplessness, hopelessness, and loneliness.

> Oh Christ, what am I going to do? I have an ache, an ache in my stomach. An emptiness, a feeling sometimes that there's no inside to me. Like this sculpture a friend of mine made before he died of a second heart attack. It's a man with no chest, that's the way he felt. I look at that, that's the way I feel. It's a state beyond aloneness. When you lose somebody, you can have a feeling of missing the person you've lost. But then you can go beyond that, to almost a personal annihilation. And I don't know that I haven't visited that second place sometimes. Where I feel that it's not that I simply lost Carol, but that I've lost ...

I sometimes have the feeling where is she? She's coming home, this is a bad dream. It has an unreal quality to it. Maybe the process of grief is to make reality out of what doesn't feel real. It seems like it couldn't have happened. In the mornings, it feels so strange to be ... Often, we would have tea together. In the evening, we would have something to eat. We would talk to each other—you know—and I miss her. I miss her desperately. I mean, there's no mystique to the nuts and bolts of living alone for me. But I miss her, I miss her presence, I miss her physically, I miss her, I miss, I mean I want to, I want, when something has happened, I want to talk to her, I want to tell her something, usually something very funny, and sometimes I talk to her, but I usually start to cry when I do, very quickly. (Campbell & Silverman, 1996, p. 33)

This voice of pain belonged to George, a widower, and is an excerpt from an interview presented in the book *Widower* by Scott Campbell and Phyllis R. Silverman (1996). Although the book focuses on gender differences and tends to be biased in favor of the ways most women grieve and against male grievers (Martin, 1988), it contains many vivid descriptions of bereavement. George describes most of his experiences as feelings, such as "I sometimes have the *feeling* where is she?" and "Maybe the process of grief is to make reality out of what doesn't *feel* real." For George, his inner life is primarily one of feeling. Like most intuitive grievers, George responds more to internal cues, which are experienced as feelings, rather than to thoughts. In fact, for the intuitive griever, thoughts and feelings are one and the same. In this way, intuitive grievers are probably more "in touch" with their feelings than instrumental grievers.

There is a tremendous depth and intensity of feeling in George's reflection of his wife's death. An intuitive griever's feelings are dominant, powerful, and enduring. They are the primary features of grieving. In his classic children's work, *Charlotte's Web* (1952), E. B. White described Wilbur's response to hearing of Charlotte's impending death: "Hearing this, Wilbur threw himself down in an agony of pain and sorrow. Great sobs racked his body. He heaved and grunted with desolation. 'Charlotte,' he moaned. 'Charlotte! My true friend!'" (p. 165).

Intuitive grievers are also unable or unwilling to distance themselves from feelings expressed by others. These grievers cry right along with other grievers who may be crying while telling their story. In this way, intuitive grievers may experience feelings either directly or vicariously from sharing the feelings of another who is expressing his grief.

The Expression of Grief: A Grief Expressed Is a Grief Experienced

The outward expression of the intuitive griever mirrors his or her inner experience. The pain of loss is often expressed through tears, and ranges from quiet weeping to sobbing to wailing. Additional features include depressed mood, confusion, anxiety, loss of appetite, inability to concentrate, and anger and irritability.

It has been said, "Grief isn't real until it's shared with someone else." This speaker certainly had the intuitive griever in mind. So did William Shakespeare when he wrote, "Give sorrow words: the grief that does not speak/Whispers the o'er-fraught heart and bids it break" (*Macbeth*, Act IV, Scene iii). These are commonly expressed sentiments. For example, most mental health professionals subscribe, at least in part, to the "talking cure" for the treatment of grief. Likewise, bereavement support groups foster sharing one's burden of grief with others, discussing it openly and often. Of course, these same bereavement support groups can be social outlets as well. Simply being with other people can be comforting. Thus, we are making a distinction between "social behavior," which encompasses vast numbers of activities and experiences, and "social disclosure" of one's inner experiences. It is possible to maintain privacy about feelings and still benefit from the company of others.

Intuitive grievers want and need to discuss their feelings. They often do this by "working through" their grief. Summarizing the traditionalists' (Bowlby, 1980; Parkes & Weiss, 1983) position on "working through," Wortman and Silver (1989) make the following point:

> Implicit in this assumption is the notion that individuals need to focus on and "process" what has happened and that attempts to deny the implications of the loss, or block feelings or thoughts about it, will ultimately be unproductive. (p. 351)

For the intuitive griever, talking about his or her experience is tantamount to having the experience. This retelling the story and reenacting the pain is a necessary part of grieving and an integral part of the intuitive pattern of grieving. It also represents the intuitive griever's going "with" the grief experience.

Primary Adaptive Strategies: Going "With" the Experience

Going "with" the experience means centering activities on the experience of grief itself. Intuitive grievers structure their actions by responding to their feelings. The intuitive griever's need and desire to talk about his or her feelings is the most prominent example of this. Other examples include the griever's efforts to find time and space for tears, seeking help, sharing time with others who are bereaved, and offering heartfelt condolences to those grievers whose losses may be more recent. This is not to say that intuitive grievers neglect their responsibilities toward others. For instance, intuitive grievers still find enough energy to care for their families, friends, and other dependents. But this means putting their grieving on hold. Thus, intuitive grievers must supplement their primary adaptive strategy of going with their experience with channeling sufficient energy to accomplish meaningful and necessary goals.

Intuitive grievers expend most of their energies coming to terms with and expressing their feelings; this may mean diverting energy from normal activities. They may require more time to rechannel their energies to routine activities, such as self-care, work, and volunteer activities. For example, D. G. Cable (personal communication, February 13, 1998) provided the following instance illustrating how neglecting one's health is potentially dangerous and may need to be discussed with the griever.

Theresa sought a counselor's help after her husband died suddenly. As the counselor listened attentively to Theresa's story, he noticed how pale she was, how her hands trembled, and how short of breath she was. He asked several times if she had seen her physician. The woman seemed not to hear the question. Finally, as their first session came to a close, the counselor confronted Theresa with her physical condition. He stated, "Before I will see you again in counseling, you must make an appointment with and see your doctor." The woman stared at him for several seconds and then, in a sheepish tone replied, "I am a physician, and I know you are right. I just haven't cared or wanted to know about the state of my own health."

Intuitive grievers are also less likely than instrumental grievers to "problem find," to seek out potential problems and solve them. Because so much of their energy is focused on their internal experience, intuitive grievers may appear to outwardly adjust more slowly to their losses. This is not necessarily so. Intuitive grievers are adapting to their losses by going with their feelings. The following case example illustrates how intuitive grievers find outlets for expressing their feelings.

Nathan had a secret: his twice-weekly visits to a therapist's office where, for 50 minutes, he sobbed. He needed to keep this activity from his coworkers and friends (who were primarily one and the same) in order to keep his job.

Nathan had always wanted to be a fireman and, unlike most kids, he followed his dream. He began volunteering as a "fire scout" when he was 12 years old, washing his beloved trucks and running errands around the firehouse. As soon as he turned 18 he applied and was accepted to his state's fire school. Now, at 25 years of age, he was living his dream as a professional firefighter. His only problem was that he had always been "sensitive," and sensitivity was not one of the attributes expected—or tolerated—by his fire chief (an ex-Marine who honestly believed that tears were for "sissies"). When his mother died unexpectedly, Nathan found himself overwhelmed with feelings. Several weeks after her death, he was sobbing alone in the station locker room when the chief walked in. He ordered Nathan to "pull yourself together" and warned him that if he (the chief) was not confident that Nathan could handle a crisis that he would suspend him. Unfortunately, home was not a sanctuary either, since Nathan shared an apartment with two other firefighters.

Desperate to gain control of his feelings, Nathan sought help. After explaining his dilemma to the therapist and sobbing while talking about his mother the two made a contract that permitted Nathan as much of the session time as needed for him to simply cry. Knowing that for at least 50 minutes a week he had a safe haven for his tears gave Nathan the strength to hide his feelings from others.

Nathan's adaptive strategy was successful, since it afforded him the opportunity to grieve openly. Nathan found a way to go with his grief.

Secondary Adaptive Strategies: Handling Problems, Meeting Challenges

Since the majority of grief energy infuses the intuitive griever's feelings, there is less energy available to activate the cognitive and physical domains of experience. (Spirituality, both as it is experienced and practiced, is highly individual and is not a useful tool for discerning patterns.) Nonetheless, intuitive grievers do have cognitive and physical responses to loss and must find ways to express these facets of their experience.

Cognitively, intuitive grievers may experience prolonged periods of confusion, lack of concentration, disorientation, and disorganization. This often impairs their ability to work or complete complicated tasks. In fact, intuitive grievers must find ways to master their thinking in order to fulfill important roles and activities such as parenting or settling an estate.

Physically, intuitive grievers experience grief energy in any number of ways; however, two physical experiences seem to dominate. First, the griever may feel exhausted. Intense expressions of feelings like crying or venting anger can fatigue the griever, as can unusual responsibilities, such as preparing for the funeral or single parenting. Likewise, fitful sleeping and a poor diet can contribute to fatigue.

Second, intuitive grievers may be aware of physical energy manifesting as increased arousal. This is the hallmark of anxiety—an individual's awareness of a heightened sense of arousal. In turn, anxiety that remains unchecked may exacerbate the griever's fatigue. Thus, intuitive grievers should explore ways to augment their energy stores. They must also develop strategies for coping with heightened anxiety.

In summary, the following describes the behaviors associated with the intuitive pattern of grief:

1. Feelings are intensely experienced.

2. Expressions such as crying and lamenting mirror inner experience.

3. Successful adaptive strategies facilitate the experience and expression of feelings.

4. There are prolonged periods of confusion, inability to concentrate, disorganization, and disorientation.

5. Physical exhaustion and/or anxiety may result.

☐ Notes

1. A loss could be appraised as positive—an end to extreme suffering—in which case the grief reaction would be modulated as well.
2. Remember that the use of the term "emotion" reflects the modalities of the individual's response tendency. Affect (feelings) is just one component of emotion. The other components are cognition, physicality, and spirituality.
3. Some colleagues have expressed misgivings about the potential outcomes for instrumental grievers. This concern involves the question of whether instrumental grievers are better at hiding from their own feeling or are simply better than intuitive grievers at hiding their feelings from others. If so, does this lead to successfully resolving and adapting to one's losses? Kagan (1994), points out that the major problem in studying emotion regulation is to separate the intensity of the emotion from the effectiveness of the regulatory effort. Thus, a suggestion would be to reframe any questions about the prophylactic effects of instrumental grief in the following way: Are instrumental grievers better at regulating their feelings about their losses or are their feelings simply less intense to begin with, or both?
4. Other authors have used different terms, e.g., antecedent-focused, response-focused (see Gross & Munoz, 1995).

CHAPTER

Instrumental Grief

Although the traditional picture of grief mirrors the intuitive pattern, a second pattern is emerging as important in the lives of many grievers—the instrumental pattern.

☐ Characteristics of Instrumental Grievers

Identified so far are three key elements associated with the instrumental griever:

1. Focus on cognition/moderated affect

2. A desire to master feelings along with a general reluctance to talk about feelings

3. Problem-solving activity

As with the intuitive style, these elements function together as a system. Readers should not assume that they operate independently of one another.

☐ Experience of Grief: Focus on Cognition/Moderated Affect

Instrumental grievers are more comfortable in dealing intellectually with their losses. Conceivably, this might indicate that grief is experienced more in the cognitive domain than in the affective domain. Perhaps instrumental grievers respond initially to thoughts explaining the circumstance of their losses, rather than to affective cues. This also suggests that instrumental grievers may perceive their losses somewhat differently than intuitive grievers. Generally, this means that the thoughts they process are less vivid and more neutral in content. Also, instrumental grievers may have a different worldview—one that emboldens them with a sense of control, a belief that they can eventually master the crisis. In cognitive terms, an instrumental griever may view adaptation to his or her loss as more of a challenge than a threat (Meichenbaum, 1977). Whether he or she can rise to the challenge depends on his or her choice and effective use of adaptive strategies.

Given that the chief experience for the instrumental griever is cognitive, it should come as no surprise that many of the most initially troubling aspects of grief involve impaired cognitive activity. Confusion, disorientation, an inability to concentrate, and disorganized thought are major handicaps to the instrumental griever whose fundamental manner of interacting with the environment is through cognition.

Instrumental grievers do not experience feelings associated with grief as intensely as intuitive grievers. These grievers often report that they cannot cry and cannot remember the last time they cried. In fact, some instrumental grievers do not feel as if they need to cry. Thus, instrumental grievers may appear to have a difficult time expressing feelings relative to intuitive grievers when, in fact, the feelings are simply less intense (Bohannon, 1991; Carroll & Shaefer, 1994).

This is not to suggest that instrumental grievers do not react affectively to their losses; they do. Instrumental grievers share common feelings experienced by intuitive grievers such as sadness, anxiety, loneliness, and yearning (see Worden, 2009). What is different is the strength of these feelings. For the intuitive griever, feelings are vibrant, intense "colors"; for the instrumental griever, they are pastels.

Whereas intuitive grievers confuse thoughts and feelings, instrumental grievers can differentiate between the two, separating specific thoughts from feelings. "Whenever I think about how she used to fuss at me for my choice of clothes, making fun of my color combinations, I feel sad." Being able to "think about thinking" implies that instrumental grievers may do best with adaptive strategies that stress management of thinking over the purging of feelings. However, instrumental grievers must also find appropriate outlets for their feelings. Whereas intuitive grievers are more in touch with their feelings, as the following case illustrates, instrumental grievers are more comfortable with their thoughts, though they find ways of expressing their feelings as well.

Leonard, a psychologist, and his wife Sheila each lost both of their parents within an 8-month period. Ironically, both mothers' deaths had been anticipated, but both fathers died unexpectedly. Sheila could not talk about any of the deaths without sobbing. When she was not crying, she sat in front of the television in a stupor. She could not concentrate. Three weeks after the last death (her mother's), Sheila tried to return to her job as a city engineer. That afternoon, she walked out of an important meeting after she choked up while trying to give a report. Her colleagues offered to pool their vacation and sick leave so that she could remain at home; she gratefully accepted. Four more months passed before she tried again to go back to work. This time she succeeded, although several times every day she would be forced to close her office door to weep in private. Two years later, she felt that she had recovered.

Leonard immediately went back to his busy practice. He saw patients, negotiated a new contract with a nursing home, and returned to teaching others about his hobby of photography through a community adult education program.

Leonard sought an internal explanation for his losses, stating that "I was always being reminded of the good times, memories of how important my parents were to me. Yes, I had feelings, but they were a kind of backdrop to my thoughts. It was similar to having a low-grade fever, uncomfortable, but not debilitating." He confessed that he wondered if his feelings would overtake him—that he would eventually "crash." Sheila shared his concerns and pleaded with him to share his feelings with her. He chose instead to shut himself in his den and listen to the big band sounds of Tommy Dorsey, his parents' favorite music, and reminisce. Leonard did not crash. As he later explained, "I guess I simply accepted the fact that all people die, including parents."

Thinking about experiences without feeling them deeply is not easy for the intuitive griever. This contributes to the communication problems often seen between different grievers. The griever who feels intense sorrow may misconstrue the reaction of one who responds intellectually to a loss. The following example illustrates how a griever who experiences a loss as an almost total affective event may not understand a griever who reacts intellectually to the same loss.

The nightmare started with a "thump" in the middle of the night. Robin was immediately awoken. Her first thought was that her 6-year-old son, Stephan, had fallen out of his bed. Stephan had already missed the previous 3 days of school because of a bad cold. Robin then thought of her 17-year-old son, Eric, who had also been home from school. Eric had been complaining of headaches for the past several weeks. His parents were not alarmed; after all, Eric had been anxiously waiting to hear whether his application to Penn State University had been accepted. Eric had always been "a worrier." Once Eric worried that he had failed his soccer teammates and his entire school when, as goalie, he had missed an opposing player's last–second, winning goal. That time, too, he had stayed home from school for several days while complaining of a headache. His headache disappeared when he learned that he had been named to the All-County Soccer Team.

Hearing nothing else, Robin lay back down and promptly fell asleep. Her husband, Jack, never stirred. The next morning, after Jack had left for work, and while Stephan was taking his bath, Robin knocked on Eric's door. There was no response. Robin returned to help Stephan bathe. Ten minutes later, she knocked on Eric's door again. Again there was no response. Although she had always respected Eric's need for privacy, this time Robin decided to walk on into his room. She had decided it was time to confront him about his "malingering" of the past several days. She discovered him lying half out of bed, his face to the floor. He was not moving or breathing. Desperately, Robin turned him over and screamed at him. Then she dialed 911.

Eric was dead. Although he was not pronounced dead until he arrived at the hospital, he had apparently died sometime during the night. An autopsy revealed a ruptured aneurysm in his brain stem. Later, the doctors concluded that he had been born with the weakness in his brain.

Robin was devastated. She stopped working, and spent her days in bed staring blankly at the television. Jack tried to comfort her by suggesting that she "get busy," but to no avail. Two months after Eric's death, and after a serious attempt at suicide, Robin voluntarily entered a psychiatric hospital.

Jack returned to writing computer programs at work immediately after the funeral. Although he had always helped out around the house, Robin's condition forced him to get more directly involved in Stephan's care and the management of the household. Jack felt heartbroken by his son's death, but while he wept at the funeral, that was the end of his tears. He had always been "unemotional" and dealt with previous losses and disappointments by keeping busy. This time, he had no choice but to keep busy.

Several months later, Robin and Jack separated. With the aid of psychotherapy and medications, Robin had resumed her life but felt that she could not forgive Jack his lack of emotion following Eric's death. Jack, in responding to Robin's accusations that he had failed to validate her grief, declared, "I couldn't allow myself to miss my son until I figured out how our family was going to survive this. I mean, how could we continue to pay our bills until you got a handle on things and returned to work? By then, I had accepted the fact that God had a purpose for Eric in heaven. Anyway, how do you know what I was feeling? Believe me, I felt plenty miserable those first two months!"

Jack and Robin reunited. Two years later they separated for good. Robin never forgave Jack his apparent lack of feelings about Eric's death.

Jack and Robin failed each other. Jack did not acknowledge Robin's pain and provide appropriate measures of comfort; Robin misunderstood Jack's stoicism as a lack of feeling and caring and negated his efforts to preserve the family.

The key point is that instrumental grievers can and do experience feelings. Although they may not experience them as intensely or be as directly responsive to them as intuitive grievers, they address some of these feelings by redirecting their energies and resolving the issues generated by their thoughts and feelings. As Robin and Jack demonstrated, conflicts arise when feelings are experienced and expressed in ways not seen as appropriate.

This can be true in professional as well as personal settings. For instance, after speaking to a group of hospice nurses about the differences between the intuitive and instrumental patterns of grief, one of the authors was approached by two of the nurses. They appeared visibly relieved. Apparently, they had both recently considered getting out of nursing, or at least hospice nursing. They offered the author copies of recent evaluations given by their nursing supervisor (who did not attend the training). The supervisor's negative evaluations were not based on their skills as nurses (in fact, she recognized that they both seemed more committed to their patients than many of their peers) but as she cited, "for failure to actively participate in staff support group." In this weekly group their peers openly wept about losing certain patients. For this pair of nurses, there were no tears to be shed. In fact, they felt extremely uncomfortable when the other nurses cried. Apparently, neither of them had ever cried easily, nor did they feel overwhelmed when one of their patients died, yet both believed that they got close to their patients and were saddened at their deaths. But they were also beginning to question their effectiveness as nurses, since they did not experience the intense pain expressed by their colleagues. When questioned about their overall responses to their losses, each described ways that they acknowledged the deaths. One of them wrote poetry that they often shared with the families of their patients, while the other (unbeknown to her peers) took a single rose to the graves of almost all of her patients. In these ways, they were able to "feel" grief. They were also able to actively decide when and how they wanted to experience their feelings.

☐ The Expression of Grief: Mastering the Environment

Instrumental grievers are often identified by the absence of behaviors—notably crying and help seeking—rather than their actions. In a sense, the instrumental griever is most often defined by a lack of expression. Since most of their psychic energy is infused into the cognitive realm of inner experience, instrumental grievers often sit quietly, contemplatively, expressing energy through thinking and planning activities. However, some instrumental grievers do show heightened levels of arousal through restlessness, rote behaviors, pacing, impaired concentration, insomnia, and muscular tension.

Since their feelings are neither as intense nor as overwhelming as they are for their intuitive counterparts, instrumental grievers do not show a great deal of affect. This often reflects the instrumental griever's desire to master or control his or her feelings. It also points to the simple fact that it is less difficult to master feelings if the feelings are lower in intensity to begin with.

Instrumental grievers do seem to be more willing to express anger than other feelings. For the intuitive griever, anger reflects an overall intensity of affect. Instrumental grievers express anger when their efforts to implement their chosen adaptive strategy are thwarted. Anger is also a way to discharge excess psychic energy. Finally, anger does not threaten the griever with as great a threat of loss of personal control. Thus, while both styles express anger, they generally do so for different reasons (see Sidebar 4.1).

SIDEBAR 4.1: Anger

> And when He had looked round about on them with anger, being grieved for the hardness of their hearts. (Mark 3:5)

The word *anger* appears 228 times in the Bible. Yet, even here, we find ambiguity when commanded, "Be ye angry, and sin not" (Ephesians 4:26). The literature on grief views anger as a normal though not universal response (Bowlby, 1980; Shuchter & Zisook, 1993), but beyond a distortion of normal grief (Raphael, 1983) if excessive. What is anger? Are some individuals more prone to anger than others? Is there a gender connection?

Spielberger (1988) differentiates between *state anger*, a brief, acute, situational-specific response, and *trait anger*, an enduring dimension of personality (though individuals with high trait anger generally experience more frequent, intense, and lengthy states of anger). Hence, though anyone may become angry, some are much more prone to do so. Applying this to patterns of grief, anger is both an emotional response as well as an adaptive strategy. Although all grievers are capable of anger, some use it productively (motivation for adaptive action), whereas others discharge it in inappropriate and unhealthy ways (aggression, self-destructive behaviors).

Nor is anger the province of one gender. Whereas a number of studies found that outside of anger and guilt, men had a difficult time expressing affect (Glick, Parkes, & Weiss, 1974; Goldbach, Dunn, Toedter, & Lasker, 1991; Lang & Gottlieb, 1993; Schwab, 1990), others have begun to challenge the conventional link between anger and gender (Deffenbacher et al., 1996; Sharkin, 1993). Deffenbacher et al. (1996), for instance, concluded that "men and women are angered by similar things, and to similar degrees, express themselves in similar ways, and suffer similar consequences" (p. 146).

Thus, irrespective of gender, patterns of grief may differ on the experience and expression of anger. Intuitive grievers, with their immense capacity for intense affect, would seem the more likely candidates for experiencing deep anger. Yet instrumental grievers may express anger just as frequently. Why is this so?

Anger may be an easier choice for the instrumental griever if perceived as a way to generate activity and to master the environment. Since most of their grief energy is cognitive, expressing anger becomes a useful secondary strategy to bolster solving problems and achieving goals.

However, given anger's identification with men, male intuitive grievers searching for an acceptable vehicle for expressing powerful affect are more likely to choose anger.

Instrumental grievers value maintaining control over their behaviors. Although this may be interpreted as controlling feelings, it represents a greater goal—personal control. These grievers find satisfaction in mastering their own feelings. They also seek ways to master their environment. Thus, the desire for mastery affects all facets of the instrumental griever's life. It begins with a predisposition to control one's inner experiences. This is more easily accomplished for instrumental grievers since they have a reduced capacity for experiencing intense feelings. Also, instrumental grievers develop strategies to master their situations including minimizing affective expressions and solving problems created by their losses. Again, it is important to remember that instrumental grievers do have feelings.

Instrumental grievers are also usually uncomfortable sharing whatever feelings they have with others. This feature of instrumental grieving has been referred to as a "desire for solitude" (Doka & Martin, 1998; Martin & Doka, 1996, 1998). The reluctance to self-disclose about feelings of grief has been confused with a wish to remain isolated from others. Many instrumental grievers benefit from the company of others.

When his wife Nancy died, Rob found solace by spending time with his neighbors. Every Tuesday and Wednesday evening, Rob, along with three other neighbors, would descend on John's garage. There they would be joined by Frank, Jeff, and Susanne (who had been the only girl among six children and had always described herself as "one of the boys") and spent several hours constructing an ultralight aircraft. Occasionally, someone would ask Rob how he was handling Nancy's death. He would usually respond with "fine." A few times Rob would share his concerns about some issue involving his teenage daughter. Susanne would offer useful suggestions about parenting a teenage girl. Most of the time, the silence would be punctuated with statements like "Hand me that torque wrench" or comments such as "Do you think this bird will ever fly?" Rob found the time he shared with the group therapeutic. He believed that the others understood him and were responding to his needs.

The point is that Rob not only chose to be with others, but he shared his grief-related issues with them without self-disclosing his feelings of grief. Instrumental grievers distinguish between talking about problems and discussing their feelings. In fact, the instrumental griever's degree of introversion is more important when he chooses solitude over sociability than his style of grief. Earlier it was shown some intuitive grievers preferred sharing their feelings with a select few rather than a larger group. Instrumental grievers are the same. Shy, introverted instrumental grievers tend to limit their disclosure of issues related to their losses to one or two others.

Instrumental grievers may discuss grief-related issues as part of their primary adaptive strategy, yet avoid disclosing their feelings. Since many instrumental grievers are men, most hospice bereavement coordinators struggle in vain to get them to participate in hospice bereavement programs. This is especially true of bereavement support groups. Perhaps their well-intentioned concern is misplaced. In fact, Tudiver, Hilditch, Permaul, and McKendree (1992) concluded that a facilitated mutual support group had no effect (and possibly a negative impact) on widowers' recovery from conjugal losses. This aversion to seeking help from support groups is often misinterpreted as isolation, when, in fact, it is not the company of those present that the instrumental griever is avoiding; it is the nature of the discussions.

Willie's wife died after a long illness, and the hospice bereavement worker called weekly to invite him to groups or to ask if he wanted counseling. He attended a group once, hoping to discuss the practical concerns he had in raising his 9- and 10-year-old daughters. But every time Willie tried to talk about his children, the group leader would interrupt and ask, "What about your feelings?" Willie, quite frankly, was uncomfortable with the question. There were times (rare, to be sure) when Willie experienced painful feelings. Alone in his car he would put on a tape with "Earth Angel," their song, and he would weep. But most of the time, he was focused on holding his job and raising his children.

Willie chose not to return to the support group because of the pressure he sensed to self-disclose his feelings. In fact, one of the fundamental social rules about self-disclosure is the "rule of reciprocity" (our term)—if I tell you my feelings, you should tell me about your feelings. Instrumental grievers (assuming they are not introverts) are comfortable in reciprocating about issues and events but not about their innermost feelings. This hidden rule of reciprocity is illustrated by the following example.

Patricia found herself in the unenviable position of avoiding her closest friends. For years, the "Tuesday night group" had gathered at one of their homes (they rotated each week). They discussed their children, their husbands, books they had read, plans they had made. They mostly just enjoyed talking with one another. True, Patricia was a little uncomfortable whenever their talks seemed more gossip than discussion, but she looked forward to Tuesdays.

Then Harold was diagnosed with a particularly virulent strain of melanoma. Four months later Patricia was a widow. After several weeks of focusing her energies on coping with a number of financial and legal issues created by Harold's death, she realized how lonely she felt and decided to resume her membership in the Tuesday night group.

The pain of grief became a topic of discussion. Patricia found herself reluctant to talk about her own feelings, yet tried to listen attentively as, in turn, each of her friends talked about their own painful feelings associated with past losses. Eventually, Patricia became very uncomfortable with the intense feelings shared by the other members of the group; she became even more uncomfortable at the not-so-subtle pressure to share her own feelings. At the conclusion of that first Tuesday meeting, one of her closest friends suggested that she should seek professional help to overcome her "denial" and to "open up and let it out."

Confused about her reactions, Patricia did seek help and discovered, to her relief, that she was not in denial of her Harold's death; she was simply handling it differently. She chose not to return to the group and began seeking out and forming new friendships.

In summary, instrumental grievers do not like discussing their feelings. They may, however, be comfortable in disclosing their concerns about issues. Whether they choose to remain solitary or to socialize depends on their degree of shyness or extroversion. Hence, the instrumental griever's expression of his or her grief may, at first glance, appear to be a lack of expression. But instrumental grievers do express their grief. They may demonstrate feelings; they just do not show the depth and intensity of feelings that intuitive grievers do.

Also, like their intuitive counterparts who choose a primary strategy of centering on their grief experience, instrumental grievers express their grief through their choice of a primary adaptive strategy—active problem solving.

Primary Adaptive Strategies: Directed Activity and Problem Solving

Since instrumental grievers convert more psychic energy into thinking rather than feeling, it is not surprising that they find expression for this energy by channeling it into activity. Becoming and remaining active are key features among the instrumental griever's adaptive strategies.

However, movement (or action) alone is usually not enough. Instrumental grievers adapt best to their losses through planned movements. These planned actions may accomplish any number of the following goals:

1. Action is a way that instrumental grievers sometimes channel excessive affective energy. However, it is important to remember that expressions of grief and adaptive strategies that are primarily driven by feelings are far more common among, and important to, intuitive grievers. Examples of using action to channel excess psychic energy include activities like running, weightlifting, martial arts, and "mindless" work like mowing grass or stacking wood. Less intense ways of displacing energy include needlepoint, knitting, sewing, gardening, painting, walking, and low-impact sports like golf or horseshoes.

After several years of treatments, remissions, and relapses, Jordan succumbed to her lymphoma. Her husband, Ken, had been at her side throughout the years of valiant struggle against the disease. After Jordan's death, Ken felt lost. He had devoted so much of his energy to caring for Jordan, he found himself experiencing moments of restlessness, or as he described it "cabin fever." Ken had always described himself as "low-key" and "not very emotional." Yet he found himself with feelings with which he had no previous experience. He could not cry, although there were times he thought he should. He tried talking to his friends about his feelings but as he described it, "I simply felt stupid talking about it. Talking didn't bring her back." The restlessness persisted. Since he did not have a job to return to (he was retired), Ken decided that he needed to do something to combat his discontent. He consulted with his minister, who suggested that he look into finding an outlet for his excess energy, perhaps a hobby.

Ken and Jordan had often camped together, especially after he had retired. Of course, Jordan's idea of camping was spending the evening quietly reading in their Winnebago while Ken's was to mingle with the other campers sharing their RV campground. As a widower, Ken found himself isolated from others. He craved human contact but wanted it to center on shared activities, not discussions about life without Jordan. He rejected the idea of camping alone since that had always been something he shared with his wife.

Eventually, his brother-in-law invited him to join a group that regularly went white-water rafting. Ken agreed and, to his surprise, discovered that the physical challenges of rafting and the shared sense of danger and adventures with his fellow rafters

> left him feeling tired but content. He also recognized that he was embarking on a different path than the one he had shared with Jordan.

2. Activity is also used as a way to memorialize the deceased. Carving an urn, digging a grave, chiseling a tombstone, planting a memorial tree, and beginning a memorial fund or scholarship are just a few of the ways action becomes mourning. In particular, rituals surrounding the death may be used as outlets for emotional energy (see Chapter 9).

> Mike's mother was worried about him. Although his father had died in a diving accident just 3 weeks earlier, Mike did not want to talk about his dad's loss. The 12-year-old boy had shown little emotion at his father's funeral and had rejected any offers of help or comfort from his mother and other family members and friends.
>
> In fact, Mike's only expression of feeling was intense anger at his mother when she brought his father's ashes home in an expensive marble urn. That evening Mike went to his father's workshop, where he remained alone for several hours. When his mother questioned him about his activities, he maintained a sullen silence. He repeated this pattern for the next several days. Finally, Mike surprised his mother with the gift of a beautifully carved wooden urn. Together they placed his father's ashes into the urn. Afterward, with tears on his cheeks, Mike read his favorite story that his father and he had shared, "Casey at the Bat."

3. Solving problems created by or associated with the loss provides the instrumental griever with an effective outlet for action. Examples include

   a. taking over a business left by the deceased,

   b. beginning or joining an organization promoting a cause associated with the death (e.g., MADD [Mothers Against Drunk Driving]), and

c. making restitution for damage or injury in the wake of the death.

One of the proudest moments in Ted's life was also fraught with trepidation. Ted experienced both on the day his daughter Karen received her driver's license. Karen had failed the driving portion of the driver's examination on her first and second attempts. It was Ted's gentle instruction and encouragement that gave Karen the courage to try a third time.

Two weeks later, tragedy struck. On the way home from afterschool band practice, Karen lost control of her car, ran through a picket fence, and died instantly when her car struck a telephone pole. Ted was initially overwhelmed with a sense of confusion and numbness. He paced restlessly and could neither eat nor sleep. He also began blaming himself for Karen's death. Realizing that he was floundering, Ted made a conscious decision to survive his daughter's death. When his wife had died 4 years previously, Ted focused his energies on getting Karen and her younger brother the emotional support he believed he could not provide. He then directed his attention to the challenges of raising a 12-year-old daughter and 9-year-old son on his own.

Now Ted chose to deal with his grief by carefully rebuilding the fence destroyed in Karen's accident. After he explained his circumstances and gained the owner's permission to rebuild the fence, Ted purchased the necessary materials and began to work.

4. Activity becomes a way to restore normalcy and a sense of security in the wake of a loss. In particular, returning to work or to school, or completing a project interrupted by the loss are examples of this.

Jack was always helping somebody. When his best friend asked his help in repairing a leak in his roof Jack did not hesitate. Tragically, Jack slipped while descending the ladder from the roof. His skull was crushed when he struck the concrete sidewalk below.

When his widowed mother, Becky, heard of his death, she felt numb with shock. Within an hour, her shock was replaced by an overwhelming sense of urgency to do something, anything. She temporarily closed the antique shop that she and Jack had run together and threw herself into making the funeral preparations. During the funeral, friends comforted her as she wept. Two days later, much to everyone's surprise, Becky reopened her shop. When friends expressed to her their concern at her quick return to work, Becky explained. "Jack was such a huge part of my life after his dad's death that I thought that I would miss him a little less if I surrounded myself with his memory. I feel as if Jack is still here."

☐ Problem Finding and Problem Solving as Directed Activity

Problem solving is often seen as an effective method of confronting personal issues. Indeed, the ability to solve problems resulting from the death of a significant other is one of the characteristics differentiating between intuitive and instrumental grievers. For intuitive grievers, problem solving is at the core of secondary adaptive strategies and may present a formidable challenge to recovery. But the instrumental griever confronts problems instinctively. This suggests that problem solving is a primary adaptive strategy. In clinical psychology, researchers have concentrated on the role of emotions in problem solving (D'Zurilla & Goldfried, 1971; D'Zurilla & Nezu, 1982). Since he or she is not overly focused on affective responses, the instrumental griever in confronting and solving issues presented by the funeral allows a sense of control over a seemingly chaotic and random world. After the funeral, dealing with practical issues and problems associated with daily living comes relatively easy.

However, to focus only on problem solving as an effective primary adaptive strategy would overlook the critical role that problem finding plays in problem solving (see Sidebar 4.2). Problem solving implies a certain degree of passivity (in order to solve a problem, the problem must first present itself). Anticipating future issues requires us to be proactive, not passive, to respond rather than react. Most would agree that prevention is better than cure.

With their focus on cognitive activities, instrumental grievers are more naturally problem finders.

When her only two children, Brenda, 14, and Justin, 17, were killed when Justin rolled his jeep over a steep embankment, Grace was inconsolable. Her husband, Jerry, while grieving his children's deaths, focused most of his attentions on Grace. His initial behaviors that enabled Grace to simply be mindful of her pain entailed planning the funeral and finding accommodations for out-of-town family members and friends. Later, he realized that Grace would need to recapture, what for her was a defining personal quality, her ability to nurture. He began researching foster parenting. Two years later, he and Grace accepted the first of what became several foster children into their home.

By anticipating what Grace would need to adapt in the future, Jerry used his instrumental skills to enable Grace to more fully heal.

Many people problem find without realizing that they are doing so. If you are a person who anticipates potential problems (for example, building the possibility of flight delays into a travel itinerary) you possess at least one quality of the instrumental griever. If your style is to deal with issues as they arise, often with affective reactions, you probably are not a natural problem finder.

☐ Intellectualizing as a Primary Adaptive Strategy

In 1937, Anna Freud first discussed intellectualization's central role as a defense mechanism during puberty. For Freud, and her more famous parent, Sigmund, intellectualization was seen as a somewhat dangerous form of defense against the anxiety prompted by threatening ideas and feelings.

Yet, using one's intellect to solve a problem is a time-honored form of rationalism, a school of philosophy that states that reason plays the key role in understanding the world. Far from being seen as pathological, using one's intellect to solve life's problems is as important as being aware of one's sensory experiences. This further highlights the basic differences between instrumental and intuitive grievers.

Instrumental grievers base their responses on an intellectual inquiry into understanding their experiences. As stated before, instrumental grievers do feel, but value thinking and other cognitive behaviors over affect. For the instrumental griever, intense feelings interfere with cognitive functioning. Indeed, clinical psychology researchers have focused on the role of emotions in problem solving (D'Zurilla & Nezu, 2006), showing that poor emotional control can disrupt focus on the task at hand and impede problem resolution.

This has important implications for counselors: When individuals treat emotionally difficult situations in logical (and seemingly "cold") ways, it does not necessarily mean that they are emotionally stunted. They may find ways in the future to experience and express their emotions.

SIDEBAR 4.2: Problem Finding

Problem finding is defined as "the way problems are envisaged, posed, formulated, and created" (Getzels & Csikszentmihalyi, 1976). It is also seen as a key component of achievement. Indeed, most Nobel Prize winners look at the same phenomenon that others have observed—sometimes for decades or longer—and see gaps of understanding, offering new perspectives that often lead to creative solutions. Getzels and Csikszentmihalyi (1976) identified key psychological attributes of artists who were outstanding problem finders. These individuals were willing to switch direction when new approaches presented themselves. They were open to reformulating challenges as they experimented with different perspectives. They also were slow to judge their work as absolutely finished. In a follow-up study 14 years later, these same artists who had been judged exceptionally creative achieved a higher degree of professional success than did their less creative colleagues (Csikszentmihalyi, 1990).

Whereas problem solving is generally passive and reactive in nature, problem finding is proactive and responsive. While both are important attributes, problem finding is generally preferable, especially since prevention is better than cure. Most people problem find but often do not realize that this is what they are doing. Brainstorming with ourselves and others as to how best decorate the house differently this Christmas is a common example of problem finding. Anticipating impediments to our travel or vacation plans (flight delays, weather issues) is another example. So is continuing to search for new means of streamlining our work processes to improve efficiency.

☐ Planned Activity as a Secondary Adaptive Strategy

Choosing an adaptive strategy that involves planned activity facilitates the expression of the instrumental griever's primary inner experience. It can afford secondary benefits as well. In addition to becoming an outlet for affective-driven energy, certain activities may also provide a way to express feelings while maintaining mastery over them. Many instrumental grievers who have difficulty crying have discovered that certain experiences unrelated to their losses enable them to shed tears. In particular, watching certain movies seems to trigger such a release. Thus, grievers can control how their affective energy is expressed by discovering and pushing their own buttons, or cues that are associated with tears. Shedding tears while watching a stirring moment on a television screen or in a darkened movie theatre permits instrumental grievers to experience and express their feelings, while remaining in control. Again, the reader is reminded that the ability of instrumental grievers to effectively master their feelings is largely due to their lesser capacity for intense feelings.

Additional Characteristics of Instrumental Grievers

In contrast to his or her intuitive counterpart, the instrumental griever experiences grief physically as augmented energy. This energy can take the form of restlessness or nervousness. It can heighten the griever's desire to "do something." Physical energy can also translate into arousal. However, instrumental grievers, unlike intuitive grievers, may not be consciously aware of feeling aroused. That is, they may report feeling calm when, in fact, their heart rate, respiration, and blood pressure all indicate a state of arousal. (This is discussed further in Chapter 6.)

Instrumental grievers may become confused, disoriented, disorganized, and unable to concentrate. However, in contrast to the intuitive griever, these cognitive reactions are generally of a much shorter duration. This is because the instrumental griever is more adept at processing events cognitively than affectively.

☐ Characteristics of Blended Grievers

Blended patterns have elements common to both instrumental and intuitive patterns, but with a greater emphasis on one or the other. Of course, the "pure" blended pattern would be a perfectly balanced combination of instrumental and intuitive grief. Just as pure intuitive and instrumental patterns are rare, so too is the perfect blended pattern. Since no one pattern is superior to the other, this includes the pure blended style. The reader will recall that it is the individual's choice of adaptive strategies and how these strategies fit with the various patterns that determine the eventual adjustment to the loss.

Earlier it was suggested that there are probably more blended grievers than intuitive or instrumental, with most leaning more toward the intuitive end of the spectrum. This should not suggest that blended–intuitive styles become the standard of healthy grief. It merely reflects what patterns dominate at this point in time.

Since blended grievers experience and express grief in ways characteristic of both patterns, it follows that blended grievers would need a greater variety of adaptive strategies from which to select. Since these grievers straddle both instrumental and intuitive experiences they may already possess a larger repertoire of strategies. Of course, the opposite might also be true: the blended griever whose experiences are widely varied and whose storehouse of adaptive strategies is severely limited. Thus being a blended griever has it strengths as well as its weaknesses.

☐ Patterns of Grief and Anticipatory Grief

The literature presupposes that being forewarned of a potential loss may affect the quality and intensity of one's grief. There remains, however, some question as to just how anticipation of a loss affects postdeath grief and what terms best describe this phenomenon (see Rando, 1986).

The meaning attached to a particular loss still remains the most important variable in determining the character of the grief response, including choice of adaptive strategies, *within the bounds of a particular individual's pattern of grief.* Intuitive grievers will still grieve intuitively and instrumental grievers instrumentally whether the loss is sudden or unexpected. What will most likely differ is the general strength of their responses and how it affects their adaptive strategies.

Where sudden or unexpected deaths seem to exert their greatest influence is among blended grievers. The following example illustrates the impact of anticipatory grief (or mourning or bereavement) on the blended pattern.

Susan remained calm and objective while caring for her mother during her mother's long battle with ovarian cancer. Although she was distressed by her mother's apparent physical discomfort, she kept her concerns and feelings to herself. Susan experienced satisfaction in her role as caregiver and found her mother's death a godsend. Following the funeral, which she had arranged, Susan spent several months settling her mother's estate. Although she missed her mother, there were only a few times she openly wept.

Three years later, Susan's response to the accidental drowning of her favorite 13-year-old nephew shocked her family and friends. When she learned of his death she felt shocked and numb. She then became disoriented and struggled to keep busy caring for her three teenage children. During the nephew's funeral Susan suddenly burst into tears and rushed out of the church. She became listless and withdrawn for several weeks after the death. She finally attended her church-sponsored support group and shared how upset she was at the unfairness of the death, how much her nephew had to live for, and how much she would miss watching him mature and develop into a young man. Her mood improved and she began to feel more in control.

Susan responded to her mother's death in an instrumental way, whereas her grief over her nephew's death reflected the intuitive pattern. What differed was her interpretation of the two losses. Her mother's death, while difficult, came at the end of a long life and released her mother from her suffering. Her nephew's death seemed unnatural and prematurely ended a promising life. Here it was her perception of the unexpected nature of the loss coupled with the death of someone so young that channeled Susan's grief more toward the affective modality and away from the cognitive. She also chose different strategies to adapt to her losses, goal-directed activity in the case of her mother, and "going with" and sharing her feelings following the death of her nephew. Given

Susan's wide range of experiences and expressions, we would conclude that she was a blended griever.

☐ Summary

The following describes the behaviors associated with the instrumental pattern of grief:

1. Thinking is predominant to feeling as an experience; feelings are less intense.

2. There is general reluctance to talk about feelings.

3. Mastery of oneself and the environment are most important.

4. Problem solving as a strategy enables mastery of feelings and control of the environment.

5. Brief periods of cognitive dysfunction are common.

6. Energy levels are enhanced, but symptoms of general arousal go unnoticed.

Again, patterns occur along a continuum. Those grievers near the center who demonstrate a blending of the two styles experience a variety of the elements of both patterns, although one is somewhat more pronounced than the other. This suggests a need for more choices among adaptive strategies than the griever whose style is more toward the extreme.

5

Dissonant Responses

What happens when grievers consistently choose adaptive strategies that do not fit or complement their style of grief? Is this tantamount to complicated mourning? In this chapter maladaptive responses to loss are identified as *dissonant*. In some cases, these reactions may become semipermanent ways of responding to loss and may sometimes serve as cornerstones for complicated mourning. This chapter begins by looking at the initial responses that may cloud the distinction between intuitive and instrumental grievers. Again, remember that patterns exist on a continuum, and those nearer the center are a blending of both styles.

☐ Initial Responses

It is important to remember that, with a few rare exceptions, the redirection of psychic energy from the griever's initial pattern of behavior to his or her enduring pattern of adaptation to loss occurs gradually and over time. The speed with which energy is channeled into the pattern that is customary may vary as an individual develops and matures. It may also vary from situation to situation. Thus, it may be difficult to categorize an individual griever's global response immediately after a loss as either intuitive or instrumental.

While models may vary somewhat, most of the literature identifying reactions to death-related loss presupposes an initial period of disorganization (see, for instance, Bowlby, 1980; Rando, 1993; Worden, 2009), where responses may include shock, numbness, hysteria, and confusion. These initial features are especially evident following sudden and traumatic losses. Taken together, these responses may represent an atypical expression of grief for a particular griever. In other words, initial responses may not be indicative of the individual's customary pattern of grieving. During this period, it may be virtually impossible to distinguish instrumental grievers from intuitive grievers or blended grievers.

Intuitive grievers may initially focus on suppressing intense, painful feelings and controlling their grief-related behavior. The following case illustrates how an individual's initial responses may reflect adaptive strategies typical of the other pattern of grieving, yet differ from his or her enduring pattern of intuitive grieving.

When Glen's 24-year-old daughter was killed in a boating accident he was overwhelmed by pain. His previous experience with bereavement included the losses of both of his parents, a younger brother, and a stillborn infant son. Through these encounters, Glen had learned that for him, grief was a profoundly painful, overwhelming feeling experience. Glen's eventual adjustment to his losses required that he focus and refocus on his feelings and that he share these feelings with others. Glen described himself as highly emotional and very sensitive.

Despite experiencing crushing agony, Glen took charge, as events unfolded over the next several days. He made the initial identification of his daughter's body, arranged her funeral, and provided transportation for the scores of relatives and friends who traveled from a distance. He comforted his wife and two children and cooperated with the police investigation into his daughter's accidental death. He later identified his strategy for coping with his daughter's death as "absolutely shutting down my feelings."

It was not until the funeral was over and the relatives and friends were ferried back to local airports that Glen, as he described it, "imploded." He became dejected and cried incessantly. He withdrew from others and contemplated suicide. Finally, he joined the local chapter of The Compassionate Friends, a support group for bereaved parents, and began his long, torturous journey to recovery. Today, he is a local chapter president of The Compassionate Friends.

It may take hours or even days for the person's true pattern of grieving to dominate his or her behaviors. In Glen's case, he might easily have been identified as an instrumental griever when, in fact, he had always followed the intuitive pattern for grieving.

Glen illustrates how intuitive grievers may initially choose adaptive strategies that typify an instrumental response to allow them to manage both their experiences and expressions of grief. These grievers may choose to manage their feelings by avoiding certain thoughts. Many grievers choosing this form of adapting manage by effectively *dosing* feelings by managing pain-eliciting thoughts (Shuchter & Zisook, 1993). They accomplish this by selectively displacing some conscious thoughts into their subconscious. This pain inventory remains in subconscious storage until they choose to reintroduce some or all of its contents into consciousness, reexperiencing the affective component of their grief. This usually occurs at times and places that do not interfere with the griever's self-defined goals and tasks.

Other ways that grievers may attempt to distract themselves include forcing painful thoughts from consciousness and substituting pleasant memories. In fact, it is the effective management of memories and thoughts that enables most grievers, regardless of their pattern, to eventually adapt to their altered worlds.

Generally, intuitive grievers revert to their customary pattern of grieving and choice of primary adaptive strategies—in this case, going with their intense feelings and openly expressing those feelings.

Instrumental grievers use these same strategies (dosing, distraction), but are generally less conscious of choosing them and invest less energy in maintaining them. Instrumental grievers naturally perceive and interact with the world through their cognitive systems. Readers should recall that however similar their behaviors are, intuitive grievers differ from their instrumental counterparts in the relative intensity of their feelings and in their motivation for dealing with their feelings.

Whereas intuitive grievers may express stoicism in the face of loss, instrumental grievers may show evidence of feelings such as crying. They may also show signs of cognitive impairment, becoming confused, disoriented, and disorganized. Eventually, instrumental grievers' cognitive control, their desire for mastery, and the muted intensity of their feelings lead to their adapting strategies usually identified with the instrumental style. Such was the case of Jim in the following illustration.

Jim was holding Alice's hand when she died after a long fight with lymphoma. He was surprised at his intense feelings of grief since he had been anticipating this moment for months. When the hospice nurse arrived just a few minutes later, she found Jim sobbing. He looked up at her and said, "I don't know what I should do." She replied that she would take care of everything and then began making the necessary calls. Fifteen minutes later, she was surprised when Jim walked into the kitchen and said, "Can I fix you a cup of coffee?" He made the coffee and then sat down and asked the nurse whom she had called and what arrangements had been made. As she described it later at the hospice interdisciplinary team meeting, "It was like he threw a switch that said 'Okay, I'm over that and back to my old self.'"

By the time the funeral staff arrived to remove Alice's body, Jim was fully back in charge. He insisted on carrying Alice down the three flights of stairs to the waiting vehicle. He then threw himself into whatever needed to be done. He contacted relatives, cleaned the house, and ordered food for the anticipated onslaught of relatives and friends. He arranged for the medical supplies company to pick up Alice's hospital bed. He did not cry again. He returned to work the day after the funeral. He politely refused offers of help from the hospice bereavement coordinator, although he did have lunch with the nurse, where they laughed and shared funny stories about Alice.

One year later, Jim became a hospice volunteer and arranged several fundraising events. He chose, however, not to be involved in direct patient care.

In this case, if the hospice nurse had left before witnessing Jim's transformation, she would have assumed that Jim would be having a very rough time of it and, even if he refused it, would probably need whatever help could be given to him. Jim's initial choice of discharging his feelings as an adaptive strategy would have identified him as an intuitive griever, when in fact, he was most comfortable with resolving losses by mastering his feelings and remaining active.

☐ Dissonant Patterns

Some grievers may be unable to alter their initial strategies; it may be maladaptive for these grievers to persist in managing or giving into their feelings and behaviors beyond the initial period of loss. These grievers are not only expressing grief differently than it is experienced, they are truly at war with themselves.

For example, male intuitive grievers are often at odds with societal norms for gender-stereotyped behaviors. For the male intuitive griever whose identity is determined solely by societal stereotypes, intense feelings of grief are more than a mere inconvenience; they represent a threat to the self. For these grievers, their need to express their feelings and share them with others is overshadowed by a rigid definition of manliness. In disenfranchising their own grief, these unfortunates may contribute to the stereotype of the poker-faced male griever. Being at odds with one's feelings has its consequences, and those who choose this method of coping might best heed the warning implicit in an ancient Chinese proverb: Expression of feelings leads to momentary pain and long-term relief; suppression leads to momentary relief and long-term pain.

The term *dissonant* is used to describe a persistent way of expressing grief that is at odds with the griever's primary internal experience. The choice of this term is consistent with the theorizing of Festinger (1957), who defined one's awareness of a contradiction among two or more elements of the mind and the resulting discomfort as *cognitive dissonance*. In most cases, individuals are motivated to behave and think in ways that reduce dissonance. This is why most grievers experience disharmony at one time or another in their grieving, yet eventually achieve resolution through expressing their experiences of grief. Unfortunately, for some, this lack of harmony between an inner state and an outer expression persists, resulting in dissonance.

☐ Dissonant Response: Suppressing Feelings

Earlier it was discussed how grievers manage their expressions of grief through the dosing feelings. This usually involves manipulation of thoughts and memories, that is, cognitive management. For instrumental grievers, the management of their thoughts and memories becomes a cornerstone of their adaptive strategy. Since most of the psychic energy is channeled into the cognitive rather than the affective realm, instrumental grievers do not need to rechannel as much energy from other realms of inner experience to manage their cognitions as do intuitive grievers. This allows instrumental grievers to harness more energy for activities— both planned and unplanned. Instrumental grievers commonly employ dosing and other cognitive strategies, such as repression, as they adapt to their losses.

On the other hand, intuitive grievers are usually not as adept at managing their cognitions; thus, they expend more energy reining in their feelings. As seen previously by Glen's experience after his daughter's death, this can be an effective strategy if employed temporarily. Unfortunately, some grievers confuse dosing with suppression and attempt to permanently contain their strong feelings. (Here the distinction between *suppression* and *repression* is made. Repression is seen as an autonomous way of adapting to loss; suppression is seen as the ongoing conscious and deliberate act of avoiding painful feelings by pushing painful thoughts aside.)

This is risky business, particularly if the grief is intuitive—that is, of primarily a feeling nature. The more intuitive the griever, the greater is the danger. Thus, perpetual suppression of feelings, where the griever's expression of grief is incongruent with his or her inner experiences, becomes a way to avoid the reality of the loss as well as a way to avoid feelings. As the following case illustrates, self-deception extracts a price from the griever's mental and emotional health.

After 12 years of loving companionship, Tim decided it was time to say goodbye to his canine best friend, Zeus. Over time, Zeus had grown increasingly feeble. For the previous several months, Tim had been forced to lift the dog's hindquarters off the ground so that Zeus could stagger into the yard to relieve himself. Zeus became disinterested in food. Then the dreaded day arrived, when Zeus had his first accident in the house. After three consecutive days of cleaning up messes and carefully bathing Zeus, Tim and his wife reluctantly decided that the dog's quality of life did not warrant the additional time with Zeus that Tim and his wife desired.

Tim carefully and deliberately arranged to take Zeus to his veterinarian the following morning. Both Tim and his wife remained at Zeus's side, stroking him, and talking to him as the vet administered the drug. As Zeus drew his last breath, Tim began sobbing. He cried uncontrollably, unwilling to leave his companion behind. It was not until he was seated behind the steering wheel that he forcibly regained his composure. The rest of that day and into the evening, Tim distracted himself from thinking about Zeus. He removed the food and water bowls and stored the collars and leads.

During the next several weeks, Tim ejected memories of the events at the vet's office, replacing those images with images of Zeus as a young dog, frolicking on the beach. He also increased his daily consumption of alcohol from his customary two beers to a six-pack and began avoiding his friends. Unfortunately, Tim never allowed himself to review Zeus's last months and moments. He denied himself the opportunity of realizing that he had given his old friend the greatest gift he could—release from his suffering.

Two months later at his insistence, Tim and his wife began visiting kennels, and after several months of careful researching, searching, and planning, they introduced a new puppy into their home. However, Tim could not bring himself to accept the new puppy. He would not help choose a name, avoided spending time alone with the dog, and declined to participate in any of the normal grooming and care activities that had cemented his bond to Zeus.

Eventually, Tim's wife confronted him with his lack of interest in the puppy, and the resulting conflict stressed the marriage. When the puppy died from an accidental poisoning, Tim was initially relieved, but then experienced intense feelings of guilt and began withdrawing from others. He drank himself to sleep every night. At his wife's prodding, Tim sought counseling for his depression. In reviewing his previous losses (father, high school best friend), Tim recognized that he had always allowed himself the luxury of his feelings and had sought the support of friends and family during times of emotional crisis. Eventually, Tim began to understand how concerned he was that his friends and coworkers would find his intense grief over a dog "silly." He also gained insight into his habitual ways of maintaining the approval of others at the expense of his own feelings. Confronting his unresolved grief over Zeus and expressing his deep feelings over the loss finally bore fruit and led to Tim's consequent recovery.

In Tim's case, one can trace the redirection of his affective energy to a cognitive strategy (avoiding all reminders of the loss, suppressing feelings) as he began removing all of Zeus's possessions. Although choosing suppression as an adaptive strategy may have been wise initially (enabling Tim to drive home), it soon disenfranchised him from his true experience of grief, which remained primarily affective. As Tim suppressed more and more affective energy, he estranged himself from his grief and established the enduring pattern of avoidance and suppression for adapting to his loss—in this case, Tim's grief became dissonant.

Intuitive grievers adapt to their losses by actively experiencing and expressing their feelings. Complicated grief responses may result if the intuitive griever's initial adaptive strategies, which temporarily enabled them to control their feelings and behaviors, persist.

Instrumental grievers, too, must find ways to express the grief energy experienced as feelings. They are often at a disadvantage since their strengths usually do not include being comfortable with an uninhibited expression of feelings. Whatever the limits of an individual's capacity to experience vivid feelings, that person will become increasingly uncomfortable as the ceiling of that boundary is approached. This fact reinforces the notion that the experiences and expressions of grief exist on a continuum.

This may severely limit the choices of secondary adaptive strategies. For instance, if the only way an instrumental griever has learned to express feelings is through anger, he or she will most likely find himself or herself in difficulty with his or her environment. Stated differently, what is initially a time-limited pattern of grieving may become an ongoing dissonant response to a specific loss.

What could motivate a griever to ignore his or her disharmonious behavior? Are certain people predisposed to use suppression as a response to bereavement? The answer may lie in exploring the concept of *impression management* (Goffman, 1959).

☐ Preexisting Pattern: Image Management

Comparing Tim's responses to Glen's reveals that the key difference between the brief and benign nature of Glen's efforts to suppress his feelings and Tim's ongoing, deleterious attempts to accomplish the same is that of motive. Whereas Glen temporarily suspended his feelings to handle the immediate aftermath of his wife's death, Tim was concerned with how others would view his grief over a dog. Tim was responding in his habitual way of needing to control the impression that he presented to the world. Thus, rather than temporarily suspend their customary pattern of grieving to accomplish necessary tasks, some grievers may be motivated by a desire to preserve their self-image, especially the image they display to the public. These *image managers* carefully screen their behavior for content that corresponds with the image the person believes is needed at the time. Despite primarily experiencing grief as painful feelings, these grievers cope by suppressing and disguising their feelings.

The concept of image management is consonant with the research on impression management, which is defined as "attempts to control images that are projected in real or imagined social situations" (Schlenker, 1980, p. 6). Whereas most people are motivated by the twin needs of getting along with others and thinking well of themselves, some people carry this to extremes. Individuals who consistently try to control others' reactions to them are identified as *high self-monitors* (Snyder, 1974). Whereas *low self-monitors* maintain consistency in their behavior from one audience to another, high self-monitors modify their behavior to please their current audience. As one might expect, high self-monitors care more about social norms and conformity. Thus, image managers are grievers who are high self-monitors and whose outward reactions to their losses are motivated by their desire to control how others think of and respond to them.

This may be particularly true of the male intuitive griever, who may tailor his behaviors to match gender role stereotypes that he believes will match the expectations of his immediate audience. For example, the male image manager might hide his sorrow and grief from those he believes would judge the open expression of these feelings as weak or effeminate. He might also suppress his feelings in order to maintain his own self-defined image to himself. This is an example of extreme self-deception.

Women, too, can be image managers. In fact, if the motive is to portray oneself in control of a situation, gender matters less than the need to be seen a certain way. Recall that image managers carefully screen and guard against any behaviors that they believe may give another a "bad" impression of them. Bereavement presents a formidable challenge to high self-monitors.

Suppressing powerful feelings requires constant vigilance and conscious control of all publicly observed actions—a taxing task at best. Some grievers expend huge amounts of energy in an effort to preserve their highly prized public image. Public expressions of grief are carefully tailored to the situation and are often counter to how the griever actually feels. If stoicism and self-control are deemed appropriate at the time, the griever becomes a true member of the "stiff upper lip" crowd.

This is not to suggest that image managers are the only grievers influenced by their immediate environment. Even the most extreme intuitive or instrumental grievers sometimes base their actions on the people around them at the time. The difference is in whether one is primarily motivated by a consistent desire for approval from others or driven by a need to respond effectively to specific environmental responsibilities. Although some grievers may initially respond in ways not consistent with their patterns, most eventually reestablish harmony between their behaviors and their internal representations of themselves. Image managers are social chameleons; their public personas are transitory and their grief behaviors are responsive to whatever role they are playing for others.

Although image managers may use some of the same strategies for managing affective expression (dosing, distraction) as other grievers, they differ in two ways. First, image managers are motivated to protect their self-images, while the others manage feelings in order to accomplish specific tasks (childcare, work environment). Second, image managers tend to continue to suppress their feelings even when others are not present, attempting to stem the tide of affective energy that needs expression. In other words, the image manager eventually seeks to hide his or her true feelings from his or her potentially most dangerous critic—himself or herself.

Since image managers depend on others to define appropriate behaviors for them, they are not grounded by a secure sense of identity. Consequently, they often experience anxiety that they carefully hide from others. When death takes a loved one, it often robs them of a primary source of self-definition. This often exacerbates their anxiety and generates intense feelings of pain and loneliness.

Unfortunately, image managers have learned only to channel energy into maintaining their public persona. With most of their efforts focused on their projected selves, they are often ineffective problem solvers. They have little reserve energy with which to assimilate and adapt to their changed worlds.

When an image manager finds that specific situations, people, and places threaten his or her control over feelings, he or she will avoid them. This is not the same as temporarily shielding oneself from painful feelings. Many grievers—both intuitive and instrumental—employ avoidance as a temporary solution and are usually motivated by a need to accomplish a specific task. However, the image manager evades certain things to avoid damaging the image he or she is trying to project to others. In some cases, these may be people who previously played a central role in the griever's life. Unfortunately, some image managers not only lose the support and comfort that others may provide, but also terminate lifelong and important relationships.

Similarly, some image managers avoid feeling-eliciting situations by remaining alone. They do not choose solitude as a way of harnessing energy to problem solve or engage in mourning-related activities; rather, they shun situations that threaten their control over their feelings of anxiety, anguish, and anger. Again, they are not consciously choosing to redirect their feelings into adjusting to their changed circumstances; they are hiding those impulses, which might overwhelm them and tarnish the image they want to project.

One strategy image managers select to control their public expression of grief is to outwardly deny the importance of the loss. Unfortunately, this public denial may extend to a private denial of the significance of the loss—a true act of self-deception. Although using self-deception occasionally may have a role in maintaining one's self-image, it is a risky mechanism to employ, especially for the individual motivated by a desire for social approval. For example, pretending that the death of one's parent is not significant because "they were old and sick" can result in a denigration of the relationship one had with the parent. Because the image manager already has a weakened sense of self, redefining a relationship to enable him or her to control public expressions of grief may deepen the estrangement from his or her true feelings about the deceased.

Another way of suppressing feelings is to anesthetize them. For most people this means using mood-altering substances. Again, there is a difference between image management and the initial numbness that is characteristic of an uncomplicated grief response. Although there are a variety of both prescription and nonprescription drugs that can generate the quiescence associated with a more desirable feeling state, the most popular choice—alcohol—is also the easiest to obtain (see Sidebar 5.1).

☐ Gender Role Conflict (or Strain) and Image Management

Gender role conflict (GRC) or strain (O'Neil, 1990) is believed to result from gender role socialization and creates distress and conflict, resulting in a wide range of negative consequences for men as well as those who populate their environment. There is a body of literature suggesting that the negative effects of GRC result from the conflict men experience when they attempt to live up to masculine expectations. These negative consequences include

- Low self-esteem (Cournoyer & Mahalik, 1995)

- Heightened stress levels (Sharpe & Heppner, 1991)

- Substance abuse (Blazina & Watkins, 1996)

- Shame (Durham Thompkins & Rando, 2003)

There is some criticism of GRC that suggests psychological distress among men is not related to gender role strain but to a man's ability to solve problems (Good, Heppner, DeBord, & Fischer, 2004). Thus instrumental grievers' innate ability to solve problems presented by their loss might provide immunity to the distress associated with GRC. Also, since most studies of the consistency between real and ideal GRC use college-age men, rigid conformation to gender role ideals may reflect the importance of solidifying one's identity during this period of life rather than exploring different ways of being a man. This concurs with both Jung's (1964) concept of anima and animus as well as Gutmann's (1987) research on cross-cultural similarities and gender role development. Both Jung and Gutmann point to the fact that men and women are most different in late adolescence and early adulthood and become increasingly similar in middle age and late life.

Perhaps the concept most important to a discussion of dissonant grief responses is *restrictive emotionality*. Restrictive emotionality has been defined as "having difficulty and fears about expressing one's feelings and difficulty finding words to express basic emotions" (O'Neil, Good, & Holmes, 1995, p. 176). The Gender Role Conflict Scale included a 10-item subscale, the Restrictive Emotionality scale, in an attempt to demonstrate the consequences of restrictive emotionality. Restrictive emotionality competes with several other constructs of emotional inexpressiveness including suppression (Gross & Levenson, 1993), repression (Weinberger, Schwartz, & Davidson, 1979), inhibition (Pennebaker, 1997), and alexithymia (Krystal, 1982). One way to clarify the differences between these various concepts, as well as which might differentiate the behavior of an instrumental and a dissonant griever, is applying the cognitive-evaluative model of emotional expression and nonexpression (Kennedy-Moore & Watson, 1999). This model describes the steps leading to overt emotional expression from covert emotional experience.

In Step 1, there is preconscious processing of emotional information and automatic physiological arousal resulting from emotion-provoking stimulus. At this juncture, nonexpression can occur simply because a person has little or no primary affective reaction to the stimulus. This represents one of the cornerstones of instrumental grief.

Step 2 involves the individual attempting to consciously perceive his or her emotional state. Disruption can occur when the person is motivated to block the experience of negative emotions. This is *repressive coping.* Not only have attempts to find a relationship between emotional expression or nonexpression and disease failed, Bonnano (2001) provided empirical validation for the potential benefits of emotional inexpressiveness for people who have been bereaved or experience another kind of significant trauma.

Step 3 of the model entails labeling and interpreting one's affective response. Here, nonexpression may occur because the person lacks the skill to label or interpret his emotional processing. This is also known as alexithymia (Krystal, 1982), a deficit in one's ability to put emotions into words. Since most instrumental grievers value intellectual abilities (problem finding, problem solving), it follows that they would have less experience with a vocabulary emphasizing emotions.

Step 4 involves evaluating the individual's affective responses in terms of his or her beliefs and goals. Here, it may be a negative evaluation concerning the expression of emotions. This would represent a dissonant behavior.

Finally, in Step 5, one tries to determine whether the immediate social context permits the expression of emotions. This, too, is a form of response representing a dissonant griever.

Wong, Pituch, and Rochlen (2006) created a study tool to examine the concept of restrictive emotionality based on the previous cognitive evaluative model of emotional expression and nonexpression. Their findings:

- Repression was negatively associated with restrictive emotionality.

- Negative attitudes toward emotional expression were strongly associated with restrictive emotionality.

- Men with high emotional restriction are probably able to express their feelings but choose not to.

Thus, the concept of emotional restrictiveness lies at the core of the first of the two forms of dissonant grief: image managers.

Why are most image managers—especially male grievers—found toward the intuitive end of the continuum? Why are there not more instrumental image managers?

1. There are probably more intuitive grievers and blended–intuitive grievers in the population to begin with.

2. Managing one's expression of feelings and projecting a sense of control remain consistent with the male role.

3. Over time, intuitive grievers may lose support for their public expressions of grief. As others tire of comforting them, they may be forced into an image management role.

In summary, most image managers experience their losses in the affective domain, but because of their habitual need to seek approval of others, they are burdened immensely by their grief as they struggle to hide their true feelings. This differs from another dissonant response in which grievers may not actively attempt to alter their expression of grief, but may experience intense guilt because they believe that their inner experience and outer expression should be different from what they are.

☐ Dissonant Response: Penitence

Whereas image managers are usually intuitive grievers who hide their feelings from others by censoring their expressions of grief, *penitents* are often instrumental grievers who condemn themselves for not having feelings to hide. The two responses are outwardly similar except that in the former, grievers experience anxiety at the potential failure to cover up their feelings, while in the latter grievers experience intense guilt because they cannot pretend to have feelings that they believe they should have. They also differ in that image managers are simply continuing a habitual way of handling general stress, whereas bereavement may precipitate the inner crisis of the penitent.

SIDEBAR 5.1: Alcohol—Balm or Bane

Although intense debate has often centered on using psychoactive medications to treat normal bereavement (see Rando, 1993), there is generally a consensus that alcohol is the most frequently chosen agent for self-medication, especially among men (Hughes & Fleming, 1991; Parkes & Weiss, 1983; Stroebe & Stroebe, 1993). What remains clouded is the question of when, outside of the disease of alcoholism, is imbibing either help or hindrance to the griever?

For the past 5,000 years humankind has been participating in a largely uncontrolled natural experiment of the relationship between alcohol and health, with few conclusions reached. Partly, this is due to ambiguous counsel from normally unimpeachable sources. For instance, as Noah stepped from the Ark, God bid him to plant vineyards, and Proverbs (31:6–7) reads: "Give strong drink unto him that is ready to perish, and wine unto those that be of heavy hearts. Let him drink, and forget his poverty, and remember his misery no more." Of course there is admonition to the contrary: "For he shall be great in the sight of the Lord, and shall drink neither wine nor strong drink, and he shall be filled with the Holy Ghost, even from his mother's womb" (Luke 1:15).

Likewise, advice about using alcoholic products from the American Medical Association (AMA) is equally ambivalent. For instance, the AMA warns that drinking can cause a whole series of health problems including heart disease, certain types of cancers, liver disease, and of course, alcoholism. At the same time, a recent issue of *JAMA* (*The Journal of the American Medical Association*; January 6, 1999) included a finding that moderate consumption of alcohol actually reduces the risk of stroke and heart disease. (This effect is not limited to red wine as previously thought.) However, there is little debate that habitually consuming too much alcohol is not a good thing.

In our own work we have found that people who already drink alcohol tend to increase their intake following the death of a loved one. This behavior does not seem to be related to any particular pattern. Different grievers may use alcohol in different ways. For example, intuitive grievers may use alcohol to anesthetize grieving, while to instrumental grievers drinking might be an activity. To dissonant grievers, alcohol may permit the release of pent-up emotion. For the vast majority of grievers, however, alcohol consumption returns to preloss levels within a year of the death. Although we would not recommend beginning or increasing drinking, we are not clear about whether alcohol interferes with grieving or simply makes it more bearable. Stay tuned.

Unfortunately, some penitents attempt to conjure up such feelings by using various substances, such as alcohol. Here, alcohol is employed in an attempt to elicit feelings versus being used to numb or suppress feelings. Other penitents share concerns that are common to image managers and may avoid or withdraw from people. The difference, of course, is that penitents fear that others will discover that they have no feelings to express. This may be especially true of the female instrumental griever, as seen in the following case.

> Anyone who knew Shirley described her as "low key." She was also very bright, finishing at the top of her graduating class from Georgia Tech. She began her career as a chemical engineer for a Japanese firm. Within 6 years she had been promoted several times and became a senior vice president of her company. She then met Marshall.

She and Marshall were opposites: he was moody, passionate, and excitable; she was stable, cerebral, and controlled. In fact, when she calmly accepted his proposal for marriage, he became upset that she wasn't more "excited."

After 3 years of marriage, Shirley finally gave into Marshall's pleas for a baby. Although she was happy being pregnant, Shirley could not begin to match Marshall's euphoria. His recently widowed mother was equally excited, believing that her first grandchild would give her a reason to go on living.

Tragedy struck when the baby's umbilical cord wrapped around its throat. It was born dead.

As one could expect, Marshall and his mother were devastated, weeping constantly. Shirley was hurt and disappointed by her loss, but reasoned that she and Marshall could have another child. Marshall and his mother were aghast at her lack of reaction. Even many of her coworkers, especially the women, suggested to Shirley that she seek help for her repressed grief. Her mother-in-law refused to speak to her. When Marshall threatened to leave her, she began to wonder and feel guilt at her own lack of feeling. She found that being with others exacerbated her guilt so she began avoiding people. She also discovered that after two large glasses of wine, she would become depressed and begin to cry. Soon, two glasses of wine became three, and then four. Although he at first encouraged her drinking since it enabled her to "feel," Marshall became alarmed as Shirley's drinking increased. She was also confronted at her office with her frequent lapses in judgment. Eventually, Marshall, along with her employer, convinced her to enter an alcohol rehabilitation center. Fortunately, one of her therapists recognized her as an instrumental griever and was able to validate Martha's tempered feelings as normal for her. Two years later, she and Marshall had another baby and the family is still intact. Sadly, the mother-in-law withdrew from her son and her new grandson as she had from Shirley.

Although Shirley had never experienced intense feelings, it was not until her baby's death and the responses from her family and friends that she became penitent.

Male instrumental grievers are also vulnerable to excessive self-criticism as highlighted by the following:

As his wife, Helen, lay dying, Peter grew increasingly alarmed at his own lack of feelings about her impending death. He began experiencing a profound sense of guilt. Peter's guilt deepened when Helen herself accused him of not loving her. She, too, could not understand how he could calmly sit by her bed as she wrestled with her anxieties about dying and her grief at having to say goodbye. As he searched his soul, Peter realized that he had never felt that deeply about either of his parents' deaths. Consequently, he began to drink more heavily, as he later described it "to feel something." The alcohol relaxed him but did not generate any feelings other than additional guilt about his drinking. Peter asked for and received a referral to a counselor from the hospice providing services to Helen and him.

Peter shared his sense of guilt with the counselor. Rather than focus on how Peter felt, the counselor asked Peter to describe what he was doing for Helen. As it turned out, he was doing practically everything. Peter cooked Helen's meals, changed and washed her linens, managed her medications, and cleaned her room. He provided personal care as well, including washing Helen's hair, ferrying her to the bathroom, and when there were accidents (and there were many), wiping and washing her bottom.

Peter's sigh of relief was clearly audible when, with the counselor's assistance, he finally realized that he was expressing his love and concern by "solving problems" rather than by expressing feelings.

What is so remarkable about Peter's case is how blind he was to the significance of his caring actions toward Helen. Peter did not have or share deep feelings, yet he tenderly performed tasks that most others would find repugnant.

☐ Identifying Dissonance

When does a response become dissonant? Without knowing the individual's history and patterns of behavior it is difficult to identify dissonance. Often, grievers themselves will recognize the clash between their feelings and their behaviors.

In general, the twin compasses of movement and direction may serve as beacons of adaptation. For example, some grievers become "stuck" in their grief. Examples include image managers who do not find appropriate ways of discharging affective energy and penitents who become mired in guilt. And while the path from acknowledging a loss to a final reconciliation is rarely direct, there is an overall progression. Often, others may notice improvement before the grievers themselves. In short, a recovery that becomes stalled for an extended period, or a pronounced regression that cannot be attributed to the usual causes (anniversary dates, specific events, additional losses, and the like), may signal a dissonant response. In particular, any behaviors that interfere with the overall health and functioning of the individual should be suspect and viewed as possible indicators of a dissonant response (see Sidebar 5.2).

To summarize, image managers act in ways to suppress or avoid their true feelings, whereas penitents experience guilt because they do not have feelings they believe that they should. Both of these responses represent immature or maladaptive strategies and, if persistent, are dissonant ways of responding to losses. It is important to explore a griever's motivation for responding in a dissonant fashion. Whereas image managers and penitents are motivated by the fear of damaging their public and private self-images, other dissonant responses may represent attempts to avoid accepting the reality that a loss has occurred. This presents an interesting question: When does a dissonant response become complicated mourning?

☐ Complicated Mourning

Therese Rando's remarkable text, *Treatment of Complicated Mourning* (1993), remains the standard for the field. Rando defined complicated mourning as "some compromise, distortion, or failure of one or more of the six 'R' processes of mourning" (p. 149). (Rando's "R" processes are listed in Chapter 2.) Rando further explicates complicated mourning as hinging on the mourner's "attempts to do two things: (a) deny, repress, or avoid aspects of the loss, its pain, and the full realization of its implications for the mourner, and (b) hold on to and avoid relinquishing the lost loved one" (p. 149). Although every dissonant response does not lead to complicated mourning syndrome, many do. In this respect, dissonant responses may be precursors to complicated mourning.

SIDEBAR 5.2: Grief and Health Promotion

Stroebe and Stroebe's (1993) longitudinal research has found that men may be more at risk for health difficulties during the course of bereavement. That research looked at gender rather than grieving patterns. It is difficult to determine, therefore, what patterns may truly incur more of a health risk. Nevertheless, Carverhill's (1995) suggestion that therapists promote health with male grievers is sound advice, regardless of the individual's grief pattern. Both Worden (2009) and Rando (1993) have theorized that conversion reactions, where grief manifests itself in another way such as illness, often occur when other responses are deemed unsuitable and blocked. Dissonant patterns, particularly since affect is suppressed, may be especially vulnerable to health problems.

But the very experience of grief threatens health. Grief and the inherent change accompanying loss generate enormous stress. Eating and nutritional patterns as well as exercise regimens and adherence to medical treatments may suffer. Counselors are wise to assess changes in health, alterations in daily routines, and to suggest to clients the prudence of a health examination with a physician who knows the patient's medical history as well as their current status, and who is aware of the health risks inherent in bereavement.

A dissonant response represents the griever's failure to effectively discharge grief energy over time. Since it requires energy to restrain energy, dissonant responses may delay or inhibit the griever from resolving his or her losses. This is especially true of the image manager who consciously suppresses and avoids deep loss-related feelings.

Dissonant responses meet Rando's (1993) requirement of avoiding aspects of the loss, particularly the pain. These responses may also represent a failure on the griever's part to complete Worden's (2009) second task of experiencing the pain. Recall, however, that complicated mourning must involve the griever's refusal to let go of the lost love. Not all dissonant grievers are motivated by their desire to cling to the deceased. As seen previously, some image managers are motivated to protect only their public personas. While this may rob them of the opportunity for comfort and support, it is not necessarily a way of clinging to the deceased or avoiding the reality of the death. Penitents, too, may experience self-doubt and self-condemnation at their perceived lack of feeling but not deny the reality of their loss.

Other dissonant grievers may suppress their thoughts and feelings to avoid acknowledging the reality and finality of the loss. For instance, image managers may continue their deceptions even absent of an audience. And some grievers use penitence as a way to generate discomfort, viewing their pain as the only link they may have to the deceased. These grievers fit the definition of complicated mourning.

☐ Summary

Since it is natural for an organism to return to a state of homeostasis, grieving becomes an adaptive response that attempts to adjust to the external and internal changes wrought by a loss. Unfortunately, these adaptive strategies do not guarantee success (see Sidebar 5.3). By choosing a strategy that permits an unfettered expression of grief congruent with the inner experiences of loss, the griever can promote healing and recovery. Likewise, persistent incongruity between the individual's inner experiences and his outward expressions of grief often inhibits recovery and increases the griever's vulnerability to complicated forms of mourning. However, choosing an adaptive strategy congruent with inner experience does not necessarily guarantee success; even effective strategies fail if the individual does not possess the necessary skills to implement them.

SIDEBAR 5.3: Grieving and Violence

In some cultures or even subcultures, the grieving rules may allow or even encourage violence as an adaptive strategy. For example, in certain cultures or subcultures, there may be norms that allow "blood feuds" or encourage revenge slayings. Here, the death of someone by violence necessitates taking another's life. That person might be the suspected perpetrator of the initial act, a member of their family or group, or perhaps any bystander.

Barrett (1997), too, notes the relationship of homicide violence as an expression of grief in subcultures of urban adolescent males. He emphasizes that in such subcultures, violence becomes a rite of mourning when the violent death of a friend or family member occurs. In this culture, the retaliatory violence has the same role as other mourning rituals, that is, it reasserts control, expresses respect for the deceased, reaffirms the loyalty of the group, and allows the ventilation of feelings such as anger.

Parkes (1996a), in his research on violence in Rwanda, speculates that such violence may arise when affect is repressed, as is the case in Rwandan society. However, anecdotal evidence as well as Barrett's (1997) research suggests the answer may be more culturally complex. In an essay, the rapper Ice-T (1995) describes the violence evident in his community of South Central Los Angeles: "When you see these drive-bys and kids are hitting five or six people on the street, they are retaliating for the murder of one of their boys. I've seen crying men enter cars and when the doors shut, they go out and murder" (p. 180).

Perhaps in cultures where violence is an accepted form of expression, it can serve instrumental or intuitive grievers equally well. For those with an intuitive pattern, it allows ventilation of affect. For instrumental grievers, it offers action as a way to reassert a sense of control. Even dissonant grievers can find a culturally acceptable way, consistent with the male role, to ventilate at least one acceptable feeling—anger. In fact, one can speculate that violence, for that reason, is a likely response of grievers with dissonant patterns. Their affect can be channeled to anger and discharged through violence. The answer to violence as an expression of grief may lie less in changing the individual's way of adapting to loss, and more in constraining and ultimately changing cultural norms that allow or encourage violence.

Pathways to the Patterns

Why are some people more instrumental than intuitive in their grief, while others are the opposite? Why is not everyone a true blended griever? That is, being equally instrumental and intuitive in his or her grief? In the next section, several potential answers to these questions are offered. In Chapter 6, the role played by the individual griever's personality in shaping his or her pattern of grief is explored. Chapters 7 and 8 deal with concepts of culture and sex role socialization and the ways these variables shape patterns of grief.

Although personality, culture, and gender role socialization are assigned to separate chapters, there is a true interactive nature of the shaping agents. Personality is strongly influenced by culture, which in turn is influenced by personality. Individuals are active participants in shaping cultural norms, including gender role expectations.

Given that the majority of instrumental grievers are men and that women are generally more intuitive, the role that gender, as a cultural factor, plays in influencing behavior is highlighted. While acknowledging that gender is an important element in determining patterns of grief, readers are encouraged to remember that there are other equally important elements, namely, personality and culture.

There are other potential explanations for patterns of grief that are not considered. For instance, some might suggest that the instrumental pattern has survival value; that is, at a more violent time, men who were more instrumental might fight off raiders rather than succumb to feelings of grief.

In sum, there are many different, but interactive pathways, leading to a particular pattern of grief. Yet one should never forget the primary premise of this book: Different patterns are just that—different, not deficient.

CHAPTER

Personality as a Shaper of Patterns

Why are some people instrumental in their grieving while others are intuitive? The search for answers begins by exploring the role that personality may play in shaping patterns of grief. Although there are many constructs of personality, our investigation is concerned with the three that best relate to grief: type theory, trait theory, and heredity (see Part II introduction). We begin by defining personality. Next, the instrumental and intuitive patterns of grief are related to the personality type theory of Carl Jung. Then, the influence of one particular personality trait, repressive coping, is examined as a shaper of grieving patterns. Finally, the role played by biology and heredity in shaping personality and, thus, patterns of grief is evaluated.

☐ Personality Defined

Every person has his or her own implicit definition of personality. From early childhood, many people have already developed a schema for classifying and predicting the behavior of others: "He's not very handsome but he does have a nice personality." In addition, many people still link personality with charisma and view it as a quality that outstanding athletes, popular entertainers, and (occasionally) politicians have in abundance, while others must make do with less. Even psychologists usually cannot agree on a single, global definition of personality; however, most definitions of personality emphasize three major characteristics.

First, personality reflects what is unique about each of us. Whatever psychological qualities are seen as making up the individual, they set him apart from other individuals or groups, and they describe that person or that "type" of person as someone different from other types of persons. Second, these qualities differentiating individuals are relatively consistent over long periods of time and across varying situations. In fact, much of the understanding people have of others is based on an assumption that their behavior will remain fairly stable in most circumstances. Third, an individual's personal qualities link the person to the social and physical world and reflect the individual's pattern of adaptation to the environment.

Thus, simply put, personality is the sum of the individual's distinguishing personal qualities that remain relatively consistent over time and across situations, and serves as the person's instrument of adaptation. Personality, along with the influential role exercised by culture and gender role socialization, determines the degree to which one is more of an instrumental or an intuitive griever.

☐ Ways of Looking at Personality

Jung's Typologies

Carl Jung published *Psychological Types* in 1920, a book that was the culmination of more than 20 years of effort in exploring the nature and problems of individual differences. Although Jung's typologies are often viewed as overly simplistic, a closer look reveals the richly variegated patterns that highlight individual (and group) differences. Although a comprehensive treatment of Jung's theory of typologies is beyond the scope and aim of this book, a brief summary is in order (see Sidebar 6.1).

Jung's personality typology has become so popular that many people do not realize he made any other contributions. His typology consists of four functions and two attitudes that begin with the attitudes, broad and general ways that people process life and respond to living. Jung makes the distinction between introversion and extroversion, with introverts being those who prefer their internal world of thoughts, fantasies, feelings, and dreams, and extroverts favoring the external world of things and people. Introverts act primarily to understand what they perceive, while extroverts seek to express and communicate their experiences.

Jung suggested that each person has preferred modes of dealing with the inner and outer world—ways they are comfortable with and good at. These are the functions of personality, thinking, feeling, sensing, and intuiting. These are the alternative ways that individuals absorb or experience situations.

SIDEBAR 6.1: The Myers–Briggs Type Indicator

The Myers–Briggs Type Indicator (MBTI) is a widely used and well-known tool for identifying an individual's psychological make up. It was developed in the United States early in the 20th century during a period when Carl Jung's theory of personality types was receiving growing interest. The MBTI is based on Jungian theory of psychological development and evaluates people's preferences with regard to Introversion and Extroversion, Sensing or Intuitive preference, and logical (Thinking) or values-based (Feeling) preference in decision making. It also analyzes an individual's preference for making decisions (Judging) or taking in information (Perceiving). These latter functions are additions to Jung's theory. Thus, each person receives a four-letter code, which indicates that individual's preferences, E or I, S or N, T or F, and J or P. There are 16 possible combinations.

The Myers–Briggs is one of the most popular, and most studied, tests of personality available. According to the MBTI what type you are says quite a bit about you—your career preferences, your likes and dislikes, which of the other types would make good mates, and so on. For example, if you happen to be an INTP (introverted thinking with a secondary ability to take in external stimuli through their intuition), you are most likely a bookworm, a philosophy major (or "wannabe"), and absent-minded. On the other hand, if you are an ESTP (extroverted sensing with thinking and the inclination to perceive the motivation of others) you probably could double for James Bond, since, while charming and suave, you can be ruthless and crave action.

While many people are wildly enthusiastic about the MBTI (from license plates to T-shirts and coffee mugs), the test itself, although inherently fair and nonjudgmental about the types, suffers from the same fatal flaws of most subjective measures of self. For instance, "How do I respond to questions concerning me when I'm not sure whether they describe me at the moment, the past, or my wished-for future?" Additionally, "How much of the time must I feel, act, think this way in order to select it from my other ways of feeling, acting, and thinking?" Also, the Myers–Briggs moves well beyond the theoretical underpinnings of Jung's theory of types with its addition of a judging and perceiving function. Finally, the MBTI meets with considerable resistance among scientists studying personality. For example, two highly respected personality researchers (McCrae & Costa, 1989) found the Myers–Briggs failed to measure distinct types, but did measure four independent dimensions of personality. They concluded that either Jung's theory of types was wrong or the MBTI fails as a measure of the theory.

While the functions are the key to determining the individual's general pattern of grief, the attitudes play a pivotal role in the griever's choice of adaptive strategies. For instance, introverts who are primarily intuitive grievers will restrict the number of others to whom they express their experiences of grief, whereas their instrumental counterparts will choose more solitary ways of mastering their feelings and expressing their experiences through activity. Likewise, intuitive grievers, who are extrovert, will seek large numbers of individuals or groups to process their feelings, while extroverted instrumental grievers will want to share activities that enable them to solve problems and master feelings.

Jung's four functions of personality operate in pairs of opposites, with one pair dominating and its associate pair serving an auxiliary function. Sensing and intuiting are one pair of contrasting functions and are the ways people encounter situations directly without regard to responding to them. In a sense, sensing and intuiting function as portals to experience, without filtering or refining incoming data. The sensing function focuses on details, while the intuiting function gathers impressions.

The second pair of functions, thinking and feeling, are regarded as being one step beyond the initial awareness of an experience. These functions actively process environmental information. They, too, are opposites.

When Jung used the word *type* to describe an individual's personality, he meant that one of the functions tends to be used more frequently in a given situation. Thus, combining the four functions results in the following types (with the dominant function listed first):

Thinking–sensing

Feeling–sensing

Thinking–intuiting

Feeling–intuiting

Sensing–thinking

Sensing–feeling

Intuiting–thinking

Intuiting–feeling

Hence, whether one is primarily a thinker or a feeler determines the nature of his or her experiences and influences his or her expressions of those experiences. Also, the pairings of functions also influence experience and expression. Complementary pairings would include

Thinking–sensing

Feeling–intuiting

Sensing–thinking

Intuiting–feeling

These complementary combinations of functions enhance the degree to which one is an intuitive or instrumental griever. While the thinking–feeling or feeling–thinking functions influence the pattern of grieving, the other pair of functions plays an important role in the initial awareness of loss. Grievers who have sensing as either their dominant or associative function are more likely to focus on the details of the event, while intuiting types get a general impression of the loss.

For example, grievers whose primary function is thinking and subordinate function is sensing (or the reverse) are more likely to experience and express grief near the extreme of the instrumental pattern since, as thinkers, they cognitively process the details of the loss presented by their sensing function. These grievers are less likely to rely exclusively on cognition as they process the loss, since the initial awareness is grounded more in an impression than in detail.

On the other hand, grievers with feeling as the dominant function, complemented by intuiting (or vice versa) will digest the loss mostly as an affective experience, since their initial awareness of the loss is based on an impression instead of centering on details. However, while sensing and intuiting influence patterns of grief, it is important for the reader to view thinking and feeling as the functions most important in determining the individual's pattern of grief (see Figure 6.1).

In Figure 6.1 the eight Jungian types are arranged along the patterns of the grief continuum. Grievers whose dominant function is either thinking or feeling are found near the extremes of the instrumental and intuitive pattern of grief, respectively. Blended grievers have either sensing or intuiting (with thinking or feeling serving as associative functions) as their dominant functions and are found more toward the middle of the continuum. These grievers still follow one of the patterns, but their reactions—experiences, expressions, and primary adaptive strategies—do not as easily identify them as either instrumental or intuitive grievers. But pairing the associative function of thinking with

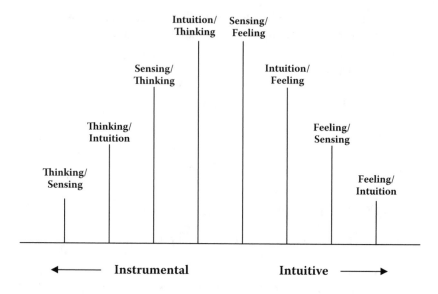

FIGURE 6.1 Eight Jungian types are arranged along the patterns of grief continuum.

sensing will intensify those elements of the blended pattern of an instrumental nature. The same is true if the pairing is intuiting–feeling rather than intuiting–thinking.

Thinking Versus Feeling: Instrumental and Intuitive Grief

Although the way in which one takes in his or her losses may affect the initial awareness of the loss, it is *where* the event is processed—either in the thinking or the feeling system—that determines how it is experienced. Hence, the feeling and thinking functions (along with additional personality, biological, and cultural factors) dictate to what degree one is an instrumental or intuitive griever.

This does not mean that instrumental grievers do not have a feeling function, nor that intuitive grievers do not think. For the instrumental griever, feelings are underdeveloped and relatively unconscious. A griever whose superior function is feeling has an underdeveloped thinking function, and his or her use of logical analysis to process losses is largely unconscious. The existence of thinking as a subordinate function to feeling, or feeling as the subordinate function to thinking, has important implications for the griever's choice among adaptive strategies.

It is important to stress the significance of intuitive grievers discovering outlets for cognitive-driven action, while instrumental grievers must find ways of discharging affective energy. Thus, intuitive grievers who have a number of adaptive strategies for expressing both feeling and action (and have the skills or abilities to implement them) will usually fare better than those whose selections are limited. Likewise, instrumental grievers who have choices among various vehicles for expressing feelings will adapt sooner and better than those whose tools for expressing feelings are confined to one or none.

Which requires more energy: thinking intensely about something or feeling it deeply? Although there is plenty of evidence that expressions of feelings like crying, wailing, or raging burn more calories than sitting contemplatively, it is debatable which internal experience requires more fuel. However, grievers who have feeling as their primary function may initially channel more psychic energy into expressing their grief than do their instrumental counterparts. Strong feelings need to either be expressed or suppressed; both processes require a large amount of energy. Thus, the intuitive griever who chooses wisely among adaptive strategies discharges enough energy into venting his or her feelings to restore a balance between the experience of grief and its expression.

For the instrumental griever, the situation is very different. The energy channeled into thinking (rather than feeling) allows mastery of feelings and finds expression in planned activities. Thus, the instrumental griever who expresses grief by carving an elaborate urn for his father's ashes or who chisels a stone for his son's memorial is channeling thinking into action. Likewise, the father who rebuilds a fence as a way to grieve his daughter's accidental death or a widow who assumes the reins of her husband's business is dispersing grief energy. The homeostasis between creating and expending energy is regained and balance is restored.

Extroverted instrumental grievers may also choose to expend energy by affiliating with others, especially in shared activities, whereas their introverted counterparts may select solitary activities, such as running, writing, or lifting weights. In many cases, these grievers redirect their energies into their work. This explains why instrumental grievers tend to return to their jobs and their previous levels of performance sooner than intuitive grievers.

To summarize, instrumental grievers have thinking as their superior function, whereas intuitive grievers have feeling as their superior function. Those grievers for whom either sensing or intuiting is their dominant function are a blending of both patterns. The complementary pairings of thinking with sensing, and feeling with intuiting influence how ardently one is either an instrumental or an intuitive griever.

☐ Repressive Coping as a Personality Construct Related to Patterns of Grief

While efforts continue to reconcile traits with types, a trait is defined as "a relatively stable aspect of mind that predisposes one to behave in a certain way." In this way, traits become part of the person rather than part of the environment. One such trait or predisposition is repressive coping. Those possessing this trait are classified as *repressors*. Repressors report less anxiety, depression, conflicts, illness, pain, and stress than nonrepressors. Ironically, repressors show higher levels of physiological reactivity to stressful laboratory procedures (Bonanno & Singer, 1990; Weinberger, Schwartz, & Davidson, 1979). Some studies report a possible correlation between repression and immune system suppression (Schwartz, 1990) and cancer (Jensen, 1987); however, Bonanno and Singer (1990) have questioned whether this is so. In fact, Paulhus and Reid (1991) suggested that repression is positively associated with adjustment.

How might the trait of repressive coping relate to patterns of grief? One such association involves the discharge of grief (psychic) energy as physical energy. Since the physical represents one of the fundamentals of human experience, what happens to the physical energy generated by loss? In the intuitive griever, it manifests as affect-related behavior such as crying. It is also experienced as an energy reduction such as fatigue. In addition, it increases arousal (such as anxiety) that is consciously experienced.

For an instrumental griever, grief discharged as physical energy augments the levels of energy already available for physical activity (Plante & Schwartz, 1990). It also may increase physiological arousal that is not consciously experienced as arousal. The latter is a classic example of repressive coping. Bonanno, Keltner, Holen, and Horowitz (1995) believe that repressive coping may be an autonomous adaptive strategy that is effective in adjusting to bereavement.

The researchers in the Bonanno et al. study (1995) investigated how grievers adapted to losing a spouse during midlife. Their purpose was to challenge the widely held assumption that emotional avoidance is a maladaptive response to loss (Bowlby, 1980; Deutsch, 1937; Doyle, 1980; Raphael, 1983). They viewed emotional avoidance as a maladaptive response when it resulted in either delayed grief (overt symptoms of grief that eventually surface), prolonged grief (the mourning process is extended), or delayed somatic symptoms (grief that eventually manifests as physical problems). The researchers characterized repressive coping as a discrepancy between a participant's subjective feelings of grief and increased cardiovascular activity.

After their results were tabulated, Bonanno et al. (1995) found no support for the standard hypothesis that avoiding or minimizing feelings associated with grief is maladaptive at either 6 or 14 months after the loss. As the authors noted, this is consistent with Shuchter and Zisook's (1993) findings that a griever's ability to regulate or "dose" the amount of feeling he or she can bear is beneficial. It also verifies the work of Kaminer and Lavie (1993), which found that those Holocaust survivors who were able to avoid thinking about and remembering their experiences were the best adjusted. Thus, the Bonanno group concluded that "the findings were consistent with the competing hypothesis that emotional avoidance during bereavement may serve adaptive functions" (p. 983). They added the following cautionary note: "If the conclusions suggested by the present data are correct, and avoiding unpleasant emotions during bereavement is in fact not such a bad thing, then a number of important implications for clinical interventions are apparent" (p. 986).

Consequently, while remembering that personality traits are found along a continuum, the degree to which one is a repressor influences whether one is an intuitive or instrumental griever, with instrumental grievers possessing a high degree of repression. From a theoretical perspective, this can be interpreted in one of two ways: Elevated levels of repression either reflect learned response tendencies or indicate a higher threshold for stimulation (see Chapter 5).

Accordingly, in addition to Jungian-type theory, the personality trait of repressive coping may be an important variable in any discussion about the role played by personality in shaping a particular pattern of grief.

☐ The Biology of Patterns of Grief: Temperament, Personality, and Affect Intensity

The final look at personality is from the perspective of heredity and biology (see Sidebar 6.2). Beginning with the work of Thomas and Chess (1977), child development specialists identified constitutionally based differences in emotional reactivity among infants. These broad, general patterns of individual differences in the intensity and duration of expressions of arousal and emotionality are defined as *temperament* (Campos, Campos, & Barrett, 1989). One of the original nine temperament characteristics was the intensity of emotional response and was defined as "the energy level of response, irrespective of its quality or direction" (Thomas & Chess, 1985, p. 219). Since differences in emotional reactivity strongly affect the kinds of experiences children have, these differences become the cornerstones of personality development. Personality evolves as the individual's unique biology elicits responses from the environment—the interaction between "nature" and "nurture."

SIDEBAR 6.2: Sociobiology

Thanks to testosterone, males are larger and more muscular. Bolstered by data that consistently link aggression to males, sociobiologists might argue that our male forebears were naturally selected to defend hearth and family. For these ancestors, emotionality may have inhibited survival. For example, when the community was under attack, men who could ignore their dismay at the deaths of comrades could focus on repelling the invaders. Afterward, the task of rebuilding could begin only if shock and grief could be laid aside. Likewise, the case could be made that conforming to society's rules, especially those involving conflicts and disputes, could be accomplished only if males curtailed their aggressiveness, perhaps through controlling, even suppressing emotions.

While such arguments are interesting and may be compelling, they are also highly controversial and are not supported by available data. Biology plays a multidimensional role in shaping patterns of grief: genetic factors, *by way of temperament*, interact with culture and are important in determining personality; while gender interacts strongly with both personality and culture in producing behavior. Differences in temperament are an established fact, whereas the link between historical social conditions and human genetics is still considered speculative.

Affect Intensity

One dimension of temperament receiving recent attention is affect intensity, which is defined as "stable individual differences in the strength with which individuals experience their emotions" (Larsen & Diener, 1987, p. 2). Larsen and Diener (1987) have summarized the following assumptions about affect intensity:

1. Affect intensity is unrelated to whether individuals feel negative versus positive affect more frequently but is, instead, related to how deeply they feel them.

2. "What goes up must come down," or affect intensity "generalizes across specific emotions such that, for example, individuals who experience their positive emotions more strongly will, over time, experience their negative emotions more strongly as well" (p. 2).

3. Affect intensity is not only the subjective experience of strong feelings, so is the physiological and cognitive responses as well, including increased heart rate, arousal, ability to concentrate, and ability to control thoughts and actions.

4. Individuals who experience high affect intensity tend to view others as having emotional responses that are strong and difficult to control.

5. Women score generally higher than men do on measures of affect intensity.

6. Affect intensity decreases with age.

Thus, a difference in one's capacity to experience feelings is an element of personality that appears to be biologically influenced. However, the role exercised by the individual's environment, particularly culture and gender role socialization experiences, is pivotal in determining the final expression of this trait.

SIDEBAR 6.3: Pattern Development From a Life Cycle Perspective

There are many questions about how and when the various patterns begin, and how they might change over the course of a life span. Although it is suggested (Chapter 3) that most grievers remain relatively consistent in their patterns, one must acknowledge that there may be a shift toward the opposite end of the continuum with age.

One of the reasons this book has not examined how patterns begin and how they change as people age is that, at this point, one cannot confirm whether these patterns are cohort specific. Stated differently, it is not known if differences among patterns can be attributed to advancing age or to the sociocultural conditions that existed during a particular historical period. For instance, people who were 85 years old at the turn of the millennium were born in 1915. They were children during the Roaring Twenties and emerged as adults during the Great Depression. They also lived through, and may have served, during the Second World War. They saw the advent of the television, space travel, and the personal computer. How much did any or all of these experiences affect their patterns of grief?

A related concern is discerning whether the key ingredients for the patterns are present at birth, evolve gradually during childhood, or occur in response to when an individual experiences his or her first significant death? Could losing a parent in childhood, especially during critical periods of personality, gender role development, or both, determine whether one is more intuitive or instrumental in grief? While attempting to provide some evidence to answer these and other questions (studies of temperament, gender role socialization, cultural changes), the definitive answers have yet to be uncovered. It may take a large, well-designed longitudinal study to answer many of the questions.

Finally, development does not occur in a vacuum. Though it may be well and good (as well as easy) to differentiate between physical, cognitive, social, and personality, in the real world these influences on behavior are constantly interacting with one another. Urie Bronfenbenner (1989) proposed adopting an ecological approach to understanding life span development. He suggested that there are four levels of the environment that simultaneously influence the individual and his behavior.

The microsystem is the immediate and everyday environment in which people lead their lives. Caregivers, friends, family, and coworkers are examples. The second level is the mesosystem, which promotes connections between the various parts of the microsystem. This system bonds children to parents, coworkers to coworkers, and students to teachers. The exosystem includes broader influences. Examples include societal institutions such as local government, schools, places of worship, and the community itself. Finally, the macrosystem represents the larger cultural influences on people. Types of government, religious systems, political thought, and society in general are contained in the macrosystem.

We will leave further exploration of the role of development to those following who are intrigued by the existence of different patterns and would like to confirm or disprove their existence.

To summarize the implications of differences in affect intensity on patterns of grief: First, affect intensity does not determine whether a griever feels. It does, however, influence how deeply he or she may feel. Second, the observation that intuitive grievers show a greater range of feeling responses in general—from despair to euphoria and everything in between—reflects differences in affect intensity. Instrumental grievers seem more "even-keeled" but less "colorful" than intuitive grievers. Third, the level of affect intensity seems inversely related to the griever's ability to concentrate, make decisions, plan, and control thoughts and feelings, all variables defining the instrumental pattern of grief. Intuitive grievers are not as adept as instrumental grievers in mastering their thoughts and feelings.

Fourth, misinterpretations of behavior and misunderstandings of intent between grievers may result from differences in affect intensity. In particular, intuitive grievers may interpret the muted display of feelings so characteristic of instrumental grievers as "covered up" or, worse, as indicating a casual dismissal of the lost relationship by the griever. Instrumental grievers may view the lavish (to them) display of affect common to intuitive grievers as evidence of irrationality or poor self-control. In either case, individuals with opposite patterns may not be able to understand and support each other if they fail to recognize the inherent strengths of their respective responses.

Finally, differences in affect intensity found between men and women highlight both basic biological differences and sex role socialization experiences. It reinforces our belief that the extremes of either pattern are influenced heavily by gender.

☐ Summary

In this chapter personality was defined and three aspects of personality that may influence styles of grieving were examined. Jung's type theory, the trait of repressive coping, and temperament-based affect intensity are constructs of personality development and function that may act either individually or in concert to produce the intuitive and instrumental styles of grief. The following are characteristics of the patterns:

Intuitive Pattern

1. The most pronounced example is the feeling–intuiting type, with intuiting–feeling more toward the center of the continuum.

2. Less use of repressive coping as a defense.

3. High levels of affect intensity.

Instrumental Pattern

1. Most pronounced among thinking–sensing types; less so with a sensing–thinking combination.

2. High degree of repressive coping.

3. Low levels of affect intensity.

Blended Pattern

1. Either sensing or intuiting (with thinking or feeling serving as associative functions) is the dominant function.

2. Moderate amount of repressive coping.

3. Moderate levels of affect intensity.

CHAPTER

The Role of Gender

☐ Introduction

There is a sculpture titled *Dark Elegy* commemorating the destruction by a terrorist bomb of Pan Am Flight 103 over Lockerbie, Scotland. The sculpture attempts to depict the agonizing grief of the 33 mothers who lost children on that flight. In many ways, the memorial also illustrates the paradox of male grievers. On one hand, they are expected to be strong; their grief is largely, as in the sculpture, silent and formless. On the other hand, they are castigated for not demonstratively showing their grief, a fact touched upon in Chapter 1.

Throughout earlier chapters, it has been argued that there are, along a continuum, two patterns of grieving—one labeled intuitive, the other instrumental. These patterns differ in the experience, expression, and adaptation to grief. In the last chapter, several factors that contribute to the reasons that different individuals exhibit these different patterns were explored. Clearly, gender role socialization is another of these factors. As Thompson (2001) notes, gender is critical to one's sense of identity. One of the first ways that even young children differentiate themselves is by gender. Often the very first self-identification that toddlers make is to define themselves as "boys" or "girls." Hence, the social norms that define these roles are learned early and play a significant role in a child's emerging sense of identity and the ways that child interacts with others and views the larger world. Gender role socialization becomes a major influence in, among other aspects, the expressions of grief and adaptation to loss.

Men and women, because of their socialization into sex roles, are likely to exhibit different grieving patterns. Men are more likely to be found on the instrumental end of the continuum, whereas women are more likely to exhibit an intuitive style. Yet gender role socialization is but one factor that influences a pattern of grief. This leads to a critical affirmation that *although patterns of grieving are certainly influenced by gender, they are not determined by gender.* Put simply, a counselor, caregiver, or any reader would be well advised not to assume without assessment that any given male is instrumental or any female intuitive. In fact, one can find male intuitive grievers, female instrumental grievers, and dissonant grievers of any sex. However, because of the constraints placed on the male role, males who experience grief in a strongly intuitive way may be limited in their expression and adaptation to a greater extent than females. Although dissonant grievers can be either intuitive or instrumental, they are more likely to be those who, because of constraints, cannot freely express feelings.

☐ Gender and Grief: Lessons From Research

Therapists' Perspective and Research on Therapy

Both clinicians and researchers have long noted that men and women exhibit differences in the ways they grieve. Stillion and McDowell (1997), for example, surveyed a random sample of counselors and educators who were certified by the major professional organization within the field— The Association for Death Education and Counseling. Their sample of both male and female counselors and educators agreed that there were significant differences between men and women grievers. Men were viewed as less likely to exhibit strong emotions and more likely to evoke distractions such as work, sex, play, or alcohol. Men were also seen as more likely to respond cognitively, or when affect was experienced, to show anger. Women, on the other hand, were seen as more expressive and willing to seek out the support of others. Their grief tended to be experienced on a deep, affective level. These counselors also expressed a belief that men needed less time to grieve.

This sample of counselors and educators noted that these reactions often correlated with social expectations based upon gender roles. Most noted were the expectations of friends and acquaintances that males would be strong and get over it quickly. Counselors also perceived that women received more social support for the expression of grief. Ironically, these counselors also noted that although women were more likely to be offered comfort, their grief made them more of a social risk. Conversely, men were seen as harder to comfort but more likely to function acceptably in social situations. In other words, counselors felt that the type of support offered men and women differed. Women could expect emotional support, but lessened opportunities for normal social activity and contact. Men, because they were seen as less likely to be "emotional," were more likely to be invited to resume their normal social contacts. Research by Kubitz, Thornton, and Robertson (1989) suggested that those who respond in ways conforming to their gender role are more likely to receive social support.

Nevertheless, although counselors saw clear differences in men's and women's expressions and experiences of grief, they did not see clear differences in outcome, that is, that women or men did inherently better with their grief. Instead, they perceived that each of these grieving styles ran different risks. For men, it was believed that this failure to grieve predisposed them to the risk of more complicated grief reaction or health issues, while women were seen as more vulnerable to depression and chronic mourning (Stroebe & Stroebe, 1983). The opinions of these experts were far different from those often expressed in the self-help literature (Staudacher, 1991; Wolfelt, 1990).

Schut, Stroebe, van den Bout, and deKeijser's (1997) research possibly suggests another opinion. These researchers randomly assigned a group of widows and widowers to two treatment approaches—one emotion focused and the other problem focused. Contrary to expectations, the men benefited more from the emotion-focused treatment while the women seemed to profit from a more problem-focused approach. Though this research may show the value of a more androgynous approach that allows the extension of a coping repertoire by offering assistance in coping with less familiar strategies, it should be noted that these subjects volunteered and their initial grieving style is unknown. It may be that these individuals may have had difficulty in coping because of a more dissonant pattern.

Research Perspectives

The perspective of these counselors and therapists, explicitly or implicitly, is grounded in much research that clearly does describe differences in the ways that men and women grieve. This research has shown that these differences exist in a wide variety of losses, including that of a spouse, parent, or child.

Spousal Loss

Much of the research has shown that the experience of grief differs for both widows and widowers. Naturally they faced distinct problems. For example, many of the widows reported financial problems and greater emotional dependence on the husband (Gilbar & Dagan, 1995). Men were more likely to talk about the loss as "dismemberment," whereas women tended to use words such as "abandonment" (Glick, Weiss, & Parkes, 1974). This is not to imply that men did not experience grief. In a self-selected sample of men receiving hospice services, these men indicated that they were emotionally involved with their dying spouse and experienced grief (Brabant, Forsyth, & Melancon, 1992).

Widowers also tended to stress the need to be realistic about the loss and to show a narrower range of affect than widows (Campbell & Silverman, 1996; Glick et al., 1974). Whereas women tended to seek emotional support, men found solace in exercise, religion, work, poetry, or in some more destructive patterns such as alcohol (Campbell & Silverman, 1996; Silverman, 1997). Men were more reluctant to reach out to others (Brabant et al., 1992), but they were more likely to return to work, date, and remarry (Campbell & Silverman, 1996). In a study of resilient widowers, Moore and Stratton (2002) noted that these widowers used strategies that included cognitive reorganization (i.e., interpreting adversity to find benefit or make meaning of the loss); taking pride in developing new skills necessitated by the loss, and in supporting and helping others; readjusted role priorities; and increased social involvements. Their advice to new widowers reflected these strategies—stressing staying active, involved in interests, maintaining companions, and relying on faith.

The research on outcome has varied considerably. Some research has indicated that men generally fare better on measures of mortality and physical and psychological morbidity (Carey, 1979; Gilbar & Dagan, 1995; Lopata, 1973; Parkes, 1970; Parkes & Brown, 1972), while other research has suggested women fare better (Bowling & Windsor, 1995; Cumming & Henry, 1961; Sanders, 1989; Stillion, 1985; Stroebe, 1994).

Loss of a Child

Many of these same differences were found in the loss of a child. Studies have shown that mothers tended to experience a more intense level of grief or distress than fathers (Carroll & Shaefer, 1994; Conway &

Feeney, 1997; deVries, Dalla Lana, & Falek, 1994; Schwab, 1990, 1996). Similar patterns were observed in perinatal loss (Boch Hughes & Page-Lieberman, 1989; Kavanaugh, 1997) though Goldbach, Dunn, Toedter, and Lasker (1991) found that these patterns tended to converge over time. In Kavanaugh's (1997) study, mothers expressed a greater need to talk about the loss than fathers. Both Boch Hughes and Page-Lieberman (1989) and Conway and Feeney (1997) speculated on the greater level of attachment that mothers invested in the child.

Strategies for dealing with the loss also differed. Mothers were more likely to seek outside support and ventilate feelings (Conway & Feeney, 1997; Kavanaugh, 1997). Fathers were less likely to express affect (Carroll & Shaefer, 1994) and felt a need to continue to provide for and protect their families (deVries et al., 1994). Conway and Feeney (1997) found that women were inclined to use strategies that were more emotion focused and support seeking. And they noted that seeking support from others might not always be effective since the quality of support offered may vary (see also Morgan, 1989). Men tended to use more problem-focused strategies. Men also controlled affective expression and intellectualized grief (Lang & Gottlieb, 1993). Where they did show affect, it was generally in anger or aggression (Lang & Gottlieb, 1993).

Unsurprisingly, these differences were evident as well in the loss of an adult child or grandchild. Goodman, Black, and Rubinstein (1996), in their sample of older men who had lost an adult child, found that most of their sample tended to intellectualize the loss. Diversion in work and humor also served as strategies. The authors suggested that some of the attributes of men—often negatively viewed by clinicians—such as individualism and self-sufficiency seem to facilitate their grieving. Fry (1997), too, found differences in grandparents who had lost a child. Grandfathers tended to offer practical assistance, while grandmothers were more likely to focus on spiritual tasks, such as helping their adult children find meaning in their loss or lives. Grandmothers also sought more affective outlets, while grandfathers found outlets in active ways.

Naturally, these differences in the experience, expression, and adaptation to grief can affect marital relationships. For example, a number of studies have considered the effect of the death of a child on sexual relationships and marital intimacy. Although the range of sexual expression varied extensively, many bereaved parents indicated that there was a breakdown or decline in sexual relationships (Gottlieb, Lang, & Amsel, 1996; Peppers & Knapp, 1980; Rosenblatt, 1997). Some of the reasons for this breakdown included a lack of energy or interest, and depression in the aftermath of the loss. But there were other reasons as well. For many, the very act of intercourse was problematic—it meant inappropriate pleasure, evoked memories of the deceased child, or created anxiety over the prospect of a new child. In other cases, sexual intimacy was welcomed for the emotional comfort it offered, for the affirmation of life it provided, or for the creation of a new child. These meanings were not necessarily shared with the partner in the relationship. One partner may seek intimacy for support, while the other partner sees it as inappropriate. Gottlieb et al. (1996), for example, found that men sought to express intimacy through sexual intercourse with their wives, but their wives did not necessarily interpret that as a need for emotional release and support.

This illustrates the larger problem. Without effective communication and information about the ways that individuals grieve, relationships can suffer. Men may experience concern and helplessness in dealing with their wives' grief. Women may feel a similar sense of bewilderment and helplessness as they seek to understand their husbands' grief or lack of overt affect. More dangerously, they can interpret their mate's response as a lack of love for the child.

Counselors and other caregivers can assist this process by helping couples explore the differences and similarities in their responses, and they can help couples understand that these differences are based on a wide variety of factors. Such differences do not denote that one loved the deceased any more or less. In this exploration, all aspects of the relationships, including sexual expression and the meanings attached to it, as well as other modes of communication, need to be considered. Counselors should also counter the destructive myths that the death of a child greatly increases the risk of divorce, almost making it inevitable. This commonly held assumption is not based upon evidence (Schwab, 1998). Although a child's death certainly may strain a marital relationship, divorce seems more related to prior difficulties. In such cases, the death of a child may simply remove a motivation or energy for working on resolution or staying together. In fact, one of the advantages of counseling is that it can facilitate communication and understanding that actually may strengthen the relationship.

Parental Loss

Most studies of children's reactions to the loss of a parent do not focus upon gender; however, Worden (1996) did find that girls, regardless of age, exhibited more anxiety and somatic symptoms than boys. Girls also seemed to idealize the deceased parent more and indicated an increased sensitivity to changes in the family following a parent's death. Boys were more likely to self-report that their conduct was worse, suggesting that some of their grief was manifested in acting out behaviors. The treatment of grievers also differed by gender of the child. Boys were more frequently admonished to be strong, while girls were more able to share feelings with other family members.

Such differences were also found in adult children who had experienced the loss of a father. Two studies (Moss, Resch, & Moss, 1997; Moss, Rubinstein, & Moss, 1997) found middle-aged sons experienced less grief and fewer somatic symptoms. Sons' expressions of grief tended to be active, cognitive, and private.

Gay Men and Lesbians

Comparatively, little research has been done on the grieving patterns of gay men or lesbians and almost none on bisexual and transgendered individuals (deVries, 2009). Some research has noted that because of societal constraints, significant losses of gay men and lesbians are often disenfranchised, limiting social support for gay grievers (see, for example, Doka, 1987, 1989a; Kelly, 1977; Kimmel, 1978; Murphy & Perry, 1988).

Much of the research has been done in the context of AIDS-related losses. These studies are problematic in that losses tend to be multiple, stigmatized, and developmentally unexpected. In addition, surviving partners may themselves be HIV infected. These studies did find high degrees of stress, including depression, anxiety, and guilt (Cherney & Verhey, 1996; Martin, 1988; Martin & Dean, 1993a, 1993b; Viney, Henry, Walker, & Crooks, 1992). They also did find increased use of sedatives as well as alcohol and recreational drugs (Cherney & Verhey, 1996; Martin, 1988; Martin & Dean, 1993a). However, Folkman (2001), in a study of gay men who were caregivers for their partners, found that strategies built upon active problem-focused coping and positive reappraisal (reframing the caregiving experience by stressing the positive aspects of caregiving) were associated with more positive outcomes. This complements research by Nolen-Hoeksema, McBride, and Larson (1997) that found that males who engaged in more rumination following the death of a partner experienced more psychological distress at both 1 and 12 months. Spiritual coping strategies had a more mixed result, perhaps reflecting the negative connotations that many faiths place on homosexuality. In reviewing research, deVries (2009) noted that many gay, lesbian, bisexual, and transgendered individuals had found that a lifetime of adversity had given them a sense of strength and competence in handling crises. Nonetheless, they did face difficulties. Often they were more likely to be single and childless, limiting caregiving networks, and since same-sex relationships are not recognized in many states, many were overrepresented among the medically uninsured.

Clearly, there is a need for studies of the patterns of grieving among gay and lesbian populations. While one would not necessarily expect that proportions of instrumental, intuitive, or dissonant grievers would differ among homosexual or heterosexual men and women, further research would be useful to assist homosexual grievers and to understand the varied factors that influence the assumption of a given pattern.

Research Summary

These results hardly should be surprising. The very nature of relationships, that is, the meaning a relationship has to a person and the complementary roles that people share within relationships, differs by gender. As the research indicated, time, energy, and meaning invested in relationships can very well be different for a mother or wife than for a father or husband. Silverman (1988), for example, found that widowhood in women created a crisis of identity, since they were more invested in the spousal relationship than men. It should be recognized, however, that Silverman's sample was of a content that was unlikely to have an independent career. The role of wife was at the core of their identity. Both Schwab (1996) and Bohannon (1990), for example, found lower levels of grief in fathers who had experienced the death of a child as compared to their wives. Similarly, the loss of a parent seemed to have more effect on middle-aged daughters than sons, reflecting in part, the authors believed, less of an emotional attachment to the relationship (Moss, Resch, & Moss, 1997; Moss, Rubinstein, & Moss, 1997). This certainly reflects traditional gender roles that see women as more invested in familial relationships.

In addition, every society has norms that proscribe not only behavior but feelings as well. Hochschild (1979) notes that these "feeling rules" dictate what feelings ought to be expressed in each situation. Naturally, these feeling rules can differ by gender. Since a subset of the feeling rules relates to expressions of grieving, it is understandable that research has revealed some gender differences in patterns of grief. For example, a number of studies have found that, apart from anger and guilt, men had a difficult time expressing affect (Glick et al., 1974; Goldbach et al., 1991; Lang & Gottlieb, 1993; Schwab, 1990). Conventional views of the effect of gender on the experience and expression of anger have recently been challenged (Sharkin, 1993). Deffenbacher et al. (1996) concluded "men and women are angered by similar things and to similar degrees, express themselves in similar ways, and suffer similar consequences" (p.

146). Similarly, studies support the fact—and belief—that women's grief is expressed more intensely and affectively (Bohannon, 1991; Carroll & Shaefer, 1994; Douglas, 1990; Versalle & McDowell, 2004).

Moreover, these feeling rules extend to the sympathy one expects (Clark, 1987). As Clark (1987) notes, sympathy is guided not only by circumstances but by other elements of one's biography, such as gender. This serves to create Cook's (1988) double bind. Grieving males are given little support, but they are expected to support others. These differences in experience and expression of grief are well documented in the literature that has surveyed gender differences. These differences have been found over a wide array of losses.

Researchers have also shown that men and women choose different strategies for adapting. For instance, men used self-help groups less often than women (Osterweiss, Solomon, & Green, 1984). Rando (1986) suggested one possible reason for this reluctance to attend support groups. Following the loss of a child, men saw themselves as needing to be providers, protectors, and problem solvers, making it difficult for them to accept and receive help. In addition, other studies have found men to be more private, intellectual, and introspective in the way they grieve (Cook, 1988; Hogan & Balk, 1990; Lang & Gottlieb, 1993; Moss, Resch, & Moss, 1997; Moss, Rubenstein, & Moss, 1997; Alston & Alston, 2009). And Bonanno's (1997) work suggests that such strategies may be as effective, if not more effective, than emotional expression and ventilation.

Men also appear to choose activity as a way of adapting to unpleasant feelings. For example, Glick et al. (1974) reported that widowers in their study expressed a concern with being "realistic" (i.e., focusing on solving the immediate problems of loss). They also reported that men were more likely to experience social recovery earlier, often quickly returning to work. Returning to work may be a useful coping strategy, since it allows people to become distracted from their grief (Osterweiss et al., 1984).

There may be other differences in adaptive strategies as well. Cook (1988) noted a number of cognitive strategies used by the men in her study, such as diversion and reflection. Employing activity and cognitive strategies to adapt to loss can be very effective. Powers and Wampold (1994) emphasized the critical role that cognitive and behavioral responses have in successfully adapting to loss.

Such differences have long been recognized in folk wisdom and custom. The Russian "Old Believer's" burial custom, in which men make the caskets and tell stories while women weep and wail, is echoed in many cultures.

Other methods of adaptations to loss may not be as effective. Studies of gay men responding to the loss of lovers and friends in the AIDS epidemic reaffirm the observations of some counselors (Staudacher, 1991) that males may be more inclined to use substances such as drugs or alcohol to mitigate the grieving process. These studies have shown that common patterns among gay men included both the use of sedatives and recreational drugs (Martin, 1988; Martin & Dean, 1993a). An investigation of men on skid row revealed that many of them had turned to alcohol following the deaths of their wives (Hughes & Fleming, 1991).

It is important to recognize that the type of loss or other variables, such as social class, may mitigate many of the gender differences cited thus far. Furthermore, there is most likely an interaction between gender differences in bereavement and age. Differences seem less apparent in older cohorts. For example, Feinson (1986) found that any gender differences in her study seemed to disappear when social and demographic variables were factored. Another study, exploring the reactions of older persons to spousal loss, found gender was unrelated to measures of adjustment and depression (Futterman, Gallagher, Thompson, Lovett, & Gilewski, 1990). In fact, the majority of studies reporting differences involved younger samples. This is not surprising, given the general agreement that both sexes, as they age, move toward androgyny (Huyck, 1990; Neugarten & Gutmann, 1968).

☐ Accounting for the Difference: Gender Role Socialization as a Shaping Agent

What accounts then for these differences in patterns of grief? As repeatedly noted, there is no one factor but certainly research has shown that what we label an instrumental pattern of grief is more typical of men than women. Most likely, these differences are due, in large part, to gender role socialization. However, prior to exploring how socialization in a gender role influences the adaptation of a grieving pattern, it is critical to acknowledge two points: gender roles are not static and there are differences within gender role socialization.

First, even within a culture, gender roles are not static. The content of a role is always dynamic, changing over time. What constitutes acceptable male or female behavior changes from one cohort or generation to another. For example, Rotundo (1993) historically reviews American definitions of the male role and notes both continuities and changes in male identity over the past 200 years. In studying the 20th-century male culture, Rotundo describes how mastery of one's emotions and enthusiasm was seen as a key developmental issue that separated boys from men. Boys could not control their enthusiasm; men had to teach and model self-restraint. Among both men and boys, emotional mastery and stiff-lipped courage were seen as virtues.

However, early in the 19th century, men often shared intimate, caring relationships with other men. Since men were expected to invest much time in public and social affairs, relationships between men were perceived as natural and productive. This began to change later in that century for three reasons. With industrialization, the work role becomes more fundamental to one's identity. There were limited opportunities to bond with other men outside of work. Second, the concurrent rise of individualism also isolated men from their peers. As men became older, established in their work and marriage, there was little time for sharing feelings and thoughts with other men. Congregating with other males began to be considered a mark of a boy, not a man. Finally, homophobia reared its unlovely head. Since gay men had been labeled as "unmanly," it was difficult to acknowledge feelings for other men that would allow one to build supportive connections with one another. By the 20th century, contemporary visions of the male role had taken root, emphasizing the male as a rugged individual.

Recently, these conceptions of maleness have been challenged. Bly (1990), for example, offers a poetic vision of what the male role can be. Drawing from ancient myths, he envisions a male role that encompasses a vigorous sense of masculinity with an ability to be emotionally rooted. Ironically, Bly sees the male as first having to acknowledge that lost fathers, dreams, and morality cause significant grief. Similarly, Keen (1991) also sees men forging an identity out of a struggle with grief and guilt, burdened by the demand of work and performance. To Keen, the essence of men is that they are spiritual warriors attempting to create meaning in their lives. Their quest is to fashion a new sense of male identity that allows for both emotionality and communality in some yet undefined but distinctly male way. Should the fledgling male movement succeed in redefining masculinity, it may likely change patterns of grieving as well.

Second, as mentioned previously, there are differences within gender role socialization even within a culture at any given time. For example, many of the more androgynous perspectives on socializing children into gender roles are not universally shared among each social class or ethnic group within American society. Whereas many middle-class families may socialize both boys and girls to more diffusely defined gender roles—allowing more opportunities for individual preferences in toys, play, sports, or other activities, and respecting, even encouraging sensitivity in boys—other cultural groupings, especially in lower socioeconomic groups or among varied cultural groups, may emphasize more traditional definitions of the male and female role.

Even within the larger culture, messages about appropriate roles may be both subtle and ambiguous. For example, even in groups that emphasize more androgynous rather than rigid role definitions, it is still more acceptable for girls to emulate boys' behaviors than visa versa. Just compare the connotations of the words *tomboy* and *sissy*.

In addition, gender role socialization is supported throughout the culture—in cartoons, advertisements, legends, stories, symbols, and, of course, throughout the media. Often these messages are subliminal—the token tomboy who plays on a team of boys. A *Cathy* cartoon illustrates that subtlety: Cathy, a liberated single woman is seen buying a toy for a friend's child. She is annoyed by a saleswoman's inquiry on gender and asks for a unisex toy. The saleswoman suggests dinosaurs, and as Cathy wryly comments that we have to go into our prehistory to find such a toy, the saleswoman returns with two dinosaurs—one with a makeup kit, the other with weapons. Folak and Abel (2004) stress the even national symbols such as Lady Liberty and Uncle Sam reflect these stereotypes. In their content analysis of political cartoons following the 9/11 terrorist attacks, Lady Liberty was portrayed as crying for the victims of the attack while an Uncle Sam vowed vengeance. Davies (1992) reminds that war stories from the *Epic of Gilgamesh* to war memorials assert it is the duty of males to leave the comfort of home and family to fight for honor and the community in the camaraderie of other males.

While gender role socialization, then, is neither uniform nor static, it does have broad effects. Two are most evident. Gender role socialization both frames the experience of grief and plays a significant role in the shaping of emotion.

Gender Role Socialization Frames the Experience of Grief

Earlier in this chapter, the fact that in any given society gender role rules influence the way each gender relates to varied social roles was explored, affecting the meaning they give to different attachments. For example, Silverman (1986), in her studies on widows, points out that for many males the role of husband is critical. Yet, Silverman reminds us that it is not tied to his identity as strongly as that of a wife is to a woman. Similarly, Thompson (1995) argues that men are socialized to live their lives in the "public sphere," balancing work, familial, and other community roles, while many women traditionally live life in a more private sphere, centering on family. The implication of both of these ideas is that women may be more invested in and attached to family roles. Thus, when a loss occurs it has multiple impact. A woman may lose a more central role, more critical to her identity than that of a man. In addition, there may be less opportunity for diversion in other roles or for reinvesting in such roles.

Naturally, this point should not be overstressed. Individuals' investments in roles, and the meanings that these relationships have, are affected by a number of variables, of which gender is only one. And certainly the definition of men's and women's roles, especially as they relate to work and family, continue to change.

The Influence of Gender Role on the Socialization of Emotion

In Chapter 3, the role of the family as a shaping agent was emphasized. This means that families socialize children into the need and ways to regulate emotions. Naturally, a family's definition of gender roles can very much affect this socialization of emotion.

In the past decade, there has been increasing attention to what has been labeled the "new psychology of men" (Cochran, 2006; Englar-Carlson, 2006; Levant, 2008; Levant & Richmond, 2007; Pollack, 1998; Robertson & Shepard, 2008; Smith, Tran, & Thompson, 2008). This perspective emphasizes that boys at young ages are socialized to a code of masculinity that emphasizes strength and stoicism, adventure seeking, interpersonal dominance and status seeking, and emotional restraint. This socially constructed ideology of masculinity often creates gender role conflicts for men who cannot live up to these images. This masculine ideology can result in a variety of difficulties including neglect of mental and physical health, detached partnering and parenting, substance abuse, reluctance to seek help including counseling, alexithyma, substance abuse, homophobia, and violent and aggressive behavior (Englar-Carlson, 2006; Levant, 2008).

These psychological insights on gender role socialization and images of masculinity are important in understanding the ways that gender role socialization can influence grief and in suggesting strategies for helping male clients (discussed in later chapters). Yet, a few cautionary statements are critical. First, families vary in the ways such masculine ideologies are supported. In some families, values such as stoicism, self-reliance, solitude, and an emphasis on rationality might be modeled or even sexual stereotypes ("big boys don't cry") fostered. However, in other families, children are taught to disclose their innermost thoughts, seek solace in community, and value their feelings as the guide to behavior. Yet, it should be acknowledged that despite changing attitudes and standards many adults continue to have traditional and stereotyped conceptions of sex roles and behave accordingly.

Second, the dominant masculine ideology described by many adherents of this approach (Cochran, 2006; Englar-Carlson, 2006; Levant, 2008; Levant & Richmond, 2007; Nutt, 2007; Pollack, 1998; Robertson & Shepard, 2008; Smith et al., 2008) often ignores or downplays some of the positive masculine values that are part of the dominant perspective of masculinity. Boys also are taught the value of being a team player, the importance of self-sacrifice ("take one for the team"), the importance of courage, the need to stand up for one's beliefs, and the duty to protect the vulnerable especially within the circle of friends and family. In addition, while some have seen male bonding as more superficial or "bonding without intimacy" (Englar-Carlson, 2006), others have recognized and acknowledged the "covert intimacy" that men often exhibit (Kiselica, Englar-Carlson, Horne, & Fisher, 2008). Here intimacy and caring are shared in many ways including protecting and teaching. In addition, humor and storytelling can be ways to compliment, reaffirm ties, and share the important role that another has in one's life.

These gender roles are usually acquired during a child's preschool years. That is, the child adopts socially defined behaviors and attitudes associated with being a male or a female. For example, even boys and girls as young as 3 years old show differences in the ways they handle everyday pain. At that young age, girls are more likely to show distress and seek out adult comfort than boys (Fearon, McGrath, & Achat, 1996). Beginning with the games of childhood, boys and girls develop different (although complementary) social skills. While girls are learning to interact one-on-one or in small groups, to work cooperatively, and to have empathy for others, boys are learning to compete with one another. They practice leading, following, and working with others on a team toward some common goal—usually defeating another team (Lever, 1976).

Experience and childrearing practices retain their eminence in shaping sex roles and emotional behaviors. In particular, the father plays a critical role in sex role development during the preschool years. The father's degree of masculinity seems to promote traditional sex roles not only in sons, but in daughters as well (Hetherington, Cox, & Cox, 1978). That the father's masculinity (and not necessarily mother's femininity) is associated with a girl's sex role development suggests that girls acquire sex roles through a process of reciprocal role learning (Lamb & Urberg, 1978). In other words, girls learn how to behave as females by complementing their father's masculinity—the more traditionally masculine dad is, the more traditionally feminine his daughter will be. Interestingly, the opposite is not true for boys. That is, boys tend to identify with and imitate their fathers' behavior, and those boys whose mothers are very feminine do not necessarily behave in a more masculine way.

As adults, males are attracted to sports that emphasize a competitive role. Their friendships usually center on shared activities. Men, as well as boys, view their relationships with others, particularly males, in terms of hierarchy (Gilligan, 1982).

Often, there is a tendency among males to de-emphasize emotionality, especially the more tender emotions (e.g., crying, nurturing). Socialization into the male role means learning to control one's emotions. As a result, men tend to learn active and problem-focused solutions of coping with stress. In addition, they tend to value self-reliance. Solving one's problems and facing one's difficulties alone have long been defined as hallmarks of manhood (Gray, 1992).

Women's experiences are somewhat different. From an early age, girls at play tend to be more cooperative and to have consideration and empathy for others (Lever, 1976). They are also taught to share confidences and draw support from one another. Emotional expressiveness is not repressed; in fact, females tend to learn more emotion-focused ways of coping (Barnett, Biener, & Baruch, 1987). Nothing in the female role eschews the support or nurturance of others. To the contrary, the ability to offer and accept such nurturance is a critical mark of the woman's role. As a consequence, because females are socialized to be more attuned to emotions, they may learn to pay more attention to their own emotional states as well as others' emotional states.

Yet Not Deterministic

Yet this should not be perceived in a deterministic way. Socialization experiences differ from individual to individual. And other factors such as personality, culture, or other experiences can affect the grieving pattern that an individual adopts.

For example, in certain cultures, the expression of affect is supported strongly for both men and women, while in others affect is discouraged for both. In the former culture one would likely find more intuitive grievers between both genders, while in the latter instrumental patterns may be more evident.

Patterns of grief are shaped by all of the powerful cultural forces of socialization, with the immediate family playing a most important part. Sons of instrumental grievers will, themselves, most likely model their fathers, while their sisters, based on the principle of reciprocal role learning, adopt the more intuitive response to bereavement. In families where the father is an intuitive griever, the sons will likely follow suit, while daughters learn to grieve in instrumental fashion.

There may be other factors, too, in the socialization experience. For example, comparable socialization experiences can lead certain women to grieve in a more instrumental way. Perhaps, women who are raised with strongly competitive values or given early caregiving responsibilities such as raising younger siblings may develop a more instrumental pattern for coping with loss. And boys growing up in families where affective expression is encouraged, even modeled, especially by their fathers, can show a more intuitive pattern.

Since gender role socialization is but one factor in an array of influences that delineate a grieving pattern, any combination of factors can influence whether a male or female moves toward the intuitive or instrumental end of the continuum. Thus, certain socialization experiences, cultures, or even personality traits can lead to a woman becoming an instrumental griever or a man becoming more intuitive in pattern.

This may help explain dissonant grieving patterns as well. Given the dominant images of the male role, males who do experience grief in a more intuitive way may feel constrained to express their grief or adapt to it in such a fashion that they will not be perceived as less manly or feel they are not fulfilling their own gender role expectations to care for others. It is in dissonant grievers that such gender role expectations truly can be said to contain and to constrain the expression of grief.

☐ Conclusion

It is critical, however, not to overstate the effect of gender role socialization on the grieving process. This is especially true since gender differences are often overexaggerated. Maccoby and Jacklin's (1974) landmark review of more than 2,000 studies found only a few characteristics in which girls and boys differed significantly. Highly touted cognitive differences between the sexes—girls' superior verbal ability, boys' better spatial and mathematical aptitudes—do not appear until near puberty and are very small indeed. Personality differences are few also. Girls generally cooperate more with their parents and their peers, and show greater concern for and identification with others' feelings. Yet some girls love rough play and are very competitive and impassive, while some boys hate roughhousing and are very sensitive to the feelings of others. But even by age 5, boys and girls still show an equal interest in babies and a willingness to help care for infants (Berman, 1980).

Thus, we must be careful not to overemphasize differences between the genders. Those differences that do exist are statistically small and convincing for large groups of men and women but are not as valid for individuals. For gender, even though a significant factor influencing the patterns by which men and women grieve, it is but one factor. Stated differently, gender *influences* patterns of grief, but gender does not *determine* patterns of grief.

CHAPTER

Culture as a Shaping Agent

The previous chapter considered some of the reasons why gender influences grieving patterns. A key factor or concern was the effect of gender role socialization. This naturally brings into focus the role of culture, since cultural expectations frame gender roles, that is, in every culture there are different expectations about how men and women will both feel and behave.

Gender role norms are but one way that a culture influences grief and the patterns by which grief is experienced and expressed. Culture affects other aspects of the grieving process as well. At a very fundamental level, culture influences the process of attachment. Cultural norms define kinship and regulate social relationships. Culturally based experiences even frame expectations for survival, affecting investment and attachments. Kastenbaum (1971), for example, hypothesizes that in cultures with high rates of child mortality, parental attachment, and even social valuation of children, may be limited until the child reaches puberty and the seeming likelihood of survival. Culture also defines appropriate expressions of grief, ritual practices, and subsequent mourning behavior.

This chapter explores the impact of culture on grief. It begins by first defining culture and then traces its many influences on grief and the grieving process. For culture, too, is a major shaping agent influencing the ways men and women grieve.

☐ The Nature of Culture

Culture is best defined as a way of life. It encompasses both material and nonmaterial aspects of life. Material aspects of a culture refer to all the visible artifacts—clothes, food, and technology—all the items used within the culture. Although the material aspects of a culture are most visible, it is the nonmaterial aspects that are most critical. These refer to beliefs, norms, and values—the ways of thinking, believing, behaving, and relating that truly define the culture. Berger and Luckmann (1966), for example, state that even reality is socially constructed. By that, they mean that culture determines the ways one organizes the world. For example, in cultures such as the United States, kinship is determined bilineally. In other cultures it may be patrilineal or matrilineal. In a patrilineal society, for instance, the sister of one's mother may not be defined as kin. But all aspects of reality are culturally determined from the ways one understands diseases to how one views the transcendental. And each culture will define its reality differently.

Cultures can be analyzed in several ways. One can distinguish between cultural universals, aspects of the culture that are widely shared; cultural alternates, or choices within a culture; and cultural specialties, or aspects of a culture that are shared by a more limited group. In complex cultures, although there may be some cultural universals, there are often large arrays of specialties and alternates. For example, in the U.S. culture, generally, rules of defining kinship, laws, and certain values such as a shared belief in the worth of education are illustrations of cultural universals. The wide ranges of transportation options or foods are examples of cultural alternates. In fact, some foods that still exist primarily within an ethnic group might be best defined as specialties. One illustration might be that 30 years ago Mexican foods were primarily shared only within that ethnic group or within the Southwest region. Now it has become a widely accepted alternative, readily available in malls, restaurants, and supermarkets. Other examples of specialties would be professional jargon, skills, or beliefs shared only by a small group.

One might also distinguish subcultures or cocultures, which are groups within the larger culture that share many of the universals but have their own mix of cultural alternates and specialties. Although one may often think of ethnic groups as cocultures or subcultures, cultures can also be delineated by other common factors such as class, age, religion, or shared behaviors and lifestyles. An illustration of the latter would be the presence in many urban areas of a robust gay subculture.

Persons enter a culture in two ways. Some may assimilate into a culture, gradually learning its ways. But most commonly, one is born into a culture. Agents of socialization, such as families or schools, socialize individuals into a way of life that becomes the only reality that person knows. The danger, of course, is the possibility that the way of life can become *the* way of life. Such ethnocentrism may be expressed as a perplexity that other cultures may do things differently or even a belief that one's own culture is superior, that other ways of viewing or organizing reality are foolish or wrong.

But cultures are not static. Early theorists of social and cultural change tended to view these patterns in sweeping, evolutionary ways. For example, both Hegel (1990) and Marx (1993) saw cultural change as the inevitable result of conflicts arising from contrasting ideas or interests. Sorokin (1937–1941) viewed cultural change more as an everlasting pendulum, swinging over centuries from sensate cultures that emphasized sense experience as an ultimate reality to ideational cultures that see ideas or beliefs as the core of reality. The pendulum shifts because as a culture follows the inevitable path from one pole to the other, it encompasses less of reality. Sorokin might wonder whether the current revival of interest in spirituality may be the death throes of a sensate culture now reaching a crisis point prior to beginning a cultural shift.

However, whether these grand theories account for cultural change, other factors generally have a significant role in changing culture. And as culture changes, the experiences and expressions of grief and death are modified as well.

Industrialization, for instance, has had a significant role in changing the experience of death and grief by changing the very demographics of death. No longer were women and children the most vulnerable populations; now the aged were. This may, as will be explored, influence the experience of attachment and grief. Industrialization affected attachment in other ways as well: It often separated men from the home; child-rearing, once shared, now became more the province of women; and boys no longer worked side by side with their fathers, learning both a trade as well as how to be a man.

Other changes in attachment patterns were evident as well. The communal or civic ties, necessary in an agrarian economy, lessened. Families and individuals now shared stronger ties within the family but looser ties outside. In short, people had attachments but within a small group. Bureaucratization and professionalization removed the care of the dying and the dead from the home to professional caregivers. Death became removed from the everyday experience. Increasing cultural diversity throughout the Western world meant that meanings accorded to death were no longer universally shared.

Such changes tend to breed reactions. The death studies movement has in many ways attempted to "deprofessionalize" death. Hospice, for example, has encouraged families to allow the dying to die at home rather than in institutions. The rise of the self-help movement has attempted to recreate a sense of community among persons who struggle with common issues. The men's movement has sought to redefine masculinity; yet there is a paradox. These very movements have created new sets of professionals and new norms about ways that individuals should act, die, and grieve.

Thus, culture frames the experience of grief—from who survives, to patterns of attachments, to the norms for expressing grief and mourning. Yet these patterns are not static. They, too, shift as individuals within a culture face new experiences, new ideas or technologies, or new problems.

☐ Cultures and Grief: Attachment

Implied throughout the earlier section is the notion that cultural experiences and norms affect the experience of grief. This occurs on a very basic level as cultures frame the very nature of attachment. It does this in a number of ways.

First, it may be that, from an evolutionary aspect, grief is an aspect of attachment. Archer (2001), building on Bowlby (1980), observes that grief is common not only in humans but also in other social animals. Since grief is dehabilitating, Archer and Bowlby wondered how it might arise as an aspect of natural selection—what value would it have? Their answer is in order for relationships to persist, a survival necessity, bonds must exist when the other is absent.

Second, as stated earlier, culture defines patterns of kinships and relationships. Societies may also vary in their definition of critical familial roles. For example, in many Christian religions, when a child is baptized (often near birth), the child's parents may choose godparents or sponsors who promise to take a role in assisting the child in fulfilling religious obligations and supporting the child in his or her faith journey. In many cultures, it is simply an honorary role that has little but ritual significance. But in other cultures, such as many Latino or traditional Italian cultures, the godparents are expected to play a significant role in the child's development, especially should a child be separated from a parent. A proverb expresses these expectations as well: "Life is so tough that a child needs two sets of parents." The point is that in such a society, these extra familial attachments can become exceedingly strong.

Similarly, in many subgroups there may exist other ties that bespeak a strong sense of attachment even in the absence of formal kinship. For instance, in some cultures men may be allowed or even expected to have mistresses. In the United States, among gay subcultures, the relationship of lovers or life partners is acknowledged. In short, every culture defines significant relationships, both within and outside kinship lines. These relationships help regulate patterns of attachment and, therefore, influence grief.

Third, not only does a culture define relationships, its norms define the quality and nature of relationships. This occurs on many levels. As mentioned earlier, culture has expectations about survival that may frame attachments. For example, Rosenblatt (1993a) notes that many lower income Brazilian mothers see the death of a child as inevitable. Attachments become limited then, until a child shows promise of long-term survival.

Beyond expectations of survival, culture influences attachment in other ways. Cultural norms define the very meaning of relationships. In some cultures, a wife may be defined as little more than chattel or property, her role being to serve her husband. But in other societies, the norms of the marital relationship may be more companionate. In such times, the death of a spouse has greater meaning, since one has not only experienced the loss of whatever functional role the spouse provided but the loss of a friend and lover as well. Each culture, then, defines the content of roles, affecting the meaning that people experience within the loss.

In addition to the meaning of the relationship, cultural norms influence attachment in other, subtler ways. For example, cultural norms define the amount of investment one places in varied attachments, therefore influencing the experience of grief. Parkes (1996b) provides a useful illustration: In traditional Malaysian society, children are reared within a communal setting. Many "mothers" or parental figures will rear children who are raised in this long-house culture. The loss of a parent then, Parkes suggests, is less traumatic than in a society in which a child is raised by a single set of parents. Parkes's illustration reminds us of the variety of cultural contexts that influence attachment. For example, in many Western cultures, life is organized around narrowly defined families or small intimate networks. This means that many people are connected to a small network to which they forge strong attachments. In other cultures, the organization of social life is more communal. Here, individuals have a larger number of attachments but these attachments seem less intense. Blauner (1968) notes that such forms of organization are very functional in societies where the death rate is high and unpredictable.

Thompson's (1995) work also explores the ways that culture influences attachment. Thompson emphasized that varied cultural norms divide life into tasks completed within the private sphere of the family from those done in the public sphere of the larger society. According to Thompson, traditional gender roles in Western societies meant that many men lived life in the public sphere, while most women experienced life more in the private sphere. This meant that, while family losses affected men, they had outlets and roles outside of the family. The experience, though, for women was different. The loss of a family member, such as a child, struck at the center of their world, creating a far different meaning for the loss. Thompson's observations are supported by the work of Silverman (1981, 1986), who found significant differences in the meaning of widowhood among older men and women. To men, the loss of a spouse meant the end of a significant role. But to women, the loss of a spouse and the assumption of the role of widow meant the end of the significant role of wife, causing a total reassessment of identity not often seen in men.

Naturally, as described earlier, cultures do change, and changing work patterns as well as reformulation of gender roles will lead to constant redefinitions of the meaning of a particular loss. Different generations, too, have distinct experiences that shape a particular cohort, giving rise to new ways of relating to mates, children, and other relationships, changing patterns of attachment as well as norms of expression (e.g., Rotundo, 1993).

Nonetheless, the basic point still can be made that cultures define the nature of the attachments, influencing, then, the very experience of grief.

☐ Culture and the Expression of Grief

Cultural norms not only influence the experience of grief but the expression of grief as well. Grief is a social construction (Averill & Nunley, 1993; Rosenblatt, 1993b), that is, that every society recognizes grief as a reaction to loss but also defines the privileges accorded to the bereaved as well as the obligations and restrictions placed on grieving individuals and families. Hochschild (1979) states that every society has "feeling rules" that govern the expression of emotions. Just as norms regulate behavior, feeling rules attempt to regulate the experience and expression of emotion.

A subset of these feeling rules may be called grieving rules (Doka, 1989a). Such rules define whom one may grieve, what one may grieve, how one's grief is expressed, and how long that grief may be manifested. Grief experienced outside of the parameters of these feeling rules may be disenfranchised, that is, others do not support the griever within the society.

These feeling rules determine not only what losses one can grieve, but also how an individual grieves. Cultures naturally differ in the expectation of how grief is expressed. In some cultures, intense affective displays are normative, even considered an expression of respect. Golden (2009) describes indigenous cultures where open, intense grief is considered food that sustains the deceased as he or she journeys to the afterlife.

But in other cultures, such emotional expression is avoided. For example, in Bali grief is muted because emotional agitation, it is believed, will impede the journey of the deceased, and prayers for the deceased will not be heard unless they are spoken calmly (Rosenblatt, 1993a). In other cultures, feelings are rarely expressed. For example, some cultures are known to be resistant to emotive expression. A common Midwestern joke tells of the taciturn Scandinavian farmer who loved his wife so much that he almost told her. Other cultures may even express grief in violent or angry ways (Rosenblatt, 1993a) or mandate other modes of expression. Rosenblatt (1997) cites for illustration one Pacific atoll. In that culture there is the Ifaluk concept of *lalomwieu*, which involves a grief response that encompasses sadness, loneliness, and obsessive thinking of the deceased. As Rosenblatt (1997) summarizes, "What emotions are felt, how they are expressed, and how they are understood are matters of culture" (p. 35).

Naturally, culture will influence the patterns of an individual's grief. In affectivity expressive cultures, intuitive patterns will be more common. In those that emphasize affective restraint, people are more likely to be socialized into more instrumental patterns. Golden (2009) observes that in many indigenous cultures, men are encouraged to grieve in active ways—singing, drumming, or dancing.

Culture too may create unique and sometimes gender-specific ways of offering support. In some cultures, men and women support grieving people of the same gender (Golden, 2009). In other cultures, unique ways may be developed to offer support in culturally attuned yet gender-appropriate ways. For example, for the Inupiats, a Native Alaskan people, each gender has specific roles during the funeral ritual. Since the group lives on the tundra, the ground is often frozen. Burial then takes days as hot water is continually boiled and poured on the ground to thaw it so it can be scraped. The men dig as adolescent boys bring in the continuing vats of hot water. The older men carve the memorial while the women cook and boil water. At night, the tribe feasts together, remembering and dancing. In one visit the men of the tribe decided to have a grief group in a smoke lodge—a place for purification. The men spoke of their losses—disembodied voices unseen through the smoke—offering a powerful illustration of melding old and new ways of therapeutic interaction (Doka, 1997). Rituals, too, may differ even within a society by factors such as gender. In Madagascar, for illustration, there are two huts for rituals or grieving: a "male house," where men meet to organize rituals for laying the body and a "house of tears," where women come together to wail and cry.

However, it is critical to remember that cultural influences are but one shaping agent. It is likely that other factors are equally important shapers of an individual's grieving pattern. Therefore, it is not unusual that any given individual's experience of grief will be at variance with culturally approved patterns of expression or adaptation. In such cases, dissonant varieties may be prevalent. And in such cases, individuals may pay a price as they experience this discord between their experience of grief and allowable expression. For example, Parkes (1996a) suggested that one result of affective control in Rwanda has been the outbursts of genocidal violence. Similarly, Parkes viewed the Navajos, where the deceased's name is never mentioned once they die as a form of cognitive suppression that often led to depression.

It also should be recognized that in many cultures, especially those that are diverse and complex, the grieving rules might mirror that complexity and diversity. For example, in countries like the United States, with many large cultural subgroups, individuals may be exposed to a range of grieving rules—some that allow affect and others that discourage it. These differences may even exist within bicultural families where children receive mixed messages on appropriate ways to grieve (Rosenblatt, 1993b). One of the authors comes from a Hispanic-Hungarian family. He has often commented that his Hispanic uncles would encourage tears—reminding him, even as a child, that they were signs of love. At the same time his Hungarian uncles would squeeze his shoulder reminding him "to be strong." Feeling rules, then, can be varied within a society or even a family.

In other cases, larger cultural forces that may affect subcultures differently may heavily influence expressions of grief. Anger, for example, is identified as a persistent issue in African American males—a result of persistent racism and discrimination (Franklin, 1998) that may emerge in both expressions of grief and types of support accepted (Rosenblatt & Wallace, 2005).

These grieving rules are not static but rather can change over time. Biddle and Walter (1998) note that among the grieving rules in England are two predominant patterns. Private grief is, they claim, the traditional perspective. Here the feeling rules require that people grieve in private, giving subtle hints that their grief is, in fact, deeply felt but that they are maintaining a stoical appearance to spare others. Others, in turn, are expected to admire the stoicism, especially since it comes at such a cost. Biddle and Walter suggested that this notion of private grief was the result of broad social changes such as the romantic movement that stressed the unique nature of relationships and the concept that each person's pain was unique and private. Walter (2008) suggests that this too was a natural development of the Enlightenment's emphasis on individuality that affirmed that each loss was singular. The other pattern, called "expressive grief," Biddle and Walter identified as a more recent transplant from the United States. Here, open emotional expression is valued. To Walter (2008), the women's movement was a significant factor, allowing more feminine notions of grief to be expressed within the public sphere. Perhaps the budding men's movement and the new psychology of men may have a similar impact on increasing affective expression in men. This change, it should be noted, is yet to be evidenced. Hayslip and Han (2009) in a review of the literature on cultural change find evidence that over time Americans now place greater emphasis on emotional control.

In some cases, too, the grieving rules may change throughout the course of grief. For example, in the United States emotional expression is encouraged early in the grieving period but not later. The result is that it is the instrumental griever who may experience disenfranchisement early in the loss, while the intuitive griever feels disenfranchised later in the loss when affective responses are less valued and accepted. This is evident in workplace policies. Most employers accord a period of time off for bereavement leave, generally 3 to 5 days. After this period of affective catharsis, employees are expected to quickly return to prior work patterns, compartmentalizing their grief. As time goes on, affective expression is less supported.

People who fail to follow grieving norms face community sanctions. For example, in one famous Australian case, Lindy Chamberlain claimed a dingo, or wild dog, attacked and dragged off her sleeping baby. The mother's absence of strong affect caused suspicion among police, especially since her husband responded in a more emotional manner. She was charged with and convicted of the child's murder; later, her conviction was overturned. The case still generates strong controversy in Australia and debates over the mother's actual guilt. The point of this case is simply that her failure to grieve in a prescribed manner was considered strong evidence of guilt. Similarly, someone who after the initial period continues to express affect may experience the withdrawal of support and criticism, especially at work, over the ways that person is grieving.

This raises another dimension of these grieving rules. These rules may differ by gender. Hence, in some societies women may be expected or allowed to show more emotion, while in others no such distinctions are made (Rosenblatt, Walsh, & Jackson, 1976). Those who are seen as conforming to these gender roles receive more support then those who are seen as nonconforming. The Lindy Chamberlain case was a good example of that. In the Outback of Australia, men are expected to be stoic. The fact that Michael Chamberlain was emotional and his wife was not highlighted suspicion. This shows a strange bias often evident in grief but not in other areas. In many aspects of life, at least in the United States and other Western cultures, gender-conforming behaviors are more supported in males. Compare, for example, the cultural meanings attached to terms like *tomboy* as contrasted with *sissy*. However, in grief, men who are nonconforming, at least in the initial period of grief, are accorded more freedom to be nonconforming. A man with more instrumental patterns may be seen as "stoic," while one with more intuitive patterns, at least in many social milieus, may be viewed as "sensitive." However, women with more instrumental patterns may be labeled as "cold."

Grieving rules vary, too, within a society. They may vary by ethnicity as different subcultures may have their own distinct ways that people express grief (Kalish & Reynolds, 1981). Naturally, as groups become more assimilated, these norms may lose their distinctiveness. One client, for illustration, who was Hispanic, spoke of his discomfort at the older generation who wailed at the casket of his grandmother. He was insightful enough to acknowledge that his older relatives were, in all probability, equally appalled by the absence of wailing in the younger generation.

Grieving rules vary not only by ethnicity but also by other factors such as age, gender, or class. (The issue of gender is considered in Chapter 7.) But Rosenblatt et al.'s (1976) research demonstrated that in many cultures grieving rules clearly varied by gender. In a study of 60 societies, they found that while close to 50% (32) demonstrated no differences between genders in crying in grief, the remainder (28) did allow more affective expressions in women.

Differences may also result from development and social class. Generally, societies permit the very young and sometimes the very old greater freedom in expression. As Rotundo (1993) notes, one mark of adulthood is the ability to conform to normative standards.

Social class, too, can create distinctions. In each social class, gender role norms as well as norms governing grief may encourage different responses to loss. For example, in some classes, anger, even violence, may be an acceptable expression of grief. In other classes the expectation may be that responses are more muted. Biddle and Walter (1998), for example, describe the upper-class English feeling rules that emphasize that the well-bred person gives no indication of inner emotion. Class may affect other forms of adaptation. Barrett (1998) in his work on African American funerals noted a strong class difference. Lower income African Americans were more likely to have highly emotional services, whereas middle-class African Americans preferred more formal and reserved rituals.

There may even be occupational subcultures that affirm their own grieving rules. For example, in the early and middle of the 20th century, many health professions viewed any public manifestation of grief over the death of a patient as "unprofessional." Other professions such as law enforcement may favor stoical responses. As Sue and Sue (2008) indicate, the culture of counseling tends to highly value affective expression in general but especially in grief. Rosenblatt (1993a, 1993b) notes the danger in a culturally diverse society when counselors project onto their clients their own social prescriptions of acceptable ways to grieve.

Cultures differ not only in feeling rules but also in other ways as well, such as rituals in and norms on appropriate adaptive and mourning behaviors. Every culture has distinct rituals by which death is acknowledged. In some cultures, these rituals may continue for a time after the loss, marking periods of mourning. For example, with Judaism, there are a series of rituals that take place both at points within a year after the loss as well as at other occasions. Other cultures may have rituals that recognize little beyond the disposition of the dead.

Mourning behaviors vary, too. In some cultures, people may mark mourning by wearing certain clothes for a period of time, perhaps even for life. It may be appropriate or inappropriate to speak of the deceased or to use the name again. In each society, rules and norms govern adaptation.

Naturally, individuals are socialized to these norms through a variety of socialization agents such as family, religious, and educational institutions. Nadeau's (1998) work reminds us that family often becomes the key agent in socializing individuals to the appropriate ways that grief may be experienced and expressed. It is families that employ cultural meanings as they attempt to make sense of loss and grief. And it is in the family that the experience, expression, and adaptation to grief are validated.

☐ Conclusion

This chapter emphasizes that one of the critical shaping agents in determining grieving patterns is provided by cultures. Although individuals within a culture will vary, cultural norms will strongly influence the experience of grief, as well as the patterns by which individuals express and adapt to grief. These standards may influence grieving in a number of ways. They make one pattern more dominant in a given culture, or they influence the fact that certain genders or classes or other groupings may be more inclined toward one pattern than another. But because culture is one shaping agent, individuals may find that their experience and expression of grief varies from cultural expectations. This may result in possible negative outcomes. When individuals find their experience and expression of grief varies from these cultural expectations, their grief may be disenfranchised, limiting social support and complicating grief.

SECTION

III

Implications and Interventions

Since counseling does have an affective bias, instrumental grievers may be reluctant to use counseling services or may find them unhelpful. This is unfortunate because counseling may be extremely helpful in assisting any grievers to surmount crises, particularly those who have limited support (Parkes, 1980). But, if counselors are to assist instrumental grievers effectively, they will have to examine their own biases, approaches, and interventions. Moreover, since many instrumental and dissonant grievers are men, counselors would be wise to utilize strategies and approaches that have been successfully adapted to male clients.

This section explores the counseling process, reviewing the ways that this process can work best with grieving individuals on each pole of the intuitive–instrumental continuum. Both Chapters 9 and 10 discuss counseling in a variety of contexts. Chapter 10 emphasizes the range of self-help strategies that can be used either independent of or complementary to the counseling process. Many of the interventive or self-help strategies commonly employed to assist grieving persons can work well with all types of grievers—perhaps for different reasons. The key is to assess, utilize, and validate each grieving individual's unique strengths. This point is reaffirmed in the summary conclusion of Chapter 11.

The message of this section then underlies the thesis of the book: It is not the style of grieving that is the problem—it is only a problem when counselors fail to recognize and to adapt their approaches to that style or to offer a range of appropriate services suitable to diverse groups of individuals experiencing grief.

9

CHAPTER

Adaptive Strategies
Implications for Counselors

Ever since the death of their child, Marie and Russ have gone to a counselor. While Marie continues to go, Russ stopped after three sessions. He believed that he was consistently "ganged up on" at these sessions. Whenever he started a conversation with "I think," or some other such phrase the counselor would say, "I am much more interested in what you feel." After a while, Russ ceased to say much, and then stopped going entirely.

Many instrumental grievers share Russ's experience. They often find grief counseling, with its strong bias toward affective ventilation, of limited value. In fact, many instrumental grievers may even perceive it as threatening, for their own approaches, strengths, and strategies are discounted. Also, interventive strategies may be designed such that rather than building on their strengths, they ignore them and concentrate instead on addressing what is perceived as their glaring weakness—the lack of strong affect.

This chapter's goal is to explore adaptive strategies. Since the intuitive pattern is widely recognized within the counseling community as

"normal," the focus is on adaptive strategies useful to instrumental grievers. It is hoped that counselors may find it useful to understand the repertoire of strategies different grievers will use. This can empower counselors
as they validate and explore the strategies of grievers who do seek help.
In addition, it can assist counselors as they aid other persons, such as
family members, in assessing and understanding the strategies that other
grievers may employ. This is critical because as stated earlier, differences
in patterns can cause conflict. Since many counselors themselves may
neither validate nor understand a pattern differing from their own, they
actually may exacerbate such conflicts by discounting cognitive and
behavioral approaches or become impatient with affective expression.
Many of these strategies may also serve as useful bridges, offering intervention opportunities for dissonant grievers that allow them to find safe
and compatible ways to express the grief that they do experience.

At a conference where the then-termed "masculine grief" was presented, one therapist noted during the question and answer period, "If I
understand your thoughts well enough, no one is going to get rich treating
masculine grievers (instrumental)." His observation had, in fact, great valid-
ity. Instrumental grievers are not likely to appear in therapeutic or self-help
groups, nor are they often apt to present themselves for individual counseling. In fact, when they do present themselves for counseling in either an
individual or group context, the counselor may suspect that they may not be
true instrumental grievers but rather dissonant grievers (see Sidebar 9.1).

As described earlier in Chapter 5, dissonant grievers tend to have
inconsistent patterns in the way they experience and express their grief.
Here it is the confines of social roles, expectations, or situational circumstances that may compel them to utilize ways of expressing and adapting
to their losses that are at variance with their experience. In one case, for
example, a 35-year-old woman was devastated by the loss of her husband, yet she felt she needed to be strong to provide for and protect her
children. Outwardly, she seemed like a classic instrumental griever—
stoic and rarely showing emotion. Her adaptive strategies were those of
an instrumental griever as well. She talked of her loss freely without
great emotion and devoted great energy to making her deceased husband's business a success. But she carried substantial pain and almost
every night quietly cried herself to sleep.

Randy's reaction to the loss of his adult daughter was similar. He was
a 52-year-old construction supervisor at the time of the death. At home,
he felt he needed to support and protect his wife. At work, he did not feel
it was safe or appropriate to express his great depth of feeling. Instead, he
cried in his car each day as he commuted to work. Randy exemplifies *gender role strain* found in many male dissonant grievers. Gender role strain

refers to the conflict between a male's reactions when it is inconsistent with the dominant masculine ideology (Englar-Carlson, 2006).

In both cases, counseling provided support and an outlet to express and ventilate affect. In addition, it allowed them to explore alternative strategies for expressing their grief. The cautionary note, then, is to carefully assess the grieving style and to be clear of reasons why a seemingly instrumental griever seeks counseling.

This does not mean to imply true instrumental grievers will never seek professional assistance. In fact, they often do for three reasons. First, they may simply seek validation. Since much of the self-help literature and popular wisdom about grieving emphasizes affective ventilation, many instrumental grievers may assume the lack of strong affect is problematic. The following case is illustrative.

> Marty was very close to his father; they even worked together. Throughout his father's illness, Marty took pride in the fact that he was a responsible and very present son. Often he would stay with his father at night, providing respite to his mother. During these nights, he would reminisce with his father, sharing with him his grateful memories of growing up with his dad. After his father's death, he still watches over his mother and keeps the house in good repair. He loves to share funny stories about his father with his own children. He describes feeling a sense of peace and presence when he does such active sharing. "At times," Marty notes, "I really feel my father is proud of how I'm helping Mom." But knowing his closeness to his dad, his wife is concerned that unless he cries he will have an "emotional blowout" later on. "She just feels I haven't grieved."

Marty's case is typical of instrumental grievers who simply need reassurance and validation that they, in fact, are grieving, albeit in a different way.

SIDEBAR 9.1: Counseling Dissonant Grievers

Counseling can be extremely effective for dissonant grievers. Dissonant grievers, as described earlier, are those who experience grief one way, but because of constraints fail to find compatible ways to express and adapt to their loss. Most are intuitive grievers, but perhaps due to gender role socialization, gender role strain, cultural constraints, or situational circumstances, hide and refrain from expressing their grief. Counseling is useful, as are self-help groups, since it provides a safe place where there is permission to express one's grief.

In counseling dissonant grievers, counselors should first assess whether the griever is truly dissonant. It may be useful to begin with the griever's family of orientation, exploring developmental and socialization experiences that might have inhibited emotional awareness and expression. As stated, some instrumental grievers might be concerned that they seemingly lack affect or the ability to emote. Such grievers need to explore the ways they experience, express, and adapt to loss as well as validation of their pattern.

Once a counselor is confident that a griever is truly dissonant, the counselor can assist the client in analyzing constraints to their expression and adaptation of the client's experience of grief. Counselors can also assist clients in finding safe places such as self-help groups or using interventive techniques that might allow the client to find compatible ways to express and adapt to his or her loss.

Steven provides an illustration case: Raised in an emotionally restricted family, Steven learned to hide his affect. When his mother died, he was troubled that he never told her he loved her. In counseling, he was helped to recognize his depth of feeling and appreciate the many ways he clearly, nonverbally showed his love. The counseling session became a safe and comfortable place for him to probe and ventilate his feelings. He became aware of the ways he used "doing" to avoid confronting his feelings. He also learned that he had missed the comfort of others, crying, for example, only when alone in his car. He was able to identify other safe places where he could feel free to grieve. In a final session, with his voice quivering, he read to an empty chair a letter he had written his deceased mother expressing his deep and strong feelings for her.

With male dissonant grievers, counselors should proceed with care. As Englar-Carlson (2006) warns, males who are ambivalent about expressing their experienced feelings may avoid therapy or terminate the therapeutic relationship as the work becomes more focused on emotion. Such dissonant male grievers can be eased into this emotional work in a number of ways. Counselors should begin by creating a safe, connected, and equalitarian environment. A counselor might self-disclose, modeling emotional expression. Cochran (2006) suggests using masculine metaphors. For example, it may be helpful to use a masculine metaphor for grief such as "carrying a heavy load," allowing a discussion of the varied ways, including dosing emotional experiences such as crying in a car, that lighten the load. Rabinowitz (2006) suggests coupling emotional work with more physical activities such as punching a bag or squeezing a towel.

Rabinowitz (2006) notes the value of male support groups for men. One of the authors has facilitated a grieving group for people assessed as male dissonant grievers. Previously in a group with women, many of the men felt constrained to cry or otherwise show emotion. Moreover, they tended to respond to the women's comments by problem solving rather than emotional validation. It is important to note that while these men will show deep emotion and clear support for one another, they often do it in ways that retain some consistency with their own male roles. In one illustration, a gay male named "Tom" lost his long-time companion. He asked, in intake, if the men were likely to be accepting. The facilitator noted that in this given area, many of the men were older, often of Greek or Italian descent, and had very traditional perspectives. Tom decided to attend but asked the facilitator to respect his wish to come out when he felt safe. After a few sessions, Tom began to discuss how much he missed his partner. The other men nodded in sympathy. One asked how long he had been married. Tom replied he was not married. Again the men were empathic; a prior member had mourned a mistress. Tom then shared his partner was male. There was a moment of shock as the men processed this new piece of information. The silence was broken when an older Italian-American longshoreman placed his hand on Tom's shoulder and gruffly asked "But you loved him right?" Tom tearfully nodded. He then reassured him. "This," he said, "is where you belong."

Counseling with dissonant grievers allows them to acknowledge their experiences, consider the factors that have blocked their expression of those feelings, and identify effective adaptive strategies, consistent with their own characteristics for dealing with their feelings.

Marty's case also points out a second issue that can lead instrumental grievers to counseling. When styles of grief are different within a family, family members can experience considerable conflict and stress. Instrumental and intuitive grievers may have such different ways of experiencing, expressing, and adapting to their loss that it can complicate the other's grief.

When Ted and Lisa's son died 2 years ago, Lisa found it helpful to join The Compassionate Friends. While Ted joined to support her, he did not feel that the organization met the same needs for him as it did for his wife. But Lisa was frustrated with Ted's inability and unwillingness to express affect and did not understand his need to channel his energies in administrating a scholarship fund in his son's memory.

Here, different grieving styles clearly have affected the relationship. A goal of counseling in this case is to assist each party in understanding how the other party experiences, expresses, and adapts to loss. Such recognition can lead to an acknowledgment that these differences do not mean that one party loved the deceased less or was less affected by the loss. And it can lead to a discussion of the ways family members can best support each other. In Ted and Lisa's case, Ted learned he could best support Lisa by listening to her and by allowing her opportunities to ventilate feelings. And Lisa learned to accept that support without insisting that Ted also share his feelings. She could acknowledge that her grief needed overt support while Ted needed his space respected.

A third reason instrumental grievers seek counseling is that they may need to explore their strategies, assessing their strengths and limitations. Not all strategies that instrumental grievers use are effective—no more than they are for intuitive grievers. For example, some strategies like substance abuse merely compound problems. Other strategies, such as problem-solving approaches, can at times be very useful but at other times lead to early and inappropriate attempts at premature replacement. For example, Tom was lonely and unable to care for himself when his wife died. He accepted a hospice bereavement worker's suggestion that he join a grief group. His goal, however, was to come to the group "to find a woman like my (deceased) wife" that he could marry. Here, an attempt at problem solving could push him into a marriage that simply seeks to replace. And other strategies, such as humor, can work in certain situations while in other cases they may alienate support and isolate grievers. All grieving individuals can benefit from assessing their approaches to grief—the strengths as well as the limitations of those approaches.

Intuitive grievers, on the other hand, often find value in individual or group counseling. Their affective responses are generally validated within the counseling framework, and counseling provides an outlet to express their strongly held feelings.

☐ Counseling: Approaches to Different Patterns

There are a variety of different models for grief counseling. Three of the most well known come from Worden (2009), Stroebe and Schut (1995, 1999), and Rando (1993). All these models share certain commonalties that, in fact, represent key approaches to grief counseling. They differ somewhat in their language of the grieving or, in Rando's terminology, the mourning process. Worden prefers to speak of four major tasks of grief, whereas Rando identifies six underlying processes of mourning (see Chapter 2). Stroebe and Schut view healthy grieving as oscillating between two processes: restoration-oriented processes (reconstructing a life after the loss) and loss-oriented processes (coping with the impact of the loss).

We also accept a process of grief counseling that includes three overlapping phases in the counseling process:

1. *Opening phase*—In this beginning phase counselors seek to develop trust, rapport, set the counseling contract, and understand the client's history as a way to assess the effects of the loss and the client's goals and motivation in seeking assistance.

2. *Intermediate phase*—The major work of counseling is done in this phase. Though different models may use distinct language in describing this process, it essentially involves identifying what is complicating grief and assisting bereaved individuals in finding ways to ameliorate it. So, for example, Worden (2009) would advise counselors to assess what tasks grieving individuals are finding difficult and assist them in identifying ways to complete those tasks successfully. Rando's (1993) approach would recommend assessing what factors complicate the resolution of key mourning processes, again looking toward therapeutic intervention to assist clients in successfully engaging those processes.

3. *Final phase*—This phase involves the difficult process of terminating the counseling relationship. The client and counselor review the progress that has been made and identify continuing issues that need attention, noting factors or relationships that can continue to both facilitate or complicate the grieving process. They also explore reactions that occur as the counseling relationship nears termination and set ground rules for any further contact.

This chapter assumes basic familiarity with the process of grief counseling and with current models. It does attempt, however, to stress and expand upon six central themes:

1. Assessment should always include an assessment of grief patterns, since these patterns are likely to affect motivation in seeking counseling, as well as the adaptive strategies grieving individuals are apt to find helpful. Sidebar 9.2 offers further suggestions for assessing patterns.

2. Assessment is critical. In recent years, there has been some controversy about the effectiveness of grief counseling (Currier, Neimeyer, & Berman, 2008; Larson & Hoyt, 2007; Neimeyer, 2000). Gamino and Ritter (2009) in summarizing this research emphasize that effects are positive when individuals are thoroughly assessed and interventions carefully designed and targeted.

3. In working with clients, counselors can be most helpful when they validate and utilize clients' strengths in adapting to their loss.

4. Counselors need to be intentional in their intervention, utilizing interventions that build upon existing strengths and adaptive strategies. These themes bear further exploration.

5. Counselors in all phases of counseling need to be culturally sensitive. Most individuals have multiple cultural identities including race and ethnicity, spirituality, social class, gender, and other identities possibly based on shared membership in a group perhaps based on sexual orientation (e.g., gay culture), occupation (e.g., police culture), or a shared characteristic (e.g., deaf culture). As Chapter 8 indicates, there are considerable cultural variations both in gender role expectations as well as grieving rules. Cultural sensitivity also means that the counselor is sensitive to the ways of his or her own cultural identities. This includes the culture of counseling. As Sue and Sue (2008) indicate, shared values of the culture of counseling such as encouragement of emotional expressiveness may make counselors less effective with instrumental grievers.

6. In using models—whether this model of adaptive grieving styles or other current models of the grieving process such as Worden's (2009) task model, Rando's (1993) six "R" processes, or Stroebe and Schut's (1995, 1999) dual–process model—it is important to remember that models are useful insofar as the model assists the therapist or offers insight to the client. Models are ways to understand reality. Socially constructed, they should never be confused with reality. The danger is when counselors attempt to reify models.

☐ Assessing Patterns

One of the first tasks for counselors, then, is to assess both the patterns of grief and the motivation for seeking counseling. One of the best ways of assessing a pattern is to listen to the language that grieving individuals use in describing their grief. Critical incident stress debriefing offers a cogent suggestion. By asking questions such as "How did you respond?" or "How did you react?" rather than "How did you feel?" counselors do three things. First, they allow clients to choose their domain for describing reactions. An intuitive griever may respond with comments such as "I felt terrible" or "I became anxious and depressed," which affirm the strong affective tone. Instrumental grievers are more likely to describe responses in more cognitive ("I couldn't believe it" or "I thought ..."), or physical or behavioral terms ("I felt sick," "I became restless," or "I just wanted to run away"). Remember, too, that it is critical to review reactions since the loss, as initial reactions alone may not be enough to assess grieving patterns.

Second, the use of terms such as *reaction* or *response* not only allows grievers to express grief in their own language; it also conveys a sense of validation. It offers the message that counselors are open to the range of domains that people may experience or express grief. Conversely, to ask the question "How did you feel?" implies that only the affective response is worthy of examination.

Beyond listening to the clients' language in describing grief, it is always useful to examine past experiences or losses, since initial reactions may not necessarily be predictive of long-term patterns. In such a loss review, it is critical to remember that counselors should assess clients' responses to a variety of losses, encouraging the client to move beyond any earlier deaths in the family to the wide range of losses people experience. This exploration will not only illuminate patterns; it will also provide opportunities to explore the strengths and limitations of a particular pattern.

This review helps in other ways, too. It offers a way to recall resources, both external and internal, that have been useful in the past, and it reaffirms to clients that they have survived earlier losses, offering hope that they can survive this one as well.

☐ Acknowledging and Affirming Strengths

In an insightful *Pogo* cartoon about pollution, Pogo stands in a rubbish-filled field and announces, "We have met the enemy and he is us." That can also be the case with grief, when grieving individuals or those who seek to help them fail to acknowledge and affirm their initial strengths. Reynolds (1993), for example, says that even our language can be victimizing or empowering. He prefers the use of the term *survivor* rather than *bereaved*, since the former is much more positive and affirming. Instrumental grievers, because they often pride themselves on their ability to adapt to crisis and have a strong sense of self-reliance, may be particularly sensitive to offers of help and assistance.

The counseling contract, then, has to be carefully tendered. Instrumental grievers may need to be positively motivated to accept counseling. Often appeals to assist others can be helpful. For example, Janet, a young widow with an instrumental grieving pattern, found counseling helpful as she dealt with the grief of her three adolescent children. Counseling gave her an opportunity to discuss problems. Her counselor continually reinforced the value of their work together as a way to assist her children. In other cases, instrumental grievers may see value of another voice, as in "We can work more effectively together than I can alone." But counselors themselves need to be clear on whose needs are being met—the individual's, the family's, or inappropriately, the counselor's own need to be helpful. Intuitive grievers will often be clearer on their goals in counseling, and more open and motivated in the process. Nevertheless, it is useful for counselors to review at the onset what any client seeks to achieve.

At the very least this will assist the process. And in some ways, the question of goals can clarify the grieving process. For example, it is not uncommon for grieving individuals to list closure as a goal. This can be a good time to emphasize that grief does not mean the closure of a relationship but its continuation in another form. Often the client's ambivalence about terminating that lost relationship can prove a barrier to the counseling process. Thus, for grievers of any pattern, it is always helpful to clarify goals and motivation.

All clients, too, will benefit from an exploration and affirmation of their own adaptive strategies. But this is especially true for instrumental grievers. Instrumental grievers will also benefit by affirming how the adaptive strategies they tried to employ—often cognitive and active—can be effective in dealing with loss. The recognition that these strategies are simply different, not necessarily deficient, allows a critical acknowledgment for grieving individuals and those who seek to assist them. Far too often the value of these strategies is not validated. Elmer's (1994) admonition is typical: "The problem for grief counselors is to convince a man that his feelings are valid, that grief is basically good, and that asking for help is not a sign of weakness."

The danger of such comments is threefold. First, it confuses grief with feelings, ignoring the many ways grief is manifested. Second, while acknowledging the value of certain adaptive strategies—ventilation of feelings and seeking support—such a statement ignores and seemingly discredits other strategies. Third, and perhaps most critically, it sets an inappropriate helping context, for only in a context where strengths are acknowledged and respected is it possible to explore the ways these strategies can be employed, to review any limitations, and to consider alternative approaches.

SIDEBAR 9.2: The Counselor as Griever

Counselors need to assess their own grieving pattern. Although counselors may have an affective bias (see Sue & Sue, 1990) in their approach to clients, this does not mean that they are necessarily intuitive in pattern. Anecdotal evidence points to a significant number of people who have entered the field of thanatology as a result of, perhaps even as a way of dealing with, their own losses. This pattern would be typical of instrumental grievers who often turn toward active and cognitive responses as a way to adapt to loss. This suggests that if this were the case, issues of countertransference may loom large. Given the culture of counseling, one way that it might be evident is that it may reinforce a tendency to press clients to share affect, essentially allowing clients to emote for both.

Beyond the issue of countertransference, analysis of a counselor's own pattern may lead to an enriched sense of the many strategies individuals use to adapt loss and it can facilitate self-care.

Studies of individuals who are working with the dying and bereaved emphasize the critical importance of effective self-care. Vachon (1987) found that helpers who were able to avoid "compassion fatigue" (see Figley, 1996) or burnout were the ones who were able to find suitable activities for respite. In addition, these helpers were able to validate their own grief, utilizing strategies such as rituals to mark their losses. They also understood the limit as well as potential inherent in their roles as caregivers and counselors. They also possessed a spiritual perspective, which allowed them to confront and accept the existential unfairness of life.

And finally, they also created for themselves effective support networks, finding support and opportunities both within and outside of their work organization. These studies suggest two things. First, counselors and caregivers should become aware of their own grief patterns and embrace those strategies best suited for their particular pattern. Second, it reminds organizations of the value of stressing and supporting multiple self-care activities other than the traditional biweekly support group.

☐ The Value of Cognitive and Active Adaptive Strategies

In Chapter 2, a key point was emphasized—that many current models of the grieving process stress that a variety of adaptive strategies may be useful to grievers. For example, Corr (1992), in a review of task models, notes that one of the strengths of such approaches is acknowledgment of individuality. Such approaches, as well as process models (Rando, 1993; Stroebe, 1997), affirm that each individual may find different tasks or processes more or less difficult than others and will work through the tasks or processes in his or her own idiosyncratic way. For example, to use Worden's (2009) task model, one of his tasks is "to work through the pain of grief" (p. 13). Some individuals may be able to accomplish this task, feeling the pain and finding ways over time to release it. Others may have difficulty with this task, avoiding or suppressing pain. And each individual will find his or her own way to work through the pain. To some it may be affective ventilation—sharing their feelings with family and friends. Others, though, may use different ways to deal with the pain or loss, perhaps expending energy in some physical task or through cognitive strategies. The central point, though, remains: a variety of strategies may be helpful as individuals adapt to loss.

Cognitive strategies certainly can be helpful. Such strategies can include varied approaches. For example, Moos and Schaefer (1986) describe a series of adaptive strategies that are cognitive in nature. Among these strategies are

- *Logical analysis and mental preparation*—In this strategy the crisis of loss is broken down into a series of small, manageable problems that can then be evaluated.

- *Cognitive restructuring*—Here the reality of the loss is accepted, but the individual focuses on favorable aspects such as how well they are coping or the transformative aspects of the loss.

- *Cognitive avoidance or denial*—These include strategies that deny, avoid, or minimize the loss. Other examples can include managing thoughts or selecting times and places where one avoids grief or uses diversion to avoid focusing on grief.

- *Information seeking*—Obtaining information allows the griever to understand and validate one's responses and to assess possible strategies to adapt to the loss.

Neimeyer (2001), coming out of his work on narrative reconstructive therapy, would add

- *Meaning-making*—Trying to develop a coherent narrative of the meaning of the deceased's life and death that allows bereaved individuals to understand the loss and their grief, and reconstruct a new identity in a now-changed world.

Such cognitive strategies are used extensively by the bereaved. For example, many researchers have found these typical reactions by males

(Brabant, Forsyth, & Melancon, 1992; Campbell & Silverman, 1996; Cook, 1988; Goodman, Black, & Rubinstein, 1996; Moss, Resch, & Moss, 1997; Moss, Rubinstein, & Moss, 1997). Klass (1997), in his studies of grieving parents, also emphasized the critical importance of cognitive processes as he indicated how grieving parents continually maintained an inner representation of the dead child, which assisted them in maintaining a continued and therapeutic sense of connection to the child. Similarly, Calhoun and Tedeschi (1990) noted the wide use of cognitive restructuring as their sample took comfort in their ability to cope and even to grow as they faced loss. The use of cognitive-orientated adaptive strategies is common, then, among the bereaved.

Cognitive-orientated strategies can be helpful in a number of ways. Neimeyer (1997a) and Attig (1996) emphasize that grief has strong cognitive components. To Neimeyer (1993, 1996, 1997a, 1997b), the central task in bereavement is meaning-making or reconstructing meaning. Losses may challenge earlier meanings, of self and the person who died, as well as our perceptions of our world. In grief, then, we need to review and reconstruct these meanings. Similarly, Attig (1996) stresses that the central issue of loss is *relearning*. Loss transforms one's world—the very fabric of life. In grief, then, one needs to learn new skills, review and relearn relationships with others—the deceased, as well as one's own sense of identify and spirituality.

Naturally, the judicious and skilled use of cognitive processes can facilitate meaning-making, allowing individuals to draw upon or develop spiritual strengths as they deal with the loss. As Klass (personal communication, March 1998) stated, "almost every philosophical system, save British analytical thought, are examples of masculine grief." By that Klass means that much of philosophy represents cognitive attempts to construct the meaning of life in the face of death and loss. Moreover, cognitive-based adaptive strategies can facilitate other aspects of grief— allowing individuals to redefine and relearn relationships with self, the world, and others. As a client once stated: "Since Marie [his wife] died, I think lots about her. I do a lot for the grandkids because I know that's what she wanted, what she would have done. I keep thinking what would Marie have done or Marie would really like this. And it makes me feel good about the kids we raised and about myself."

Cognitive-based adaptive strategies provide other benefits. A loss creates myriad practical problems. One now needs to adjust to a new environment, which entails learning new skills, coping with loss-related difficulties, and coping with the mundane problems of everyday life. Cognitive skills can facilitate problem solving, and they can provide opportunity to ventilate it. One of the critical recognitions that has emerged from critical incident stress theory (Figley, 1996) is that talking and thinking about loss can be as effective in ventilating and dissipating energy aroused by grief as affective-focused approaches.

It is little wonder, then, that research has indicated the effectiveness of cognitive-based strategies. Figley (1996), for example, found that simply telling and retelling the story often lowered trauma, and he noted that newer approaches to the treatment of posttraumatic stress disorder involve cognitive and physical interventions. Similarly, Powers and Wampold (1994) found that cognitive approaches were very successful in coping with loss, allowing grief to be validated, meaning reconstructed, and dosing periods of directly confronting the loss with other activities. Bonanno (1997) emphasized that cognitive approaches often worked better than affective processes, since they allowed one to function reasonably effectively and to meet ongoing responsibilities. This allowed individuals to maintain their sense of identity, in turn minimizing disruptions that might complicate their adjustment to loss, thereby reinforcing self-esteem and engendering support. Bonanno's research emphasized that those using a "positive bias," that is, a cognitive orientation, as a means to cope with loss actually had better outcomes than those who dealt with their loss by affective disclosure and ventilation of negative emotions. In addition, those who disassociated with negative emotions had lower levels of grief. There was a short-term cost in more somatic symptoms at 6 months out from the loss, but these health differences were not apparent at 14 and 28 months. Naturally, such a cost may be significant for a medically frail population such as older widows, suggesting a need for alternate interventive approaches. Other researchers (Goodman et al., 1996; Moss, Resch, & Moss, 1997; Moss, Rubinstein, & Moss, 1997) have noted both the presence of these cognitive strategies and their seeming effectiveness in their male samples. And Horowitz's (1970) work also emphasized the value of both cognitive and behavioral approaches.

But every strategy has limitations. Among the limitations of cognitive-based strategies is that the person employing them may be believed or be perceived by others to be cold and unfeeling. As Hochschild (1979) reminds us, every society has feeling rules that express a societal consensus on how one is to feel in a given situation. The feeling rules about grief often mandate overt affective expression. The absence of such overt affect can lead a person to redefine himself or herself, or lead others to define that person as not grieving effectively or as being unfeeling, which may erode support, self-esteem, and adaptation to loss. Or in other cases, persons with an overly cognitive approach might find it difficult to be sensitive to the needs of other grievers. They may find it hard to understand their adaptive strategies or attempt to "solve" the problems of other individuals as they affectively ventilate.

☐ The Roles of Humor

Humor, too, represents a cognitive strategy. Humor offers a number of benefits including tension release. The following case illustrates that point.

> "After my father died, there was that one difficult solemn moment at the funeral, you know, right before they close the casket and you go for your last look. After that we filed down to the limousine to the cemetery. No one said a word as the driver started following the hearse. Then all of a sudden my brother taps the driver on the shoulder. Now you have to understand that this was a large funeral home that had a number of funerals that day. My brother says to the driver seriously and quietly: 'Is there another hearse in front of that one?' The driver, confused, answers confused. 'No. Why?' My brother deadpans, 'That is not my father's casket.' The driver absolutely panics and we all burst out laughing and talking as we reassure the driver that he is following the correct hearse."

Not only does humor relieve tension (as it did in the previous case), it provides opportunities to express emotion and stimulates memories. Often at funerals, sharing humorous stories about the deceased provides a way past the immediate memory of loss and pain, and allows attendees to acknowledge, even celebrate other legacies in the life of the deceased. And because humor reduces tensions and invites relational response, it can often enhance social support. People are more drawn to those who respond to loss with a touch of laughter rather than a torrent of tears.

Humor provides other benefits as well. It can temporarily divert us from the pain. Humor can offer a sense of perspective that allows us to laugh at our fears and difficulties. In doing so, it can allow that positive sense of adapting that Bonanno (1997) associated with favorable overcomes. And it may even provide physiological benefits (Cousins, 1979) that can inoculate individuals experiencing a high level of stress and other negative physiological aspects of loss.

But the limits of humor are well illustrated by an episode on the sitcom *Home Improvement*. In the episode Jill's (the mother) father dies. As her teenage sons prepare to join her for the funeral, the middle son, Randy, jokes about the death. "I know how to iron for a funeral—just set it on stiff." To his consternation, his brothers walk away from him in disgust. Later, in a quiet moment with his father, Randy confesses that he does not know why he does this. His father reassures him that it is a method of adapting that they share. But he offers sage advice "Don't make jokes around anybody sensitive—do it around me."

Many of the positive benefits of humor, like any other adaptive strategy, can be negated if used insensitively or excessively. There is a fine line between diverting pain, however tempered, and denying it. And while humor can generate and cultivate support, it also runs the risk of being off-putting and striking others as insensitive, thereby negating support. Tim's advice to Randy is sagacious—one has to know when to use it.

☐ Behaviorally Focused Strategies

Instrumental grievers will often make use of active adaptive strategies as well as cognitive approaches. Such adaptive strategies can be varied. For example, information seeking is both cognitive and active as it allows one a meaningful activity at a disorganized time. Problem-solving activity is another such strategy. Here, specific steps are taken to deal with one or more aspects of the crisis. For example, one may take comfort in planning and participating in the funeral. In another strategy, identifying alternative rewards, individuals either attempt to replace the loss or to find other sources of satisfaction to compensate it (see Moos & Schaefer, 1986).

Beyond these problem-focused strategies, sheer activity may be useful sometimes. This may have a symbolic relationship to the deceased. For example, one funeral director shared how two professional football players decided to handle the death of their father. They chose to physically dig the grave. Or in another case, a mother, after the death of her daughter, placed much of her energy in an annual award given in her daughter's memory. She raised funds, interviewed candidates, and had the public opportunity each year to remember her daughter.

Sometimes these actions may not be so overtly related to the loss. For example, in the film *Basketball Diaries*, the adolescents return from the funeral of a good friend and teammate, Bobby. They sit in a park unable to articulate their feelings of loss, each attempt ending in silence. But then their grief seems to come out in a furious game of basketball played in a dark playground under a drenching rain. A similar illustration occurred in a middle school after a student died in a car crash caused by a drunk driver. In the aftermath of the death many of the students openly wept and talked about their grief, but a number of the boys were mute. However later in gym, an aggressive game of dodgeball provided an opportunity for these boys to physically ventilate. As they lobbed the ball at one another, they made direct references to the crash and the driver.

Physical ventilation is one benefit of active strategies. As an old German American pastor once shared in Idaho: "It's not just because the casket is heavy that six men lift it." In that environment, the opportunity for physical ventilation is welcome. It provides avenues for the discharge of the energy generated by grief.

But active strategies have other benefits as well. They allow one to "do something," reinforcing a sense of control in an otherwise hopeless time. Aaron, for example, was a social worker who worked with HIV-infected children in foster care. On his days off, he volunteered at an animal shelter. Here, he realized, he could assist in the adoption of pets that would not likely die within a short time after placement. In another illustration, Jim, a chaplain in a leukemia ward, donated platelets weekly, because it was something tangible he could do for the children in his ministry. One of the greatest benefits of prayer, beyond its spiritual efficacy, is that it offers a form of symbolic control in a seemingly uncontrollable situation (Doka & Davidson, 1998). Sometimes that control can be more than symbolic. Deathbed instructions, for example, can be seen as both an attempt to symbolically control the future as well as a real effort to problem solve. For example, when Mike was dying he gave instructions to his wife about raising their young son. He also had a friend promise that he would assist in raising the child. These actions gave him comfort and reassurance that his son would be well taken care of after he died. We might add that even on the cross Christ, gave instructions to his disciples and mother to care for one another.

At the time of the death, activity, too, can be helpful. Planning the funeral and engaging in ritual offer meaningful activity at a much-disorganized time. During the course of the grieving period, activity can also be helpful. Solving some of the day-to-day problems that arise as one deals with the loss can reinforce a sense of self-esteem, competence, and control. As one griever shared, "After Johnny died, I had to sell his house. I fixed it up some and handled all the details. It was funny—I felt kind of good about that—I could still handle stuff." Moreover, activities can provide structure in a seemingly disorganized time and offer opportunity for respite and diversion. This allows a person "time off" from active grieving. Sometimes it can allow one to assume a leadership role, assisting others who experience grief as more of an affective crisis. Such a role can generate support and enhance self-esteem.

And sometimes, these actions cannot only solve an individual problem but address larger social issues as well. For example, Cindy Lightner responded to her child's death, caused by a drunk driver, by founding Mothers Against Drunk Driving (MADD). MADD has played a significant role in changing the public perception of drunk driving as well as the laws that now address it. Similarly, much of the social concern about missing children arose from John Walsh's attempt to deal with the abduction and subsequent death of his young son, Adam. It is little wonder, then, that such adaptive strategies are often used (Brabant et al., 1992; Campbell & Silverman, 1996; Cook, 1988; Goodman et al., 1996; Moss, Resch, & Moss, 1997; Moss, Rubinstein, & Moss, 1997; Neugebauer et al., 1992;) and that they are effective (Bonanno, 1997; Figley, 1996; Horowitz, 1970; Powers & Wampold, 1994).

But again, any strategy has its limitations. Active adaptive strategies may be used not only to engage and ventilate grief but also to divert and to deny grief. For dissonant grievers, particularly, activity may subvert their need to find more effective ways to adapt to their loss, as well as physically exhaust them.

Problem-solving approaches can be ineffective and sometimes complicate grief. For example, attempts to cope with the problems of loneliness may involve a premature attempt to replace the loss. Even avoiding such an extreme example, instrumental grievers may attempt to join support groups that are primarily therapeutic merely for social contact.

In other cases the activity can complicate relationships with others. For example, sexual activity can be an attempt to create a sense of intimacy in an isolating time. But partners may not understand nor share that meaning. For example, when their child died, Ryan found sex to be a source of comfort for him, but his overtures troubled his wife who felt her own sexual desires decreased in her grief.

In addition, certain behaviors are, by themselves, problematic. For example, instrumental grievers may attempt to "resolve" issues generated by the loss by the use of drugs or alcohol. Or they may engage in acting out or other self-destructive behaviors.

☐ Affectively Focused Adaptive Strategies

The forgoing should not imply, in any way, that affectively oriented adaptive strategies are not as effective. Affective strategies such as affective ventilation and acceptance can be extremely helpful, both in generating support and in exploring and resolving emotional conflicts. Affective regulation—that is, choosing appropriate times and places to share or feel deep affect—is a critical strategy since it allows individuals to exercise elements of control over their affect, permitting them to function. It is often a key adaptive strategy in dissonant instrumental grievers who may strongly believe they should not show affect except at certain times or places when they find it safe and appropriate, such as in therapy or in self-help groups or when they are alone. But almost all grievers, including instrumental grievers, use this strategy to some degree. For even in instrumental grievers, affect is tempered, not absent.

As with other strategies, affective strategies have limitations as well. Excessive affect can limit support and impair effective functioning. Again, grieving can limit the time or place when grief is shared. As noted earlier, the grieving rules of American society tend to encourage affective ventilation early in the grieving period, while discouraging it later on. For example, ever since her sister died, Jean has found it difficult to remain composed. Even small events or little reminders have led to periods where she needs to cry. Many friends have begun to avoid her and her supervisor at work has written her up for "a lack of self-control." She is aware of these difficulties and her own sense of self-worth has suffered. Affective regulation can be problematic, as well, inhibiting grievers who really do need to affectively ventilate from doing so.

Counselors should explore the role of affect as a connector. Some individuals fear that when they no longer can experience the pain of the loss, they lose their connection to the deceased. Grieving clients can be reassured that the bond transcends the pain. We often begin counseling by examining the client's goals. We can then clarify the process of grief, reaffirming the memories that will be sustained and even be more accessible as the pain of grief lessens.

Thus, affective strategies, like all others, have positive and negative aspects. Used effectively, they can provide grievers with opportunities to explore and resolve feelings and to reach out for support. Doing so can assist grievers both in coming to terms with the loss and in reconstructing their lives in the face of that loss. But while more of the literature extols the value of affective expressiveness (e.g., Elmer, 1994; Staudacher, 1991; Wolfelt, 1990), it is critical to remember that it is but one of a series of adaptive reactions, each with its unique strengths and limitations.

☐ Spiritually Focused Strategies

Spiritually focused strategies undoubtedly are the most analytically complex strategies, in that they are usually derivatives of cognitive, affective, or active strategies. For example, prayer can be a way to express emotion or process thoughts. And prayer allows one to do something, often when there are few other opportunities to do anything. The following cases illustrate the multifaceted nature of prayer, and, for that matter, other spiritually focused strategies.

> "When my son first died, I still prayed but I would use my prayers to spew anger. 'How could you do this to me?' I would rail against God daily."
>
> —34-year-old clergyman
>
> "When the doctor told me there was nothing more to do, I remember smiling and saying I can always pray."
>
> —74-year-old widow
>
> "When I pray, I think about Bobby a lot. It gives me a chance to review what happened, to remind myself that his life and death were in God's hand's, and that I just did not have the power to save him."
>
> —Bereaved mother

To Pergament (1997), this is one of the great strengths of religious or spiritually based strategies. The pathways of such strategies can utilize cognition, affect, or behavior. Like other forms of adaptive strategies, there are varied spiritual approaches that can entail a range of responses from deferring it to some higher power, to collaborative approaches that emphasize using oneself as an instrument of one's own faith or prayer, to those in which the person is totally self-directing. Pergament, too, reminds us that, as with other strategies, spiritual strategies can be both helpful and harmful. For example, reframing a loss as God's will may be perceived by some as part of a design or plan that offers a sense of comfort, while others will see it as a vindictive punishment. Even spiritual or religious communities may be perceived as helpful or unhelpful.

This does not deny the critical importance of spiritual issues in loss and grief, or the value of spiritual beliefs, practices, and rituals (see Doka, 1993; Doka & Morgan, 1993). Loss and grief are fundamentally spiritual crises, since they evoke questions of meaning. As such, spiritually focused strategies will necessarily be utilized as individuals struggle with these spiritual concerns. The goals of the counselor or the person seeking to help himself or herself is to explore and understand how their use of these approaches reveals the underlying adaptive strategies they use and, as with other strategies, when they are helpful and when they are not.

☐ How Do You Know If a Person Is Grieving?

Counselors often question how, if grief is not expressed in overt affect, they can determine whether an individual is, in fact, grieving. Might the lack of affect indicate denial or suppression? Two considerations may assist. The first is to assess activity. Individuals who can describe grief in some domain, that is, talk about ways they are thinking or behaving in response to the loss, are demonstrating grief even if not in overt affect. In short, grievers will show some activity after a loss, but it may be in one or more domains. The absence of any activity may be an indication of more complicated responses, but the absence of significant affect may only point to the fact than an individual is an instrumental griever, actively using cognitive or behavioral strategies.

A second consideration is movement. As described earlier, grief is an unclear process, a roller coaster full of ups and downs. Significant amelioration may be experienced even within the first 2 years. Nevertheless, people who are grieving ought to be able to describe the ways that they experience the process. And over time they should be able to indicate a lessening of intensity. In other words, although they still experience downs, these should be experienced as less intense, less long lasting, and less frequent than was evident in the first 2 years.

Similarly, Webb (1993) offers a notion of disabling grief, referring to the degree that grief impairs normal functioning. Again, the level of impairment may vary in the grieving process; it may even increase once one moves beyond the initial shock of loss. But again, over time, people should begin to function at levels similar to, or perhaps even better than, those earlier.

In summary, the fact that grievers are both doing something and conveying a sense of movement are clear signs that the person is grieving even if he or she does not fit some perceived stereotypes on how that person should grieve.

☐ A Note on Counseling Male Instrumental Grievers

Throughout this section, two critical points are emphasized. First, there are a number of appropriate strategies that counselors can utilize in dealing with instrumental grievers. Second, while grieving styles are related to gender, they are not determined by gender. Nonetheless, although Sidebar 9.1 addresses the particular needs and strategies useful for male dissonant grievers, it is worthwhile to add a few comments on approaching male instrumental grievers.

Much theorizing in the new psychology of men has stressed that a dominant male ideology, which emphasizes that men should not show weakness, be independent and strong, and strive for success, adversely affects men's psychological health and their ability or willingness to seek psychological counseling (Cochran, 2006; Englar-Carlson, 2006; Levant & Richmond, 2007; O'Neil, 2006; Smith, Tran, & Thompson, 2008). Yet, as this section affirms, the problem may not be with men but more with a culture of counseling (Sue & Sue, 2008) that emphasizes emotional expressiveness, self-disclosure, and the value of insight that does not fit well with male instrumental grievers who may focus more on cognitive and active strategies and focus on problem solving. Counselors therefore need to examine their own perceptions of the appropriate ways, especially regarding emotional expression, of how individuals grieve. As Rosenblatt (1993a) notes, these can vary widely not only by gender but also by cultural identification.

Counselors can begin by recognizing and acknowledging the strengths of the dominant male ideology. Such strengths emphasize self-sacrifice, protection of the weak and vulnerable, the value of courage, and the social responsibility inherent in being a team player. As stated earlier, utilizing that ideology can be useful in motivating men to begin or continue in counseling.

Throughout this section, we have sought to offer counselors a variety of counseling strategies that would work well with instrumental grievers of either gender. Such strategies can, as stated earlier, build on male-oriented metaphors such as "carrying a heavy load" or "taking one for the team."

Kiselica and Englar-Carlson (2008) suggest that adolescent male clients may react negatively to the inherent hierarchy of counseling. Among their recommendations are helpful suggestions to encourage more flexible structures for timing, model self-disclosure, create a welcoming space (for example, Nerf balls to squeeze), offer counseling in informal and natural settings, sit side by side, use cultural healings for modeling, use appropriate humor, and emphasize, particularly in early sessions, assistance with practical concerns. While aimed at counseling boys, these suggestions have general value in dealing with male clients.

Further, Thompson (1997) suggests that the male focus on problem solving may inhibit their oscillation to the alternate process of dealing with the loss. Yet we would hold this is not inherent; men may simply acknowledge the loss in ways that are more active and cognitive, perhaps in developing a memorial project. Whatever the underlying model, it is critical that counselors assess whether male instrumental grievers are coping with all the issues inherent in loss. Often men will be willing to tackle these more difficult issues when counselors assist them in reviewing their previous coping to reaffirm a sense of experienced competence (Allen & Hayslip, 2001).

☐ Couples Counseling/Family Counseling and Grieving Styles

Different grieving patterns can cause conflict within family systems. Persons with a more intuitive grieving pattern may be concerned that family members who are more instrumental in pattern may be repressing grief or question whether the lack of affect means a lack of commitment or love for the deceased. The instrumental griever may be concerned by the intuitive griever's constant need to express feelings and worry about the mate's ability to cope. Both types of grievers may feel frustrated that their pattern of adapting to loss are questioned and feel frustrated in each person's ability to help one another.

For these reasons, couples or family counseling can be very helpful for family systems where different grieving patterns are evident. There are a number of goals for such counseling. First, it is helpful for counselors to affirm the existence of different patterns and explore the different patterns of each family member, offering insight as to the reason such patterns developed.

Second, the counselor should help couples or families explore the ways that their styles inhibit or facilitate interaction and support. There are a number of factors that should be included in this assessment. One factor to assess is whether the styles in the couple or family are complementary or symmetrical, that is, whether family members have different or similar styles. Each combination has potential corresponding advantages and disadvantages. For example, sharing grieving styles may allow family members to understand and support one another. However, it also might limit support since each family member is competing with the same needs. Conversely, complementary styles can inhibit mutual support since members may misinterpret the ways that other family members are coping with the loss. Or complementary styles can be a source of strength as members can be mutually supportive.

Other factors to consider may be whether family members grieve in isolated ways or in ways that interact with others in the family system. Again neither approach is inherently advantageous. This will depend on whether family members respect these differences or see them as a source of conflict. It can be useful too to consider how these differences fit in with larger cultural implications of gender role expectations. For example, when Edie and Ron's 12-year-old son died after falling from a cliff on a hike at a state park, Ron cried often. Edie, on the other hand, focused her grief by advocating for guardrails on that particular trail. Edie's strongly instrumental grieving style especially contrasted with Ron's more intuitive style, particularly in their Western community where men were supposed to show emotional restraint. This led to a community perception that if Ron was so emotional, Edie should demonstrate even more emotion. The fact that Edie did experience or express her grief in such a manner made others in the community perceive Edie's response as cold and unfeeling.

In assessing couples, it is critical to consider not only their comfort with their current level of sexual intimacy and activity but also the meaning each individual gives to sexual intimacy, particularly in coping with the loss. A number of studies (Gottlieb, Lang, & Amsel, 1996; Peppers & Knapp, 1980; Rosenblatt, 1997) have indicated that sexual relationships can be problematic following a loss, especially the loss of a child. It may very well be that instrumental grievers find sexual intimacy both a comforting activity and a way to express emotional support, whereas more intuitive grievers may feel sexual pleasure to be a betrayal of their feelings of grief.

Once counselors assess styles, they can assist family members in finding ways to support one another. With symmetrical styles, counselors may review the ways families can use their similar styles as a source of empathy and validation. When styles are complementary, counselors can explore the ways that families can utilize these differences as strengths. For example, when one of their children died in a car crash, Wally and Carol responded in very different ways. Wally placed many of his energies in following the court case and, subsequently, in a group that sought to change laws about drinking and driving. Carol needed to speak about the loss. In counseling both were able to affirm the value of each other's approach.

Counselors can use a number of different strategies as they work with families. Certainly psychoeducational approaches that emphasize and validate different adaptive styles are useful. As teachers we have often used media as an instructional tool. Sometimes, for example, media can be an apt assignment in counseling couples or individuals. We have on occasion assigned an episode of *Home Improvement*, a situation comedy, for couples to watch. In the assigned episode, Jill, the spouse and mother of the series, experiences the death of her dad. Jill's grief is somewhat complicated since her relationship with her father had some ambivalence. Her husband, Tim, responds beautifully—getting her to the airport, taking care of the kids, and shepherding them to the funeral. At the end of the episode, Jill reminds Tim she often prods him to be more in touch with his feelings. "This time," she affirms, "I needed you to be you." The brevity of the episode (23 minutes) and the familiarity of the characteristics have often allowed a relaxed discussion of the ways that different styles can be highly supportive.

It may be useful to have couples remember the factors that initially attracted them to one another. Beyond reaffirming their earlier bonds, such a strategy often reminds them that the very factors that attracted them—perhaps sensitivity or stoicism—are now the same factors that offend. Counselors, too, should challenge inappropriate judgments when necessary, reminding couples or family members that these differences in styles are not differences in love nor are they deficiencies in character.

Counselors can assist family members to realistically assess what support they can reasonably expect from others in the family system, and they can explore alternate sources of support as well. Debra, for example, was very pleased with a support group. Her husband, Paul, did not find the group to be helpful especially since it had a strongly affective bias. In counseling, Debra expressed a need for Paul to attend. Her need was twofold. She both wished there was someone with whom she could discuss the group experience and, on a very practical level, she was sometimes so emotionally exhausted that she did not wish to drive the distance home. In counseling, she realized that the group was not helpful to her husband. Challenged to take responsibility for her own needs, she asked her sister to join her in the group.

It is important, too, for counselors to affirm that as children grow, they develop their own grieving styles. Parents can explain their ways of experiencing, expressing, and adapting to loss so children can begin to understand and interpret their personal reactions. Counselors though need to encourage parents to understand and respect the grieving styles that children may evidence. Kyle's dad died when Kyle was 4 years old. When Kyle was 8 years old, he asked a favored uncle to take him to his father's grave. His mom was taken aback by the request. "Wouldn't you," she asked, "like to see the grave with me?" Kyle explained that he knew his mother would cry while his uncle would not be so emotional. Kyle returned from the memorial site and explained that he and his uncle (his dad's brother) reminisced at the site. Kyle was especially interested in knowing what his dad was like when he was Kyle's age—information only his uncle knew. Even at 8 years old, Kyle knew his own grieving needs. Happily Kyle's mother respected and supported her son's grieving style.

☐ Grief in the Workplace: Implications for Employee Assistance Programs

There are implications of adaptive grief styles for work environments. The importance of offering support for grieving employees is both sensitive and sensible. The very nature of grief is likely to affect an employee's performance. Losses that occur within the workplace or are work related, such as a line of duty death, may disrupt not only an employee but reverberate throughout the entire work environment. Even in professions where a death is not uncommon, such as the military and police, it is critical to understand that such deaths are still perceived as sudden, unexpected, and are likely to disrupt the assumptive world of their members (Davidson & Doka, 1999).

It is clear that organizations that do not adequately offer effective care for their employees will pay a cost in decreased productivity, lower morale, and increased turnover. Conversely, empathic work environments were associated with higher employee satisfaction and increased commitment to the organization, and lower turnover (Davidson & Doka, 1999). Two key elements were that supervisors were trained and supported to respond sensitively to grieving employees and that employee assistance programs (EAPs) were available should assistance be needed.

EAP counselors though should understand the implications of varied grieving styles within the work environment. Intuitive grievers may very well, at times, be immobilized at work. Many EAP counselors are skilled at offering services to bereaved individuals such as referral to individual counseling or grief groups. Supervisors too may know and offer validation, support, and assistance in prioritizing work tasks.

Instrumental and dissonant adaptive styles may offer more of a challenge. Dissonant grievers, for example, may seek escape in work. They may return to work shortly after a loss and focus on work as a diversion from their grief. The danger is that their inability to focus on their loss may be supported and even praised within the workplace, even as it takes on a personal and family toll. Instrumental grievers too may find comfort in the routine activity of their work environment. Sensitive supervisors and EAP counselors can regularly assess how the grieving individual is responding and ask about the ways other family members are coping with the loss as this may show indications of difficulties within relationships or at home. In addition, it may be useful to offer a variety of interventions including psychoeducational interventions, such as reading materials or brown-bag lunches, that convey information about grieving styles and the grieving process.

A similar array of services should be offered when a loss occurs within the work environment. No one interventive strategy can encompass all grievers. Offering a variety of services including rituals, reading materials, debriefings, psychoeducational support, counseling, and grief groups offers employees the opportunity to find interventive strategies that are most clearly suited to their grieving style. In addition it affirms a critical message that the work organization is sensitive not only to the employee's loss but to their individuality and uniqueness.

Work organizations can find their own ways to support grieving employees in ways compatible with their style and culture. This premise was reinforced a number of years ago when one of the authors vacationed in Atlantis, a major resort on Paradise Island in the Bahamas. The very name *Atlantis* projects a magical and mystical escape, an ambiance that is the essence of the resort. Dining in one of the most elegant restaurants on the resort, one of the authors noticed on the tuxedo of the wait staff a black ribbon, a common indication of mourning within that culture. When asked, a waiter explained that a popular employee had died suddenly that week, the result of an accident. The guest indicated he was impressed with the sensitivity of the employer as it would have been easy to suppress the ribbon as inimical to the image of the resort. The employee explained that not only did the restaurant management allow the wait staff to wear the ribbons but also it had donated all food and arranged coverage so that the wait staff could not only attend the funeral but also cook and serve a postfuneral meal (a common part of the funeral ritual within the Bahamas). To this wait staff of primarily men, the waiter asserted that this activity was particularly helpful. "It allowed us to free the family to be with their kin, it made us feel that we were doing something important to help," he stated. Here the resort management not only responded in a sensitive and humane way, it also enabled a strategy that allowed employees to act on their grief and respect their deceased coworker. The pride and commitment that the staff members had for their employer was admirable.

☐ Summary: Androgyny and Beyond

In recent years, there has been a concern to move toward androgynous perspectives (see Bem, 1981). The underlying notion, which has itself emerged from sections of the feminist and men's movements, is that both the feminine and masculine sides that exist within each individual should be embraced. Inherent in this idea is the perspective that one can learn much from both the feminine ability to recognize and to express feelings and the masculine ability to persevere in the midst of a crisis.

The therapeutic implication here is that counselors and individuals should cultivate alternative strengths. The feminine griever ought to be shown the value of cognitive and active approaches, while the instrumental griever ought to confront his or her underlying feelings, however difficult that is. It is argued that only by engaging both sides of oneself can one respond to loss in a holistic manner. Certainly those with the widest range of adaptive strategies are best able to surmount crises.

There is some support for this approach. For example, Schut, Stroebe, van den Bout, and deKeijser (1997) found that men tended to benefit more from client-centered therapies, whereas women found value in more cognitive approaches. However, it is important to consider that this research used gender rather than grieving styles as the variable. The study may, in fact, indicate the value of androgynous approaches. Perhaps each gender benefited from exposure to less familiar, alternative approaches. Since there is no evidence of the styles that these grievers initially presented, or full descriptions of the therapeutic process, one can entertain alternative explanations of these results. Perhaps these grievers leaned toward the dissonant part of the continuum. For example, a male dissonant griever who experiences grief as deep affect but is constrained by his perceptions that such feeling is inappropriate for a man to express, may find safe places to express feeling in a client-centered approach. Or the chosen therapeutic methods themselves may preclude a particular style. Cognitive-centered approaches do not preclude affective exploration and ventilation. In fact, some researchers have suggested a move beyond androgyny (Stillion & McDowell, 1997), urging both individuals and clinicians to ignore any hint of sexual stereotyping and to teach individuals the widest range of adaptive strategies as they seek to ameliorate grief.

Certainly, gender is but one factor that influences grief patterns. Just as surely, individuals as well as clinicians are urged to make careful assessment of one's own or a client's grieving style. In addition, it can also be affirmed that individuals with the widest range of strategies are more likely to adapt well.

Yet in other ways, one may part company with calls to androgyny (Bem, 1981) or even admonitions to move beyond androgyny (Stillion & McDowell, 1997). Bem's (1981) recognition that calls to androgyny can be "doubly incarcerating" has value. It is a reminder that such calls pose unrealistic and unfair demands on grievers.

Furthermore, such calls to androgyny or beyond are problematic in three ways. First, any careful assessment of an individual grieving style should not ignore factors such as gender, socialization, culture, or other variations that might influence the grief pattern. Certainly, understanding how these factors have influenced a grieving pattern can be useful to individuals and clinicians. For example, when Dave, a 15-year-old boy, heard the news of the death of his mother and younger sister in a car crash, he initially expressed little affect. But after time, his grades began to fall and he did exhibit acting-out behavior. He reluctantly agreed to counseling. In counseling, it became clear that throughout his life he experienced, both as the son of a military officer and as a student in a military academy, rigorous sex role socialization. As a result, he learned to hide well the deep affect he did experience. Only by exploring these early factors was he able to acknowledge his level of affect and begin to grieve in a way more consistent with his experience of grief. But his older brother and father also recognized through similar exploration that their affect had always been tempered. True instrumental grievers, they benefited from more cognitive and active approaches.

Second, these cases that speak to androgyny and beyond ignore the fact that instrumental and intuitive grievers vary not only in the adaptive strategies they use but also in their very experience and expression of grief. To urge oneself or another to express feelings that are, in fact, not really a significant part of the grief experience is counterproductive.

Finally, such calls ignore both the basic principle of self-help and counseling—lead with strengths. Crises are poor opportunities to attempt to comply with uncomfortable or unfamiliar approaches. One is better served by effectively employing the adaptive strategies that seem most natural.

There is one other critical implication for organizations offering grief support. Since individuals are likely to have different grieving styles, no one interventive strategy will universally meet needs. Although organizations such as hospices that offer grief support do well to conduct their own local needs assessments, it seems logical to suggest that organizations that wish to meet client needs effectively ought to offer a range or menu of services. Individual counseling, or referral to counseling, grief groups, grief libraries and pamphlets, ritual events such as periodic memorial services, and psychoeducational programs that offer information and validation about grief such as "How to Handle the Holidays" programs, all have their place.

10
CHAPTER

Strategies for Self-Help and Intervention
The Need for Interventive Intentionality

This chapter in some ways has a dual focus. Although written primarily for counselors, it offers suggestions for the types of strategies that may work with a range of grievers. Hence the chapter may be used to suggest self-help strategies to instrumental and dissonant grievers.

Many of the interventive strategies discussed here have been developed for people who are grieving, and the strategies are effective with a wide range of grievers, even those with different grieving patterns. The reason for that effectiveness is that these strategies allow grieving individuals to use them in ways that are compatible to their individual patterns. They allow grieving people the ability to engage on a cognitive, affective, or behavioral level. One can express feelings or thoughts. In effectively using these strategies, counselors or grieving individuals ought to remember three critical aspects:

1. *Be intentional*—That is, understand what one is attempting to accomplish by the strategy that is used. For example, is one seeking to assist cognitive processing or empower the ventilation of feelings?

2. *Choose comfortable modalities*—Individuals are more likely to benefit when they are comfortable with the modality being used. For example,

expressive therapies and the creative arts can be wonderfully effective in assisting people who are grieving. But for someone who is uncomfortable with the arts, other approaches such as storytelling may be useful. However, people who feel awkward in speaking may not find much value in storytelling as a therapeutic approach.

3. *Build from strengths*—These strategies work well because they allow a grieving individual to adapt to his or her pattern. They work best when they illuminate and amplify the strengths of a given pattern rather than attempting to force an alternative approach. Journaling, for example, can be useful for many reasons. It can be used to assist in the reconstruction of meaning, to stimulate a continued bond, to ventilate feelings, or to allow meaningful activity. But to insist that a grieving individual with an instrumental pattern only use the journal to document feelings, both denies the value of such an exercise and creates resistance and frustration.

☐ Bibliotherapy

Bibliotherapy, or the therapeutic use of self-help literature, has grown in recent years. In fact, there is a wide range of self-help literature available. Some are firsthand, personalized accounts of grief; professionals write others. Some are general, touching all types of loss (see Rando, 1986; Sanders, 1993), while others are written about a specific type of loss, such as the death of a child (Koppelman, 1994; Rosenblatt, 2000; Sanders, 1992) or the death of a parent (e.g., Myers, 1988). Some, such as Golden's *Swallowed by a Snake* (1996) or Staudacher's *Men and Grief* (1991), are addressed to men, whereas others, such as Caine's (1974) *Widow,* are more suited to women. Some books may confront specific issues or concerns such as the spiritual (see Kushner, 1981; Lewis, 1963). In addition, there is a range of literature suitable for children.

In addition to books, there are a number of other print resources such as magazines like *Bereavement Magazine* or *Thanatos,* or a newsletter such as *Journeys.* There is also a wide range of pamphlets, many of which may be available at funeral homes, hospitals, or hospices. In addition to these print resources, nonprint resources, such as self-help videos or audiotapes, are also available.

Bibliotherapy can have much value in general. It can offer grievers three major gifts. First, it can provide a sense of validation, normalizing feelings and reactions. Second, it can offer suggestions, options for adapting to varied issues that one faces in the grieving process. For example,

Rando's book *How to Go On Living When Someone You Love Dies* (1991) provides a variety of strategies for such practical problems as facing the holidays, reaching out for support, designing therapeutic rituals, and other problems that often accompany loss. Finally, bibliotherapy offers hope and reassurance to grievers that they, too, can survive their loss. It is little wonder that bibliotherapy has been found to be an effective tool in grief (Doka, 1990; Seogin, Jamison, & Gochneaur, 1989).

Bibliotherapy may have special value to instrumental grievers. It is by its very nature cognitive and active. It is solitary. It allows dosing, that is, if the griever finds something too painful or difficult, he or she can set it aside for a while. And certainly it offers control. Grievers can choose the time and place that they use it.

Yet bibliotherapy should be treated as a prescription drug, that is, one should carefully assess what books may offer valued insights to a particular struggle. Not only do books vary in focus and orientation, they also vary in quality. More important, some, used uncritically or selected without forethought, may complicate grieving. For example, Kushner (1981) has a wonderfully written, sensitive book titled *Why Bad Things Happen to Good People*. In it he addresses a frequent spiritual issue: If God is so good and so powerful, why did this loss occur? Many grievers may find solace in his notion that God allows the world to run itself; that while this power is distant, his mercy and goodness remain. But others may find that idea troubling, finding more comfort in Lewis's (1963) acceptance of that paradox, while acknowledging the unanswerable quality and mystery behind the question.

Similarly, dissonant instrumental grievers may find Staudacher's book *Men and Grief* (1991) to offer both validation and permission to grieve using affective adaptive strategies. But those closer to the instrumental pole on the grieving continuum may find that her message invalidates their own adaptive strategies.

Happily, there is a range of resources available. One should simply choose well and read critically. The question is always a personal one; not "Are these ideas right?" but "Will they work for the grieving individual?"

☐ Online Resources

One of the remarkable events of the last quarter century has been the growth of personal computers and their use in a wide range of ways. Given that context, it is unsurprising that they have become a resource for the bereaved.

The Internet offers many online resources for grievers. Certainly a wide range of information on loss and grief is available through the Internet.

Some informational resources provide referral to grief groups, organizations, or other available materials. There are interactive possibilities as well. Online grief groups, chat rooms, and e-mail offer opportunities to interact with other grievers. And some Web sites, including Facebook and MySpace, offer opportunities to memorialize, empowering cyberspace ritual.

In fact, adolescents and young adults are likely to use the Internet as a major source of information and support for grief (James, Oltjensbruns, & Whiting 2008). Online resources can provide many of the benefits of bibliotherapy as well as other advantages. They can be validating and offer suggestions for adapting as well as providing reassurances of hope. In addition, they may offer interpersonal support. Unlike many resources, the Internet is available 24 hours a day.

Instrumental grievers, in particular, may benefit since online resources are highly compatible to their grieving styles and strategies, particularly those that are cognitive and active, such as information seeking. These resources allow a certain degree of anonymity that may be lacking in other forms of interpersonal contact while offering opportunities to connect with other grievers. Going online gives control to the griever allowing him or her to sign on or off or to not respond at all. Because of that, the griever retains the opportunity to dose pain and grief. Moreover, the very variety of online resources provides grievers opportunities to select a comfortable level of engagement as well as to choose what resources one accesses at any given point in his or her grief. Intuitive grievers and dissonant grievers, too, can find great value since going online offers safe space for ventilation.

Yet online resources carry disadvantages as well. Quality varies more widely on the Internet than one would likely find in print and nonprint resources. Cyberspace is in many ways the final frontier. Because grievers can be vulnerable, it is essential to be wary of schemes that may seek to take advantage. Online resources are powerful tools, but again, they must be used with care. Counselors, especially with adolescents and young adults, should always assess how grievers are utilizing online resources for information and support.

☐ Creative Arts

Would you know my name if I saw you in heaven? Would it be the same if I saw you in heaven? I must be strong and carry on 'cause I know I don't belong here in heaven.

—Eric Clapton, "Tears in Heaven"

When his 4-year-old son died, Eric Clapton eulogized him in the beautiful and plaintive song "Tears in Heaven." Clapton's way of dealing with loss is just one example of using the creative arts as an adaptive strategy. Examples are as varied as the arts themselves. Native American groups have often included dance within their grieving rituals. Other examples include painting, music, photography, writing, storytelling, cinematography, and the use of videos. Journaling, or writing about one's feelings or thoughts, is a well-established approach in grief counseling or self-help. John Gunther (1949) and Kent Koppelman (1994) each dealt with the loss of a son by writing extensive accounts of the life and death of the child. Another illustration, albeit fictional, is offered by S. E. Hinton's 1967 novel of class conflict among adolescents, *The Outsiders*. The book, written as the journal of Ponyboy, the adolescent protagonist, recounts the events leading to the deaths of two close friends. As this fictional journal continues, one has the sense of how healing writing the book must have been. In fact, research has supported the therapeutic value of such creative approaches. Both Lattanzi and Hale (1984) and Pennebaker, Keicolt-Glaser, and Glaser (1988) found that writing about trauma and loss was useful in ameliorating grief.

Creative arts can be useful for grievers with any grief strategy. Creative arts can allow affective ventilation or cognitive processing. All of these are active processes that allow a sense of interpretive control, allowing grievers symbolic control over a situation or loss that provides the grievers little actual control. They have other functions as well. Riches and Dawson (1998) noted that the use of photography by bereaved parents assisted them in remembering the life of the deceased child rather than the death, facilitated reminiscing with others, and introduced the child to others who did not know him or her, reinforcing a continued bond. Most current models of loss emphasize two functions in the grieving process: dealing with the loss and recreating a new life with a redefined relationship to the deceased (Stroebe & Schut, 1995; Worden, 2009). As Riches and Dawson (1998) affirm, creative arts can allow individuals outlets to fulfill both. And as time goes on, the creative expression can change as the grieving process continues (Harvey, Orbuch, Weber, Merbach, & Alt, 1992). For example, accounts and stories that are initially problematic or painful may later become more hopeful.

As with other strategies, creative arts should be used in a manner that is both intentional and prescriptive. Persons should use modalities that are comfortable for them. It makes little sense to encourage painting for someone who has little interest in it. Rather, it is worthwhile to assess which modes would be useful to the person. Similarly, these creative approaches often work best when they are reflective and amplify basic adaptive strategies. For example, intuitive grievers may find the arts to be effective approaches to ventilate affect, while instrumental grievers may use them to cognitively process memories. The goal remains to validate and respect the use of each form of creative expression.

☐ Ritual

The term *ritual* is one of those words that can have many different meanings. Any regularized activity can be said to be a ritual. For example, one can say that having coffee and reading the paper is one's regular morning ritual. But such usage trivializes the notion of ritual. Following Shorter (1996), we prefer to call such activities *ceremonies* or perhaps simply *habits* and reserve the term *ritual* to special acts that offer sacred meaning to events. As Grollman (1997) is apt to say, "Rituals make mountains out of moments."

Rituals are another powerful tool in dealing with loss. Gennep (1960) reminds us that the power of rituals lies in the fact that they are *liminal*. By liminal, Gennep means that they strike us at the threshold of consciousness, speaking to both our conscious and subconscious simultaneously. Rando (1984), too, delineates many useful facets of ritual, which include allowing individuals to act, offering legitimization for physical and affective ventilation, delineating grief (i.e., limiting grief to a certain space and time), giving a sense of control (i.e., doing something at an otherwise uncontrollable event), providing an ongoing sense of connection to the loss, allowing space to safely confront ambivalent or confused feeling or thoughts, generating social support, and offering opportunities to find meaning in the loss by applying spiritual frameworks to that loss.

Rando (1984) reminds us that these therapeutic properties of ritual make it a highly useful therapeutic instrument throughout the entire experience of grief—from the illness through the funeral and beyond. And, in fact, both theory and research have supported the therapeutic role of ritual (e.g., Bolton & Camp, 1987, 1989; Doka, 1984; Klass & Heath, 1996; Reeves & Boersma, 1990; Van der Hart, 1988).

Because rituals possess so many therapeutic properties, they can be valuable for many different types of grievers. Intuitive grievers can benefit from the opportunities rituals offer for affective ventilation. Instrumental grievers will appreciate the opportunities to act as well as to focus thoughts and assist in meaning making.

Moreover, the fact that rituals provide a space for grievers, or as Golden (1994a) states, a container to hold grief, makes it highly compatible to grievers, either instrumental or dissonant, who seek to dose or limit their exposure to grief.

Naturally, funerals and other socially shared rituals can offer therapeutic opportunities to deal with grief. Planning and participating in funeral rituals can be very helpful to grievers (Doka, 1984). As the following case illustrates, instrumental grievers may particularly benefit.

> "When my father died, it was important for my brother and me to take charge of the funeral. Everything we did was intentional. We chose oak because that was his favorite wood. All the hymns we chose had meaning. We had a meal afterwards in his favorite restaurant. This had special meaning since he had, before he became real sick, wanted to take the whole family there. He was a newspaperman, so whenever I bought something, he would always say I should have come to him since he knew someone who gets it wholesale. My friend is a funeral director so he gave us a big discount. I figure Dad was thinking, 'He finally learned that nobody pays retail.' I think about the service often. It really helped."
>
> —40-year-old clergyman

Other rituals, too, may have value. The Jewish ritual of Kaddish, prayer said for a period of time after the loss, serves as an example. In the Orthodox tradition, only males counted toward the quorum. Thus, the prayer in effect offered an opportunity for males to come together in a ritual way for companionship and support.

While funerals, anniversaries, holidays, or special occasions offer times for ritual, one of the advantages of ritual is that it can be used whenever it meets a need. Grievers may create rituals any time to deal with issues yet unresolved. Rituals provide a powerful tool to work on continuing issues.

The first question to think through is what message one wants the ritual to convey. Van der Hart (1978), for example, building on the work of Gennep (1960), discusses two types of rituals. *Rituals of continuity* are rituals that emphasize, even in the midst of loss, the continuing connection. The AIDS quilt is an excellent example. Each panel reminds us that the individual remains part of the fabric of life and will not be forgotten. A friend offers another illustration. Every holiday his family ends the meal with a toast to an eccentric aunt with her favorite drink. This simple ritual becomes a wonderful way to recount all their favorite

Aunt Carmen stories, even imparting them to a generation that barely knew her.

Rituals of transition (Van der Hart, 1978) offer another message. Here the theme is that one has entered a new place in one's journey through grief. The following case offers an illustration.

Mary is a widow in her 40s, whose husband died 7 years ago after a 5-year, debilitating struggle with multiple sclerosis (MS). Mary is at a point where she would like to take off her wedding ring and begin dating, but she seems unable to do so. In discussing her relationship with her counselor, it becomes clear that the ring has great meaning. Though the illness was very difficult for both, every night after a long day's struggle, when they lay in bed, they would put their ring fingers together and repeat their vows "in sickness and in health." The counselor acknowledged that she had put on the ring in a ritual that had great value, and both he and Mary agreed that it should be removed in another meaningful ritual. It was arranged that on Sunday afternoon, Mary and her friends and family gathered in the church where she and her husband had exchanged vows. The priest met her at the altar. There he repeated the vows, now in the past tense. "Were you faithful in sickness and in health, in good times and in bad?" he intoned. Mary could, in the presence of these witnesses, affirm that she had been. The priest then asked for the ring. As Mary later described, it came off "as if by magic." As planned, the priest arranged to have both rings interlocked and welded to her wedding picture. He returned it to her in a brief ritual of continuity.

Rituals can have other meanings as well. *Rituals of reconciliation* either ask for or extend forgiveness. A note at the Vietnam Memorial Wall provides a poignant example: "We did all that we could, I guess, but since you're here, it was not enough." *Rituals of affirmation* provide a complement to rituals of reconciliation. Rituals of affirmation simply provide ways to acknowledge legacies or say thanks. The following case provides an example.

"When my friend died, I took a special interest in Mark, his son. One day, I took him to a place where we had once fished. I had told him the story of how his dad had angered me by always losing my fishing lures. On the trail down to the stream, we found an old rusted lure. Mark got a real kick out of that and said, 'This was a gift from my dad.' We ended up doing a ritual where we thanked his dad for bringing us together. As of that ritual, Mark decided to lose the lure."

In developing rituals, it is critical to remember four principles of planning:

1. *Rituals always arise from the story*—Each ritual should be individually planned. Think about what type of ritual is needed. What elements should be part of it and who should witness it? Some rituals may be private; others shared with a few. Some, like the ritual of the wedding ring, will be very public.

2. *The elements used in a ritual should be both visible and symbolic*—Since rituals are liminal, they should include elements that both can be seen, appealing to our conscious senses but moving beyond them. The ring is not only a piece of gold but also a symbol of commitment, just as the rusted lure symbolizes connection.

3. *Rituals should be planned and processed*—Before undertaking a ritual, it is critical that it be carefully thought out. The powerful ritual around the wedding ring would have been far different if the priest had asked at that special moment when the ring was removed "Who gets it now?" Follow the planning through to the conclusion. After the ritual, individuals may need opportunities to process, or continue to think about or talk about the event.

4. *Use primal elements*—One of the lessons that churches, synagogues, mosques, and temples teach is that rituals are most effective when they employ the primal elements—water, earth (for example, flowers), wind (as in music), and fire (such as candles).

☐ Self-Help and Support Groups

The value of self-help and support groups has long been established (Silverman, 1981, 1986). They can provide opportunities for education and ventilation, places to bond with supportive others, suggestions for adapting, and hope that one can survive the loss as others have done or seem to be doing. There may be other benefits as well. Lund (1999), for example, notes that individuals within a self-help group who perceive that they are helping others experience better grief outcomes themselves, perhaps because their own self-esteem is enhanced. And the very nature of mutual support reinforces a sense of the normality of the grief experience as well as furthering self-reliance.

Groups are not only an effective but also an efficient way of assisting grieving individuals. Many more people can be helped within a group setting than through individual counseling. For these reasons, groups have become a staple of many bereavement outreach programs sponsored by varied agencies, such as hospices, funeral homes, larger self-help networks, or other organizations.

Groups can also vary in many ways. Some, like The Compassionate Friends, strongly emphasize self-help, keeping the professional's role minimal. Others are professionally led. Some are open-ended—individuals come and leave according to their own needs. Others ask for a specific commitment to attend a limited number of sessions. Once these sessions begin, others cannot join. Some are general, focusing on a wide variety of losses, while others are made up of individuals who have experienced a common loss such as the loss of a child or spouse. In some, such as Parents of Murdered Children, the focus is very narrow. Some, too, are part of larger groupings such as national or regional meetings; others simply are based in one community. Again, as with other interventions, the question is not which approach is best, but rather what best meets an individual's given need.

Although groups have much value, they are not suitable for everyone. Some individuals whose needs for help are simply too overwhelming cannot prosper in a group environment. And, as discussed in Chapter 3, some individuals are very introverted. Here the "rule of reciprocity" may make them uncomfortable, since they may feel that they need to respond to the sharing of others. This may be particularly so in some groups where that more general rule is a norm of the group. There is also the question of fit. Fit involves the somewhat tangible yet intangible way that the grieving individual experiences a sense of connection to the group. For example, when Bob died, he left his wife Lois quite well off since he was heavily insured. Although Lois was devastated by the loss, she felt uncomfortable in the widows group where much of the discussion centered on the difficulty of surviving financially. With groups that have an intake process, issues of fit and appropriateness can be addressed prior to entry.

For many grieving people with an intuitive pattern, groups can have a great value. They provide a safe, comfortable environment for sharing feelings. As such, they validate many of the difficult feelings that such individuals may be experiencing. And in addition to all the other benefits, they allow grieving individuals to identify and bond with supportive others who both share and understand their plan.

In other groups where the norm is not reinforced, some introverted individuals may experience great value in hearing their own sentiments expressed and in deriving other benefits of the group experience.

Dissonant grievers too, especially male dissonant grievers, may find great value in such groups as it gives them a safe place to validate and share their feelings. Joe, for example, has benefited much from one. A retired steamfitter in his 60s, he misses his late wife intensely. Joe believes that he needs to be tough and strong to hold his family together and support his daughter's grief. The support group provides a safe place for him to feel and share his loss. Each month as he tells different aspects of his story, his voice cracks and his eyes well with tears. But instead of the discomfort that such reactions cause when he is around friends and family, in the support group they engender empathy. As mentioned earlier, there may be value in creating special groups for dissonant males.

☐ Can Grief Groups Work for Instrumental Grievers?

One of the questions often asked is whether groups work for instrumental grievers. Often this question says more about the needs of the person raising it than it does about the instrumental griever. Most traditional self-help groups, with their emphasis on self-disclosure and affective exploration, are a poor match with the characteristics of instrumental grievers. As Chapter 3 explored, instrumental grievers tend to be uncomfortable with self-disclosure and their tempered affect may be perceived as cold or resistant by other grievers. And instrumental grievers may look to utilize such groups for problem-solving approaches, striking facilitators and other group members as inappropriate or premature. For example, they may see such groups as opportunities for respite or socialization. Dan, a 52-year-old widower, provides one such example. After his wife died, he experienced both loneliness and problems in managing daily tasks around the house. He decided to attend a widow's group with the hope that he might "meet a nice widow." As he described it, he would often come late, hoping to minimize the "raw parts" of the meeting when people shared their feelings. And he wondered why his attempts to solve others' problems, for example telling a fellow member with anger "to run it off," seemed dismissed and unappreciated. "I always liked the coffee and cake part at the end best," he stated.

Some groups may be designed especially to meet the needs of instrumental grievers. O'Neil (1994), for example, developed a network for widowers with school-aged children that provided information about resources as well as education about common problems. Men had the option to communicate in a variety of ways, including phone, fax, letter, or e-mail. Worden (2008) noted that in the Harvard Bereavement Study, young widowers seemed to benefit more from groups that focused on being a good single parent than on those that offered emotional support.

Other groups may emphasize other problem-oriented issues such as living alone. In one area, for example, the local hospice offered a program that provided classes for widowers on basic skills such as doing laundry, cleaning, and cooking. After the classes ended, the men chose to stay together, often working on projects. Their first project, evolving out of the cooking class, was to develop a cookbook for men, where they not only shared their wives' recipes but also in those recipes included reminiscences of their wives.

In addition to problem-focused groups, a number of other approaches may work as well. Other groups for instrumental grievers may utilize active approaches. For example, some groups may be focused on expressive arts while others might offer a focus on reading and discussion.

Active groups may be especially excellent modalities for adolescent males. Following a mine disaster, a bereavement network found that boys were reluctant to join grief groups. In response, the group offered an adventure-focused counseling approach for these boys. They found that this approach worked well on three levels. First, it filled a void in the boys life left by the deaths of their dads. Second, the mastery of new skills such as caving or rock climbing contributed to their self-esteem and sense of competence. Third, on camping trips, they found that as the boys sat around the fire it was a natural time to share memories of their dads with the group as well as a sense of their loss. The campfire seemed a natural setting for sharing remembrances and receiving support.

Group modalities can certainly be adapted to culturally appropriate formats. For example, the Inupiats, a Native Alaskan group, decided to have a men's grief group meet in a sweat lodge—melding the new form of a self-help group with a traditional activity where men seek healing and support.

In addition, educational seminars about grief, for example, "How to Handle the Holidays" and "How to Cope with Grief and Loss," can appeal to a range of grievers. As emphasized in the prior chapter, grief support for a range of grieving styles ought to be triadic—offering rituals, support groups, and psychoeducational information.

Approaches that emphasize problem solving or education often work with instrumental grievers; however, these groups must remember the value of truth in advertising. It does little good to advertise a group in such a manner to attract grievers uncomfortable with more traditional approaches as a way to slowly wean them into affective self-disclosure. For the reader who is an instrumental griever, a similar caution is offered. Be clear about what a group's approach and aims are, and assess whether this fits with your goals and needs.

☐ Conclusion

This chapter emphasized that there are many strategies that individuals can utilize as they deal with their grief. Effective strategies build upon, rather than deny, the strategies that grievers already count as strengths. The words of one person I once knew offer a wise conclusion. He was an older man who lived in my neighborhood, whose wife had died a few months earlier. In a chance meeting on the street, I asked him how he was doing. He thought he was doing well. But when he felt tense or lonely, he recounted, he often worked out or ran. Almost apologetically, he continued, reminding me that he had been a boxer earlier in life. "The one thing I learned in boxing was that you start with your strong hand."

Conclusion

In many ways, this project has been a journey that began with an interest in the way men grieve. It has subsequently opened up to larger patterns of grieving; ones that exist beyond gender. It would do well in the final section to summarize and briefly explore the implications of adaptive grieving styles for researchers, theorists, educators, clinicians, and those experiencing grief.

To summarize:

- Although grief is a very individual experience and the meaning of loss can vary significantly, individuals often exhibit patterns in the ways they experience, express, and adapt to loss.

- These patterns are a continuum; on one end are people who tend to be *instrumental* in their grief, whereas on the other end are individuals who may be considered *intuitive*.

- Intuitive grievers experience grief primarily as waves of affect expressing this grief in a variety of ways, such as crying or ventilating affect. Finding appropriate ways to ventilate this affect is a useful adaptive strategy that facilitates their grieving process.

- Instrumental grievers experience grief in other ways. Affect is usually modulated and they tend to describe grief more in physical, behavioral, or cognitive manifestations. Expressions of grief tend to be active and cognitive. Useful adaptive strategies for instrumental grievers will be drawn from more cognitive and active approaches.

- Many individuals will experience changes in their patterns throughout their life cycle. As individuals age, their patterns are likely to move toward the center of the continuum, becoming more blended.

- There is a pattern that might be termed *dissonant*. Here there is dissonance between the way a person experiences grief and the manner in which that person expresses and adapts to grief. This usually occurs with an individual whose internal experience of grief is more intuitive, but who, for some reason or another (such as constraint) finds it difficult to express that emotion. Hence, some males may be dissonant, that is, experiencing grief as intense feelings they are constrained from expressing.

- These patterns are *related* to gender, albeit not *determined* by gender—at least in Western societies. Other factors—temperamental, cultural, historical, generational, perhaps even biological—as well as socialization and developmental experiences may affect an individual grieving pattern.

- Counselors need to carefully assess an individual's grieving patterns. Only then can counselors offer interventive strategies that are comparable with the way an individual grieves and build on that individual's strengths.

- Within family systems different grieving patterns can complicate one another's grief. Effective counseling can assist family members in identifying where they can find the support they need while drawing upon the complementary strengths of individuals with other patterns.

- Differences in patterns are differences, not deficiencies. Each pattern, depending on the way it is utilized—as well as the societal expectations about grief—can complicate or facilitate the grieving process.

This approach suggests certain implications for theorists, researchers, educators, and clinicians, as well as grieving individuals. In many ways, this is a new approach to grief theory, but one that takes seriously the understanding that grief is a multidimensional reaction consisting of multiple manifestations of grief. Grief is not just an affective experience, but also one that touches the cognitive, spiritual, physical, and behavioral realms. This approach also takes seriously the understanding of many current approaches, such as task models (see Worden, 2009), which show that there are varied ways for individuals to express grief and adapt to loss.

Finally, this approach reminds theorists of the valued linkages, models, and insights that can be drawn from related disciplines such as psychology and sociology. There is a danger to the emergence of practice-oriented disciplines such as education, nursing, or thanatology. The danger is one of marginalization as small circles of specialists teach and educate one another. Lest thanatology's models of the grieving process become too parochial, it is essential not to lose the connections with larger models and master concepts that provide linkages between and within one's discipline (see Corr & Doka, 2001).

This is a challenge to researchers as well, but it is hoped that there are other challenges offered by this work. First, there is a need to continue to validate these assumptions of patterns and to assess the distribution of these patterns within given populations. Subsequent research could then consider the relationship of a pattern with a wide range of other variables, such as developmental factors and grieving outcomes, as well as associations with other assessments such as Myer–Briggs. In addition, a rough tool for assessment of a pattern was offered within this book. However, alternative approaches to assessment that are clearly validated are essential.

Finally, the journey taken in this book suggests to researchers that gender may not be as useful a variable as sometimes assumed. The extensive research cited here on gender simply seems to validate the old law of social physics—for every PhD there is an opposite and opposing PhD. Perhaps this is because gender itself is related to a critical variable: pattern. Researchers, then, may wish to move beyond gender.

Educators and clinicians, too, may wish to carefully examine their own assumptions. As Sue and Sue (2008) note, there is an inherent bias in counseling, one that emphasizes the ventilation of feelings as a critical value. Not only does that lead to insensitivity to cultures that do not value emotional expressiveness as much, it disenfranchises those who express their grief in a different way.

Ironically, this may place many educators and counselors in a paradoxical situation. Biographical evidence suggests that many people who specialize in thanatology (Corless, 2001; Corless & Vachon, 2003) do so after an encounter with dying, death, or grief. This may suggest an initial bias toward instrumental modes, an attempt at cognitive mastery. The irony is that in traditional counseling, they may learn to invalidate their own pattern of grief, much like our colleague, perinatal pioneer Jane Nichols, whose story is discussed in Chapter 1, invalidated her own grief. The danger is that unacknowledged, this may create considerable issues for countertransference that could harm or alienate more instrumental grievers.

Thus educators and clinicians share a joint responsibility to validate the many ways that people grieve. It is a responsibility exercised in counseling sessions, classrooms, and community educational forums. It begins, too, in the education of counselors. Perhaps an emphasis is needed on both the value of exploring and validating counselors' own ways of dealing with loss and on cultivating eclectic approaches that acknowledge the distinctive grieving patterns of their clients. Once after the public presentation of this material, one participant came up to thank the presenter. The counselor stated how valuable he found the presentation and how much he could use the techniques shared. However, he concluded with an interesting statement: "How much easier it would be if these people could only get in touch with their feelings!" Educators and clinicians, too, need to see beyond gender and beyond our own biases.

In many ways this has been a personal journey as well as a professional one, clarifying earlier experiences and reactions. One author was part of a clinical pastoral education program, working with children with cancer. Each supervisory session spent considerable time exploring the comparative lack of affect that the supervisor noted in the student counselor. Each week, in tones of exasperation, the supervisor would ask, "What do you do with your feelings? How can you not grieve?" In reality much grieving was taking place, but it was expressed in other modes—biweekly donating of platelets, numerous journal entries, talking about the children, reading, and ultimately writing two master's theses based, in part, on the experience. How much more useful it would have been had the supervisor been able to identify that grief work and to explore its strengths and limitations. Similarly, the other author conducted a series of videotaped interviews with a 16-year-old female dying from an inoperable brain tumor. After the girl's death, a graduate student in thanatology asked him: "How can you continue to teach this stuff after what you've just been through?" It was pointed out that teaching was a way of expressing grief, just as delivering the teenager's eulogy had been.

Ultimately it is that identification, validation, and exploration of their pattern of grief or adaptive grieving styles that grieving individuals will find empowering and that will allow them to deal with that loss on their own terms, with their own unique strengths.

In recent years, there has been considerable movement in the ways we understand grief and loss (Doka, 2007, offers a summary). There is an increased appreciation of cultural differences (e.g., Rosenblatt, 2008), a widening understanding of the many losses that engender grief (Doka, 2002), new models and approaches to understanding the grieving process (e.g., Neimeyer, 2000; Rando, 1993; Stroebe & Schut, 1999; Worden, 2009), an acknowledgment of the continuing bonds that persist even after loss (Klass, Silverman, & Nickman, 1996), a recognition of the possibilities for growth that exist in grief (Calhoun & Tedeschi, 1990, 2006), and, as represented by this work, a move beyond simply seeing grief as affect. Fundamentally, these approaches have moved us from looking at grief as a process whereby people experience universal stages to recognition of the very personal and individual ways that people grieve.

This book states that both instrumental and intuitive grievers are disenfranchised. Instrumental grievers are disenfranchised early in the grief process when the comparative absence of affective expression may make others believe they are untouched by the loss. Intuitive grievers may feel disenfranchised over time, when others seem to tire of their need to express and share their grief. Dissonant grievers as well may be disenfranchised when their own conceptions of their role of societal definitions of males and females constrain their expression of grief. Perhaps, as one understands these patterns of grief or adaptive grieving styles, and as one looks at grief beyond gender, these individuals may be disenfranchised no more.

APPENDIX A: GRIEF PATTERN INVENTORY

Please respond to each of the following statements using the key below. If appropriate, choose the response that best describes you in the past 2 weeks.

Key:

A = Always

U = Usually

S = Sometimes

R = Rarely

N = Never

Please circle the best response for you.

1. A U S R N I am more emotional than most people I know.

2. A U S R N It is easy for me to cry and show my feelings to others.

3. A U S R N Even though I have returned to my normal routine, I still have strong and painful feelings about my loss.

4. A U S R N Even though I feel like crying, I do not cry in front of others.

5.   A   U   S   R   N   Although I am grieving in my own way, others may think me cold and unfeeling.

6.   A   U   S   R   N   I don't seem to get as upset as most other people I know.

7.   A   U   S   R   N   I feel overwhelmed by my feelings of grief.

8.   A   U   S   R   N   I appreciate when others encourage me to share my painful feelings with them.

9.   A   U   S   R   N   I avoid highly emotional or "touchy-feely" situations of any kind.

10.   A   U   S   R   N   It is important to me that others view me as being in control.

11.   A   U   S   R   N   I have been told that I am avoiding my grief even though I don't think that I am.

12.   A   U   S   R   N   I have been controlling my painful feelings by drinking or by using other prescription or nonprescription drugs.

13.   A   U   S   R   N   I believe that a bereavement support group is (would be) very helpful for me.

14.   A   U   S   R   N   I worry that I am not as upset by my loss as I should be and feel guilty that I don't have more intense feelings.

15.   A   U   S   R   N   I resent efforts to get me to show feelings that I don't have.

16.   A   U   S   R   N   I *think* more about my loss *than feel* things about my loss.

17.   A   U   S   R   N   I believe it is very important to be aware of, and in touch with, all of my feelings.

18.   A   U   S   R   N   I find that solving problems associated with my loss helps me.

19. A U S R N Although I can sometimes control my painful feelings, they usually return and overwhelm me.

20. A U S R N Since my loss, I feel like I'm just pretending to be strong in front of most people.

21. A U S R N I find that I can't stop my grieving by thinking of other things.

22. A U S R N I have taken deliberate action to honor the memory of my loved one, even though I have not been as upset as most others who are grieving my loved one.

23. A U S R N Others seem surprised by my recovery from my loss.

24. A U S R N Although I took care of things immediately after my loved one's death, I was surprised when I eventually "crashed" and began to have intense, painful feelings.

25. A U S R N I would describe myself as more intellectual than emotional.

26. A U S R N If I am upset or sad, I don't like to show it for fear that I will be seen as weak.

27. A U S R N It does not usually occur to me to deal with my pain by talking about what is bothering me.

28. A U S R N It is easy for me to put my feelings into words and discuss them with others.

29. A U S R N I usually respond to the question of "how are you feeling" with what I am not feeling (e.g., "not too bad").

30. A U S R N I don't see the value of talking about feelings that I don't have in the first place.

APPENDIX B: ITEM ANALYSIS AND SCORING OF THE GRIEF PATTERN INVENTORY

The Grief Pattern Inventory contains 30 items with response choices ranged along a continuum: always, usually, sometimes, rarely, and never. This reflects the belief that patterns exist on a continuum from profoundly intuitive to intensely instrumental. What follows is a brief description of each question and the pattern suggested by a positive response.

1. *I am more emotional than most people I know.* The basis of the patterns lies in the individual's customary choice of feelings over thinking and vice versa. Positive = intuitive.

2. *It is easy for me to cry and show my feelings for others.* A willingness to disclose feelings is associated with the intuitive pattern. Positive = intuitive.

3. *Even though I have returned to my normal routine, I still have strong and painful feelings about my loss.* Positive = intuitive.

4. *Even though I feel like crying, I do not cry in front of others.* This is the first of seven questions where a positive response could reveal a tendency toward a dissonant response. Although this would usually point to an intuitive dissonant response, it could include instrumental grievers who have no other outlets for expressing whatever degree of feelings they experience. Positive = dissonant.

5. *Although I am grieving in my own way, others may think me cold and unfeeling.* Instrumental grievers are often perceived as lacking feelings. Positive = instrumental.

6. *I don't seem to get as upset as most other people I know.* Positive = instrumental.

7. *I feel overwhelmed by my feelings of grief.* Positive = intuitive.

8. *I appreciate when others encourage me to share my painful feelings with them.* Although this could measure a griever's tendency toward introversion, it is most likely an example of intuitive grieving. Positive = intuitive.

9. *I avoid highly emotional or "touchy-feely" situations of any kind.* Instrumental grievers rarely choose to place themselves in situations designed to elicit the experience and expression of feelings. Positive = instrumental.

10. *It is important to me that others view me as being in control.* This is especially important for intuitive grievers who may become image managers in the wake of a loss. Positive = dissonant.

11. *I have been told that I am avoiding my grief even though I don't think that I am.* Positive = instrumental.

12. *I have been controlling my painful feelings by drinking or using other prescription or nonprescription drugs.* Positive = dissonant.

13. *I believe that a bereavement support group is (would be) very helpful for me.* Positive = intuitive.

14. *I worry that I am not as upset by my loss as I should be and feel guilty that I don't have more intense feelings.* Penitent instrumental grievers feel unusually guilty about their lack of pain. Positive = dissonant.

15. *I resent efforts to get me to show feelings that I don't have.* Positive = instrumental.

16. *I think more about my loss than feel things about my loss.* Positive = instrumental.

17. *I believe it is important to be aware of, and in touch with, all of my feelings.* Positive = intuitive.

18. *I find that solving problems associated with my loss helps me.* Positive = instrumental.

19. *Although I can sometimes control my painful feelings, they return and overwhelm me.* Positive = intuitive.

20. *Since my loss, I feel like I'm just pretending to be strong in front of most people.* Positive = dissonant.

21. *I find that I can't stop my grieving by thinking of other things.* Positive = intuitive.

22. *I have taken deliberate action to honor the memory of my loved one, even though I have not been as upset as most others who are grieving my loved one.* Positive = instrumental.

23. *Others seem surprised by my recovery from my loss.* Positive = instrumental.

24. *Although I took care of things immediately after my loved one's death, I was surprised when I eventually "crashed" and began to have intense, painful feelings.* Even strongly intuitive grievers can sometimes manage certain postdeath activities before being overwhelmed by their feelings. Positive = intuitive.

25. *I would describe myself as more intellectual than emotional.* Positive = instrumental.

26. *If I am upset or sad, I don't like to show it for fear that I will be seen as weak.* Positive = dissonant.

27. *It does not usually occur to me to deal with my pain by talking about what is bothering me.* Positive = dissonant.

28. *It is easy for me to put my feelings into words and discuss them with others.* Positive = intuitive.

29. *I usually respond to the question of "how are you feeling" with what I am not feeling (e.g., "not too bad").* Positive = instrumental.

30. *I don't see the value of talking about feelings that I don't have in the first place.* Positive = instrumental.

We again remind readers that the Grief Pattern Inventory is designed to augment other methods for assessing a client's grief. In addition, it is always a sound practice to readminister the Grief Pattern Inventory after several weeks have passed. Dissonant responses, in particular, are often temporary in nature. Finally, we would advise waiting at least 2 to 3 weeks after the death to begin evaluating patterns. Suggested guidelines for interpreting a griever's scores follows:

Key: A = +2; U = +1; S = 0; R = −1; N = −2

Intuitive Pattern: Questions #1, 2, 3, 7, 8, 13, 17, 19, 21, 24, 28

Score: 16–22   Profoundly intuitive pattern

            11–15   Moderate intuitive pattern

            6–10   Blended intuitive pattern

            −5–+5   Blended balanced pattern

Instrumental Pattern: Questions #5, 6, 9, 11, 15, 16, 18, 22, 23, 25, 29, 30

Score: 16–24   Profoundly instrumental pattern

            11–15   Moderate instrumental pattern

            6–10   Blended instrumental pattern

            −5–+5   Blended balanced pattern

Dissonant Responses: Questions #4, 10, 12, 14, 20, 26, 27

Each dissonant response should be evaluated separately.

REFERENCES

Allen, S., & Hayslip, B., Jr. (2001). Research in gender differences in bereavement outcome: Presenting a model of experienced competence. In D. Lund (Ed.), *Men coping with grief* (pp. 97–115). Amityville, NY: Baywood.

Alston, N., & Alson, P. (2009). The birth of purpose. *The Forum Newsletter, 35*(1), 7.

Archer, J. (2001). Grief from an evolutionary perspective. In M. Stroebe, R. Hansson, W. Stroebe, & H. Schut (Eds.), *Handbook of bereavement research: Consequences, coping, and care* (pp. 263–283). Washington, DC: American Psychological Association.

Attig, T. (1996). *How we grieve: Relearning the world.* New York: Oxford University Press.

Averill, J., & Nunley, E. (1993). Grief as an emotion and a disease: A social constructivist perspective. In M. Stroebe, R. Hansson, W. Stroebe, & H. Schut (Eds.), *Handbook of bereavement research: Consequences, coping, and care* (pp. 77–90). Washington, DC: American Psychological Association.

Barnett, R., Biener, L., & Baruch, G. (Eds.). (1987). *Gender and stress.* New York: Free Press.

Barrett, R. (1997). Bereaved black children. In J. Morgan (Ed.), *Readings in thanatology* (pp. 403–420). Amityville, NY: Baywood.

Barrett, R. (1998). Sociocultural considerations for working with Blacks experiencing loss and grief. In K. Doka & J. Davidson (Eds.), *Living with grief: Who we are, how we grieve* (pp. 83–96). Washington, DC: Hospice Foundation of America.

Bem, S. L. (1981). *The lenses of gender: Transforming the debate on sexual inequality.* New Haven, CT: Yale University Press.

Berger, P., & Luckmann, T. (1966). *The social construction of reality.* New York: Doubleday.

Berman, P. W. (1980). Are women more responsive than men to the young? A review of developmental and situational variables. *Psychological Bulletin, 88,* 668–695.

Biddle, L., & Walter, T. (1998). The emotional English and their queen of hearts. *The Forum Newsletter, 24*(5), 13–15.

Blauner, R. (1968). Death and the social structure. In M. Truzzi (Ed.), *Sociology and everyday life* (pp. 346–367). Englewood Cliffs, NJ: Prentice Hall.

Blazina, C., & Watkins, C. E., Jr. (1996). Masculine gender role conflict: Effects on college men's psychological well-being, chemical substance usage, and attitudes toward help-seeking. *Journal of Counseling Psychology, 43,* 461–465.

Bly, R. (1990). *Iron John: A book about men.* New York: Vintage.

Boch Hughes, C., & Page-Lieberman, J. (1989). Fathers experiencing perinatal loss. *Death Studies, 13*, 537–556.

Bohannon, J. (1990). Grief responses of spouses following the death of a child: A longitudinal study. *Omega: The Journal of Death and Dying, 22*, 109–121.

Bohannon, J. E. (1991). Religiosity related to grief levels of bereaved mothers and fathers. *Omega: The Journal of Death and Dying, 23*, 153–159.

Bolton, C., & Camp, D. (1987). Funeral rituals and the facilitation of grief work. *Omega: The Journal of Death and Dying, 17*, 343–351.

Bolton, C., & Camp, D. (1989). The post-funeral ritual in bereavement counseling and grief work. *Journal of Gerontological Social Work, 13*, 49–59.

Bonanno, G. (1997). *Examining the "grief work" approach to bereavement.* Presentation to the Annual Meeting of the Association of Death Education and Counseling, Washington, DC.

Bonanno, G. A. (2001). Grief and emotion: A social-functional perspective. In M. Stroebe, R. Hansson, W. Stroebe, & H. Schut (Eds.), *Handbook of bereavement research: Consequences, coping, and care* (pp. 493–515). Washington, DC: American Psychological Association.

Bonanno, G. A. (2004). Loss, trauma, and human resilience: Have we underestimated the human capacity to thrive after extremely aversive events? *American Psychologist, 59*(1), 20–28.

Bonanno, G. A., Keltner, D., Holen, A., & Horowitz, M. J. (1995). When avoiding unpleasant emotions might not be such a bad thing: Verbal-autonomic response dissociation and midlife conjugal bereavement. *Journal of Personality and Social Psychology, 69*, 975–989.

Bonanno, G. A., & Singer, J. L. (1990). Repressor personality style: Theoretical and methodological implications for health and pathology. In J. L. Singer (Ed.), *Repression and dissociation* (pp. 435–470). Chicago: University of Chicago Press.

Bonanno, G. A., Wortman, C. B., & Nesse, R. M. (2004). Prospective patterns of resilience and maladjustment before and after the death of a spouse. *Psychology and Aging, 19*, 260–271.

Brabant, S., Forsyth, C., & Melancon, C. (1992). Grieving men: Thoughts, feelings and behaviors following deaths of wives. *The Hospice Journal, 8*(4), 33–47.

Bronfenbrenner, U. (1989). Ecological systems theory. In R. Vasta (Ed.), *Six theories of child development*. Greenwich, CT: JAI Press.

Bowlby J. (1980). *Loss, sadness and depression*. New York: Basic Books.

Bowling, A., & Windsor, J. (1995). Death after widow(er)hood: An analysis of mortality rates up to 13 years after bereavement. *Omega: The Journal of Death and Dying, 31*, 35–49.

Caine, L. (1974). *Widow*. New York: Bantam.

Calhoun, L., & Tedeschi, R. (1990). Positive aspects of critical problems: Recollections of grief. *Omega: The Journal of Death and Dying, 20*, 265–272.

Calhoun, L., & Tedeschi, R. (Eds.). (2006). *Handbook of posttraumatic growth*. Mahwah, NJ: Lawrence Erlbaum Associates.

Campbell, S., & Silverman, P. (1996). *Widower: When men are left alone*. Amityville, NY: Baywood.

Campos, J. J., Campos, R. G., & Barrett, K. C. (1989). Emergent themes in the study of emotional development and emotion regulation. *Developmental Psychology, 25*, 394–402.

Carey, R. (1979). Weathering widowhood: Problems and adjustments of the widowed during the first year. *Omega: The Journal of Death and Dying, 10*, 163–173.

Carroll, R., & Shaefer, S. (1994). Similarities and differences in spouses coping with SIDS. *Omega: The Journal of Death and Dying, 28*, 273–284.

Carverhill, P. (1995). *Hearing men's voices: The lived experience of spousal bereavement.* Presentation to the King's College Conference on Death, Dying, and Bereavement, London, Canada.

Cherney, P., & Verhey, M. (1996). Grief among gay men associated with multiple losses from AIDS. *Death Studies, 20*, 115–132.

Clark, C. (1987). Sympathy, biography, and sympathy margin. *American Journal of Sociology, 93*, 290–321.

Cochran, S. (2006). Struggling for sadness: A relational approach to healing men's grief. In M. Englar-Carlson, & M. A. Stevens (Eds.). *In the room with men: A casebook of therapeutic change* (pp. 91–107). Washington, DC: American Psychological Association.

Conway, V., & Feeney, J. (1997). Attachments and grief: A study of parental bereavement. *Journal of Family Studies, 3*, 36–42.

Cook, J. (1988). Dad's double binds: Rethinking father's bereavement from a men's studies perspective. *Journal of Contemporary Ethnography, 17*, 285–308.

Corless, I. (Ed.). (2001). Women in thanatology [Special issue]. *Illness, Crises, & Loss, 9*(1).

Corless, I., & Vachon, M. (Eds.). (2003). Lords of the manor: Men in thanatology [Special issue]. *Illness, Crises, & Loss, 11*(1).

Corr, C. (1992). A task based approach to coping with dying. *Omega: The Journal of Death and Dying, 24*, 81–94.

Corr, C. (1998). Enhancing the concept of disenfranchised grief. *Omega: The Journal of Death and Dying, 38*, 1–20.

Corr, C., & Corr, D. (2000). Anticipatory mourning and coping with dying: Similarities, differences, and suggested guidelines for helpers. In T. A. Rando (Ed.), *Clinical dimensions of anticipatory mourning: Theory and practice in working with the dying, their loved ones, and their caregivers* (pp. 223–251). Champaign, IL: Research Press.

Corr, C. & Doka, K. (2001). Master concepts in the field of death, dying and bereavement: Coping vs. adaptive strategies. *Omega: Journal of Death and Dying, 43*,183–199.

Corr, C., Nabe, C., & Corr, D. (2009). *Death and dying: Life and living* (6th ed.). Pacific Grove, CA: Brooks/Cole.

Cournoyer, R. J., & Mahalik, J. R. (1995). Cross-sectional study of gender role conflict examining college-aged and middle-aged men. *Journal of Counseling Psychology, 42*, 11–19.

Cousins, N. (1979). *Anatomy of an illness.* New York: Norton.

Csikszemihalyi, M. (1990). *Flow: The psychology of optimal experience.* New York: Harper & Row.

Cumming, E., & Henry, W. (1961). *Growing old.* New York: Basic Books.

Currier, J., Neimeyer, R., & Berman, J. (2008). The effectiveness of psychotherapeutic interventions for bereaved persons: A comprehensive quantitative review. *Psychological Bulletin, 134*, 648–661.

Davidson, J., & Doka, K. (1999). *Living with grief: At work, at school, at worship.* Washington, DC: Hospice Foundation of America.

Davies, J. (1992). War memorials. In D. Clark (Ed.), *Sociology of death* (pp. 112–128). Oxford, UK: Blackwell.

Davis, M. H. (1983). Measuring individual differences in empathy: Evidence for a multidimensional approach. *Journal of Personality and Social Psychology, 44*, 113–126.

Deffenbacher, J. L., Oetting, E. R., Thwaites, G. A., Lynch, R. S., Baker, D. A., Stark, R. S., Thacker, S., & Eiswerth-Cox, L. (1996). State-trait anger theory and the utility of the trait anger scale. *Journal of Counseling Psychology, 43*, 131–148.

Deutsch, H. (1937). Absence of grief. *Psychoanalytic Quarterly, 6*, 12–22.

deVries, B., Dalla Lana, R., & Falek, V. (1994). Parental bereavement over the life course: A theoretical intersection and empirical review. *Omega: The Journal of Death and Dying, 29*, 47–70.

deVries, B. (2009). Aspects of death, grief, and loss in lesbian, gay, bisexual, and transgendered communities. In K. Doka & A. Tucci (Eds.), *Living with grief: Diversity and end-of-life care.* Washington, DC: Hospice Foundation of America.

Doka, K. J. (1984). Expectation of death, participation in funeral arrangements, and grief adjustment. *Omega: The Journal of Death and Dying, 15*, 119–130.

Doka, K. J. (1987). Silent sorrow: Grief and the loss of significant others. *Death Studies, 11*, 455–469.

Doka, K. J. (1989a). *Disenfranchised grief: Recognizing hidden sorrow.* San Francisco: Jossey-Bass.

Doka, K. J. (1989b). Grief. In R. Kastenbaum & B. Kastenbaum (Eds.), *Encyclopedia of death* (pp. 127–131). Phoenix, AZ: Oryx Press.

Doka, K. J. (1990). The therapeutic bookshelf. *Omega: The Journal of Death and Dying, 21*, 321–326.

Doka, K. J. (1993). *Living with life-threatening illness: A guide for patients, their families, and caregivers.* San Francisco: Jossey-Bass.

Doka, K. J. (1994). *Doubly Disenfranchised: The Masculine Griever.* Keynote at Kings College Conference on Loss. London, Ontario.

Doka, K. J. (1997). Grief in the Arctic Circle. *The Forum Newsletter, 23*(4), 7–8.

Doka, K. J. (2002). *Disenfranchised grief: New directions, challenges, and strategies for practice.* Champaign, IL: Research Press.

Doka, K. J. (Ed.). (2007). *Living with grief: Before and after death.* Washington, DC: Hospice Foundation of America.

Doka, K. J., & Davidson, J. (1998a). *Living with grief: Who we are, how we grieve.* Washington, DC: Hospice Foundation of America.

Doka, K. J., & Martin, T. L. (1998b). Masculine responses to loss: Clinical implications. *Journal of Family Studies, 4*, 143–158.

Doka, K. J., & Morgan, J. (1993). *Death and spirituality.* Amityville, NY: Baywood.

Doughty, E. A. (2009). Investigating adaptive grieving styles: A Delphi study. *Death Studies, 33*, 462–480.

Douglas, J. (1990). Patterns of change following parent death in midlife adults. *Omega: The Journal of Death and Dying, 22,* 123–137.

Doyle, P. (1980). *Grief counseling and sudden death: A manual and guide.* Springfield, IL: Charles C Thomas.

Durham Thompkins, C., & Rando, R. A. (2003). Gender role conflict and shame in college males. *Psychology of Men and Masculinity, 4*(1), 79–81.

D'Zurilla, T. J., & Goldfried, M. R. (1971). Problem solving and behavior modification. *Journal of Abnormal Psychology, 78,* 107–126.

D'Zurilla, T. J., & Nezu, A. M. (1982). Social problem solving in adults. In P. C. Kennedy (Ed.), *Advances in cognitive behavioral research and therapy* (pp. 201–274), New York: Academic Press.

D'Zurilla, T. J., & Nezu, A. M. (2006). *Problem-solving therapy: A positive approach to clinical intervention* (3rd ed.). New York: Springer.

Elias, N. (1991). On human beings and their emotions: A process-sociological essay. In M. Featherstone, M. Hepworth, & B. Turner (Eds.), *The body: Social process and cultural theory* (pp. 103–125). London: Sage.

Elison, J., & McGonigle, C. (2003). *Liberating losses: When death brings relief.* Cambridge, MA: Persues Publishing.

Ellis, R. (1997). Private Communication.

Elmer, L. (1994, May). *Grief does not compute.* Presentation to King's College Conference on Death, Dying and Bereavement, London, Ontario.

Englar-Carlson, M. (2006). Masculine norms and the therapy process. In M. Englar-Carlson & M. A. Stevens (Eds.), *In the room with men: A casebook of therapeutic change* (pp. 14–47). Washington, DC: American Psychological Association.

Englar-Carlson, M., & Stevens, M. A. (2006). *In the room with men: A casebook of therapeutic change.* Washington, DC: American Psychological Association.

Faschingbauer, T. R., Zissook, S., & DeVaul, R. (1987). The Texas revised inventory of grief. In S. Zissook (Ed.), *Biopsychosocial aspects of bereavement* (pp. 111–124). Washington, DC: American Psychiatric Press.

Fearon, I., McGrath, P., & Achat, H. (1996). Booboos: The study of everyday pain among young children. *Pain, 68,* 55–62.

Feinson, M. (1986). Aging widows and widowers: Are there mental health differences? *International Journal of Aging and Human Development, 23,* 241–255.

Festinger, L. (1957). *A theory of cognitive dissonance.* Stanford, CA: Stanford University Press.

Figley, C. (1996). Traumatic death: Treatment implications. In K. Doka (Ed.), *Living with grief after sudden loss* (pp. 91–102). Washington, DC: Hospice Foundation of America.

Folak, V. & Abel, S. (2004). Boys don't cry: Cartooning, grieving strategies, and gender-based stereotypes in the aftermath of September 11. *Grief Matters* (Autumn), 12–17.

Folkman, S. (2001). Revised coping theory and the process of bereavement. In M. Stroebe, R. Hansson, W. Stroebe, & H. Schut (Eds.), *Handbook of bereavement research: Consequences, coping, and care* (pp. 563–584). Washington, DC: American Psychological Association.

Fox, N. A. (1989). Psychophysiological correlates of emotional reactivity during the first year of life. *Developmental Psychology, 25,* 364–372.

Franklin, A. J. (1998). Treating anger in African-American men. In W. S. Pollack & R. F. Levant (Eds.), *New psychotherapy for men* (pp. 239–258). New York: John Wiley & Sons.

Freud, A. (1993). *The ego and mechanisms of defense.* London: Karnac Books.

Freud, S. (1957). *Mourning and melancholia. Standard edition* (Vol. XIV). London: Hogarth. (Original work published 1917)

Fry, P. S. (1997). Grandparents' reactions to the death of a grandchild: An exploratory factor analysis study. *Omega: The Journal of Death and Dying, 35,* 119–140.

Futterman, A., Gallagher, D., Thompson, L., Lovett, S., & Gilewski, M. (1990). Retrospective assessment of marital adjustment and depression during the first two years of spousal adjustment. *Psychology of Aging, 5,* 277–283.

Gamino, L., & Ritter, R. H. (2009). *Ethical practice in grief counseling.* New York: Springer.

Gennep, A. (1960). *The rites of passage.* Chicago: University of Chicago Press.

Getzels, J. W., & Csikszentmihalyi, M. (1976). *The creative vision: A longitudinal study of problem finding in art.* New York: Wiley.

Gilbar, O., & Dagan, A. (1995). Coping with loss: Differences between widows and widowers of deceased cancer patients. *Omega: The Journal of Death and Dying, 31,* 207–220.

Gilligan, C. (1982). *In a different voice.* Cambridge, MA: Harvard University Press.

Glick, L., Parkes, C. M., & Weiss, R. (1974). *The first year of bereavement.* New York: Wiley.

Goffman, E. (1959). *The presentation of self in everyday life.* Garden City, NY: Doubleday.

Goldbach, K., Dunn, D., Toedter, L., & Lasker, J. (1991). The effects of gestational age and gender on grief after pregnancy loss. *American Journal of Orthopsychiatry, G1,* 461–467.

Golden, T. (1994a). *A man's grief.* Privately published.

Golden, T. (1994b). *Different paths toward healing: The experience and healing of a man's grief.* Privately published.

Golden, T. (1994c). *Gender and cultural differences in grief.* Privately published pamphlet.

Golden, T. (1996). *Swallowed by a snake: The gift of the masculine side of healing.* Kensington, MD: Golden Healing.

Golden, T. (2009). Gender differences in death customs around the world. In J. Morgan, P. Laungani, & S. Palmer (Eds.), *Death and bereavement around the world: V.5: Reflective essays* (pp. 79–90). Amityville, NY: Baywood.

Good, G. E., Heppner, P. P., DeBord, K. A., & Fischer, A. R. (2004). Problem-solving appraisal and masculine role conflict as predictors of psychological distress in male college students. *Psychology of Men & Masculinity, 5,* 168–177.

Goodman, M., Black, H. K., & Rubinstein, R. L. (1996). Paternal bereavement in older men. *Omega: The Journal of Death and Dying, 33,* 303–322.

Gottlieb, L., Lang, A., & Amsel, R. (1996). The long-term effects of grief on marital intimacy following an infant's death. *Omega: The Journal of Death and Dying, 33,* 1–20.

Gray, J. (1992). *Men are from Mars, women are from Venus: A practical guide for improving communication and getting what you want in your relationship.* New York: Harper-Collins.

Grollman, E. (1997). Coping with loss. In K. Doka (Ed.), *Clergy to clergy: A tape series*. Washington, DC: Hospice Foundation of America.

Gross, J. J., & Levenson, R. W. (1993). Emotional suppression: Physiology, self-report, and expressive behavior. *Journal of Personality and Social Psychology, 64,* 970–986.

Gross, J. J., & Munoz, R. F. (1995). Emotion regulation and mental health. *Clinical Psychology: Science and Practice, 2,* 151–164.

Gunther, J. (1949). *Death be not proud: A memoir*. New York: Harper & Row.

Gutmann, D. L. (1987). *Reclaimed powers: Toward a new psychology of men and women in later life*. New York: Basic Books.

Hansson, R. O., Carpenter, B. N., & Fairchild, S. K. (1993). Measurement issues in bereavement. In M. S. Stroebe, W. Stroebe, & R. S. Hansson (Eds.), *Handbook of bereavement: Theory, research, and intervention* (pp. 255–270). Cambridge, England: Cambridge University Press.

Harvey, J., Orbuch, T., Weber, A., Merbach, N., & Alt, R. (1992). House of pain and hope: Accounts of loss. *Death Studies, 16,* 99–124.

Hayslip, B., Jr. & Han, G. (2009). Cultural influences on death, dying, and bereavement: An overview. In K. Doka & A. Tucci (Eds.), *Living with grief: Diversity and end-of-life care* (pp. 2–20). Washington, DC: Hospice Foundation of America.

Hegel, G. (1990). *Philosophy of history*. Amherst, NY: Prometheus Books.

Hetherington, E. M., Cox, M., & Cox, R. (1978). The aftermath of divorce. In J. H. Stevens, Jr., & M. Mathews (Eds.), *Mother-child father-child relations*. Washington, DC: National Association for the Education of Young Children.

Hinton, S. E. (1967). *The outsiders*. New York: Puffin.

Hochschild, A. R. (1979). Emotion work, feeling rules and social structure. *American Journal of Sociology, 85*(3), 551–575.

Hogan, N. & Balk, D. (1990). Adolescent reactions to sibling death: Perceptions of mothers, fathers, and teenagers. *Nursing Research, 39,* 103–106.

Horowitz, S. C. (1970). Strategies within hypnosis for reducing phobic behavior. *Journal of Abnormal Psychology, 75,* 104–112.

Hughes, C., & Fleming, D. (1991). Grief casualties on skid row. *Omega: The Journal of Death and Dying, 23,* 109–118.

Humphrey, K. (2009). *Counseling strategies for loss and grief*. Alexandria, VA: American Counseling Association.

Ice-T. (1995). The killing fields. In L. A. Despeider & A. L. Strickland (Eds.), *The path ahead: Readings in death and dying*. Mountain View, CA: Mayfield.

Izard, C. E. (1991). *The psychology of emotions*. New York: Plenum Press.

James, L., Oltjensbruns, K., & Whiting, P. (2008). Grieving adolescents: The paradox of using technology for support. In K. J. Doka & A. Tucci (Eds.), *Living with grief: Children and adolescents* (pp. 299–316). Washington, DC: Hospice Foundation of America.

Jensen, M. R. (1987). *Psychobiological factors in the prognosis and treatment of neoplastic disorders*. Unpublished doctoral dissertation, Yale University, New Haven, CT.

Jung, C. G. (1920). *Psychological types*. London: Routledge & Kegan.

Jung, C. G. (with Franz, M. L.). (1964). *Man and his symbols*. Garden City, NY: Doubleday.

Kagan, J. (1994). On the nature of emotion. In N. A. Fox (Ed.), The development of emotion regulation. *Monographs of the Society for Research in Child Development, 59*(2–3, Serial No. 240).

Kalish, R. (1985). *Death, grief, and caring relationships* (2nd ed.). Monterey, CA: Brooks/Cole.

Kalish, R., & Reynolds, D. (1981). *Death and ethnicity: A psychocultural study.* Amityville, NY: Baywood.

Kaminer, H., & Lavie, P. (1993). Sleep and dreams in well-adjusted and less adjusted Holocaust survivors. In M. S. Stroebe, W. Stroebe, & R. O. Hansson (Eds.), *Handbook of bereavement: Theory, research, and intervention* (pp. 331–348). Cambridge, UK: Cambridge University Press.

Kastenbaum, R. (1971). *Encountering death 1: From a distance.* Paper presented at Mount Angel College, St. Benedict, Oregon.

Kavanaugh, R. E. (1972). *Facing death.* Los Angeles: Nash.

Kavenaugh, S. (1997). Gender differences among parents who experience the death of an infant weighing less than 500 grams at birth. *Omega: The Journal of Death and Dying, 35,* 281–296.

Keen, S. (1991). *Fire in the belly: On being a man.* New York: Bantam.

Kelly, J. (1977). The aging male homosexual: Myth and reality. *The Gerontologist, 17,* 328–332.

Kennedy-Moore, E., & Watson, J. C. (1999). *Expressing emotion: Myth, realities, and therapeutic strategies.* New York: Guilford Press.

Kimmel, D. (1978). Adult development and aging: A gay perspective. *The Journal of Social Issues, 34,* 113–131.

Kiselica, M., & Englar-Carlson, M. (2008). Establishing rapport with boys in individual counseling and psychotherapy. In M. Kiselica, M. Englar-Carlson, & A. Horne (Eds.), *Counseling troubled boys: A guidebook for professionals* (pp. 48–68). New York: Routledge.

Kiselica, M., Englar-Carlson, M., Horne, A., & Fisher, M. (2008). A positive psychology perspective on helping boys. In M. Kiselica, M. Englar-Carlson, & A. Horne (Eds.). *Counseling troubled boys: A guidebook for professionals* (pp. 31–48). New York: Routledge.

Klass, D. (1997). The deceased child in the psychic and social worlds of bereaved parents during the resolution of grief. *Death Studies, 21,* 147–175.

Klass, D. & Heath, A. (1996). Mizuko kuyo: The Japanese ritual resolution. *Omega, The Journal of Death and Dying, 34,* 1–14.

Klass, D., Silverman, P., & Nickman, S. (1996). *Continuing bonds: New understandings of grief.* Washington, DC: Taylor & Francis.

Koppelman, K. (1994). *The fall of a sparrow.* Amityville, NY: Baywood.

Koriat, A., Melkman, R., Averill, J. R., & Lazarus, R. S. (1972). The self-control of emotional reactions to a stressful film. *Journal of Personality, 40,* 601–619.

Krystal, H. (1982). Alexithymia and the effectiveness of psychoanalytic treatment. *International Journal of Psychotherapy, 9,* 353–378.

Kubitz, N., Thornton, G., & Robertson, D. (1989). Expectations about grief and the evaluation of the griever. *Death Studies, 13,* 313–323.

Kushner, H. S. (1981). *Why do bad things happen to good people.* New York: Avon.

LaGrand, L. (1986). *Coping with separation and loss as a young adult.* Springfield, IL: Charles C Thomas.

Lamb, M. E., & Urberg, K. A. (1978). The development of gender role and gender identity. In M. E. Lamb (Ed.), *Social and personality development*. New York: Holt, Rinehart and Winston.

Lang, A., & Gottlieb, L. (1993). Marital intimacy after infant death. *Death Studies, 17,* 233–256.

Larsen, R. J., & Diener, E. (1987). Affect intensity as an individual difference characteristic: A review. *Journal of Research in Personality, 21,* 1–39.

Larson, D., & Hoyt, W. (2007). What has become of grief counseling? An evaluation of the empirical foundations of the new pessimism. *Professional Psychology: Research and Practice, 38,* 347–355.

Lattanzi, M., & Hale, M. (1984). Giving grief words: Writing during bereavement. *Omega: The Journal of Death and Dying, 15,* 46–52.

Lazarus, R. S. (1966). *Psychological stress and the coping process*. New York: McGraw-Hill.

Lazarus, R. S. (1991). Cognition and motivation in emotion. *American Psychologist, 46,* 352–367.

Lazarus, R. S., Averill, J. R., & Opton, E. M., Jr. (1970). Toward a cognitive theory of emotions. In M. Arnold (Ed.), *Feelings and emotions* (pp. 207–232). San Diego, CA: Academic Press.

Lazarus, R. S., & Folkman, S. (1984). *Stress, appraisal, and coping*. New York: Springer.

Levant, R. (2008). How do we understand masculinity? An editorial. *Psychology of Men and Masculinity, 9,* 1–4.

Levant, R., & Richmond, K. (2007). A review of research on masculinity ideologies using the Male Role Norms Inventory. *Journal of Men's Studies, 15,* 130–146.

Lever, J. (1976). Sex differences in the games children play. *Social Problems, 23,* 478–487.

Lewis, C. S. (1963). *A grief observed*. New York: Bantam.

Lindemann, E. (1944). Symptomatology and management of acute grief. *American Journal of Psychiatry, 101,* 141–148.

Lopata, H. Z. (1973, July). Living through widowhood. *Psychology Today, 7,* 87–92.

Lund, D. (1999). Giving and receiving help during later life spousal bereavement. In J. Davidson & K. Doka (Eds.), *Living with grief: At work, at school, at worship*. Washington, DC: Hospice Foundation of America.

Lund, D., Caserta, M., & Diamond, M. (1993). The course of spousal bereavement in later life. In M. Stroebe, W. Stroebe, & R. Hansson (Eds.), *Handbook of bereavement: Theory, research, intervention*. Cambridge, UK: Cambridge University Press.

Maccoby, E. E., & Jacklin, C. N. (1974). *The psychology of sex differences*. Stanford, CA: Stanford University Press.

Martin, J. (1988). Psychological consequences of AIDS-related bereavement among gay men. *Journal of Counsuling & Clinical Psychology, 51,* 856–862.

Martin, J., & Dean, L. (1993a). Bereavement following death from AIDS: Unique problems, reactions & special needs. In M. Strobe, W. Strobe, & R. Hansson (Eds.), *Handbook of bereavement: Theory, research, intervention* (pp. 317–330). Cambridge, UK: Cambridge University Press.

Martin, J., & Dean, L. (1993b). Effects of AIDS-related bereavement and HIV-related illness on psychological distress among gay men: A seven-year longitudinal study. *Journal of Consulting & Clinical Psychology, 61,* 94–103.

Martin, T. L., & Doka, K. J. (1996). Masculine grief. In K. J. Doka (Ed.), *Living with grief after sudden loss* (pp. 161–172). Washington, DC: Hospice Foundation of America.

Martin, T. L., & Doka, K. J. (1998). Revisiting masculine grief. In K. J. Doka & J. D. Davidson (Eds.), *Living with grief: Who we are, how we grieve* (pp. 133–142). Washington, DC: Hospice Foundation of America.

Martin, T. L. & Doka, K. J. (2000). *Men don't cry...women do: Transcending gender stereotypes of grief.* Philadelphia: Brunner/Mazel.

Marx, K. (1993). *Capital: A critique of political economy.* London: Penguin Classics.

McCrae, R. R., & Costa, P. T., Jr. (1989). Reinterpreting the Myers-Briggs type indicator from the perspective of the five-factor model of personality. *Journal of Personality, 57,* 17–40.

Meichenbaum, D. H. (1977). *Cognitive-behavior modification.* New York: Plenum.

Moore, A., & Stratton, D. (2002). *Resilient widowers: Older men speak for themselves.* New York: Springer.

Moos, R. H., & Schaefer, J. (Eds.). (1986). *Coping with life crises: An integrated approach.* New York: Plenum Press.

Morgan, D. C. (1989). Adjusting to widowhood: Do social networks really make it easier? *The Gerontologist, 29,* 101–107.

Morgan, D. L. (1989). Adjusting to widowhood: Do social networks really make it easier? *The Gerontologist, 29,* 101–107.

Moss, M., Resch, N., & Moss, S. (1997). The role of gender in middle-age children's responses to parent death. *Omega: The Journal of Death and Dying, 36,* 43–65.

Moss, S., Rubinstein, R. L., & Moss, M. (1997). Middle-aged son's reactions to father's death. *Omega: The Journal of Death and Dying, 35,* 259–278.

Murphy, P., & Perry, K. (1988). Hidden grievers. *Death Studies, 12,* 451–462.

Myers, E. (1988). *When parents die: A guide for adults.* New York: Penguin Press.

Nadeau, J. (1998). *Families making sense of death.* Thousand Oaks, CA: Sage.

Neimeyer, R. (1993). An appraisal of constructivist psychotherapies. *Journal of Consulting and Clinical Psychology, 61,* 221–234.

Neimeyer, R. (1996). Process intervention for the constructivist psychotherapist. In H. Rosen & K. T. Kuchlwein (Eds.), *Constructing realities* (pp. 371–411). San Francisco: Jossey-Bass.

Neimeyer, R. (1997a). Meaning, reconstruction and the experience of chronic loss. In K. Doka with J. Davidson (Eds.), *Living with grief: When loss is prolonged* (pp. 159–176). Washington, DC: Taylor & Francis.

Neimeyer, R. (1997b, June). *Presidential address.* Association for Death Education and Counseling meeting, Washington, DC.

Neimeyer, R. (2000). Searching for the meaning of meaning: Grief therapy and the process of reconstruction. *Death Studies, 24,* 541–558.

Neimeyer, R. A. (Ed.) (2001). *Meaning reconstruction and the experience of loss.* Washington, DC: American Psychological Association.

Neugarten, B. & Gutmann, D. (1968). Age-sex roles and personality in middle age: A thematic apperception study. In B. Neugarten, (Ed.), *Middle age and aging* (pp. 58–71). Chicago: University of Chicago Press.

Neugebauer, R., Raskin, J., Williams, J., Reimien, R., Goetz, R., & Gorman, J. (1992). Bereavement reactions among homosexual men experiencing multiple losses in the AIDS epidemic. *American Journal of Psychology, 149,* 1374–1379.

Nolen-Hoeksema, S. (2001). Ruminative coping and adjustment to bereavement. In M. Stroebe, R. Hansson, W. Stroebe, & H. Schut (Eds.), *Handbook of bereavement research: Consequences, coping, and care* (pp. 545–562). Washington, DC: American Psychological Association.

Nolen-Hoeksema, S., McBride, A., & Larson, J. (1997). Rumination and psychological distress among bereaved partners. *Journal of Personality and Social Psychology, 72,* 855–862.

Nord, D. (1990). Issues and implication in the counseling of survivors of multiple AIDS-related loss. *Death Studies, 20,* 389–413.

Nutt, R. (2007). Counseling men: Necessary knowledge. *Counseling and Spirituality, 26,* 53–80.

O'Neil, D. (1994, May). *Home alone: Widowers with school age children, the need for a functional network.* Presentation to the 12th annual King's College Conference on Death, Aging and Bereavement, London, Ontario.

O'Neil, J. M. (1990). Assessing men's gender role conflict. In D. Moore & F. Leafgren (Eds.), *Problem solving strategies and interventions for men in conflict.* Alexandria, VA: American Association for Counseling and Development.

O'Neil, J. M. (2006). Helping Jack heal his emotional wounds: The gender role conflict diagnostic schema. In M. Englar-Carlson & M. A. Stevens (Eds.), *In the room with men: A casebook of therapeutic change* (pp. 259–284). Washington, DC: American Psychological Association.

O'Neil, J. M., Good, G. E., & Holmes, S. (1995). Fifteen years of theory and research on men's gender role conflict: New paradigms for empirical research. In R. Levant & W. Pollack (Eds.), *The new psychology of men* (pp. 164–206). New York: Basic Books.

Osterweiss, M., Solomon, F., & Green, M. (Eds.). (1984). *Bereavement: Reactions, consequences and care.* Washington, DC: National Academy Press.

Parkes, C. M. (1970). "Seeking" and "finding" a lost object: Evidence of recent studies of reaction to bereavement. *Social Science and Medicine, 4,* 187–201.

Parkes, C. M. (1980). Bereavement counselling: Does it work? *British Medical Journal, 281,* 3–6.

Parkes, C. M. (1987). *Bereavement: Studies of grief in adult life* (2nd ed.). Madison, CT: International Universities Press.

Parkes, C. M. (1996a). Genocide in Rwanda: Personal reflections. *Mortality, 1,* 95–110.

Parkes, C. M. (1996b). Conclusions II: Attachments and losses in cross-cultural perspective. In C. M. Parkes, P. Laugani, & B. Young (Eds.), *Death and bereavement across cultures* (pp. 233–243). London: Routledge.

Parkes, C. M., & Brown, R. J. (1972). Health after bereavement: A controlled study of Boston widows and widowers. *Psychosomatic Medicine, 34,* 449–461.

Parkes, C. M., & Weiss, R. S. (1983). *Recovery from bereavement*. New York: Basic Books.

Paulhus, D. L., & Reid, D. B. (1991). Enhancement and denial in socially desirable responding. *Journal of Personality and Social Psychology, 60*, 307–317.

Pennebaker, J. W. (1997). *Opening up: The healing power of expressing emotions*. New York: Guilford Press.

Pennebaker, J. W., Kiecolt-Glaser, J., & Glaser, R. (1988). Disclosure of traumas and immune function: Health implications for psychotherapy. *Journal of Consulting and Clinical Psychology, 56*, 239–245.

Pennebaker, J., Zech, E., & Rimé, B. (2001). Disclosing and sharing emotion: Psychological, social, and health consequences. In M. Stroebe, R. Hansson, W. Stroebe, & H. Schut (Eds.). *Handbook of bereavement research: Consequences, coping, and care* (pp. 517–543). Washington, DC: American Psychological Association.

Peppers, L., & Knapp, R. (1980). Maternal reactions to involuntary fetal infant death. *Psychiatry, 93*, 155–159.

Pergament, K. (1997). *The psychology of religion and coping: Theory, practice and research*. New York: Guilford Press.

Plante, T. G., & Schwartz, G. E. (1990). Defensive and repressive coping styles: Self-presentation, leisure activities, and assessment. *Journal of Research in Personality, 24*, 173–190.

Pollack, W. S. (1998). Mourning, melancholia, and masculinity: Treating depression in men. In W. S. Pollack & R. F. Levant (Eds.), *New psychotherapy for men* (pp. 147–166). New York: John Wiley & Sons.

Pollack, W. S., & Levant, R. F. (1998). *New psychotherapy for men*. New York: John Wiley & Sons.

Powers, L., & Wampold, B. (1994). Cognitive behavioral factors in adjustment to adult bereavement. *Death Studies, 18*, 1–24.

Prend, A. (1997). *Transcending loss: Understanding the lifelong impact of grief and how to make it meaningful*. New York: Berkley.

Rabinowitz, F. (2006). Thawing the iceman: Coping with grief and loss. In M. Englar-Carlson & M. A. Stevens (Eds.), *In the room with men: A casebook of therapeutic change* (pp. 109–127). Washington, DC: American Psychological Association.

Rando, T. (1984). *Grief, dying, and death: Clinical interventions for caregivers*. Champaign, IL: Research Press.

Rando, T. (1986). The unique issues and impact of the death of a child. In T. Rando (Ed.), *The parental loss of a child* (pp. 5–44). Champaign, IL: Research Press.

Rando, T. A. (1991). *How to go on living when someone you love dies*. New York: Bantam Books.

Rando, T. (1993). *Treatment of complicated mourning*. Champaign, IL: Research Press.

Rando, T. A. (2000). Why study anticipatory mourning?: A justification of and introduction to clinical investigation of the phenomenon. In T. A. Rando (Ed.), *Clinical dimensions of anticipatory mourning: Theory and practice in working with the dying, their loved ones, and their caregivers*. Champaign, IL: Research Press.

Raphael, B. (1983). *The anatomy of bereavement*. New York: Basic Books.

Reeves, N., & Boersma, F. (1990). The therapeutic use of ritual in maladaptive grieving. *Omega, 20*, 281–291.

Reynolds, J. (1993). Grief and the culture of victimization. *The Forum* (March/April), 9–11.

Riches, G., & Dawson, P. (1998). Lost children, living memories: The role of photographs in processes of grief and adjustment among bereaved parents. *Death Studies, 22*, 121–140.

Robertson, J., & Shepard, D. (2008). The psychological development of boys. In M. Kiselica, M. Englar-Carlson, & A. Horne (Eds.), *Counseling troubled boys: A guidebook for professionals* (pp. 3–29). New York: Routledge.

Rosenblatt, P. (1993a). Cross cultural variations in the experience, expression and understanding of grief. In D. P. Irish, K. F. Lundquist, & V. Jenkins (Eds.), *Ethnic variations in dying, death, and grief: Diversity in universality* (pp. 13–20). Washington, DC: Taylor & Francis.

Rosenblatt, P. (1993b). Social context of private feelings. In M. Stroebe, W. Stroebe, & R. Hansson (Eds.), *Handbook of bereavement: Theory, research, and literature* (pp. 102–111). Washington, DC: American Psychological Association.

Rosenblatt, P. (1997). Grief in small-scale societals. In C. M. Parkes, P. Laugani, & B. Young (Eds.), *Death and bereavement across cultures* (pp. 27–51). London: Routledge.

Rosenblatt, P. (2000). *Help your marriage survive the death of a child*. Philadelphia, PA: Temple University Press.

Rosenblatt, P. (2008). Grief across cultures: A review and research agenda. In M. Stroebe, R. Hansson, H. Schut, & W. Stroebe (Eds.), *Handbook of bereavement research and practice* (pp. 207–222). Washington, DC: American Psychological Association.

Rosenblatt, P., & Wallace, B. (2005). *African-American grief*. New York: Routledge.

Rosenblatt, P., Walsh, R., & Jackson, D. (1976). *Grief and mourning in cross-cultural perspective*. Washington, DC: HRDF Press.

Rothbart, M. (1991). Temperament: A developmental framework. In J. Strelau & A. Angleneitner (Eds.), *Explorations in temperament: International perspectives on theory and measurement* (pp. 61–74). New York: Plenum Press.

Rotundo, E. A. (1993). *American manhood: Transformations in masculinity from the revolution to the modern era*. New York: Basic Books.

Ryan, D. (1989). Raymond: Unquestioned grief. In K. Doka (Ed.), *Disenfranchised grief: Handling hidden sorrow* (pp. 127–134). Lexington, MA: Lexington Press.

Saarni, C. (1989). Children's understanding of strategic control of emotional expression in social transactions. In C. Saarni & P. L. Harris (Eds.), *Children's understanding of emotions* (pp. 181–208). New York: Cambridge University Press.

Sacco, R. L., Elkind, M., Boden-Albala, B., I-Feng, L., Kargman, D. E., Hauser, W. A., et al. (1999). The protective effect of moderate alcohol consumption on ischemic stroke. *Journal of the American Medical Association, 281*, 53–60.

Sanders, C. (1989). *Grief: The mourning after: Dealing with adult bereavement*. New York: Wiley.

Sanders, C. (1992). *Surviving grief and learning to live again*. New York: Wiley.

Sanders, C. (1993). Risk factors in bereavement outcome. In M. Stroebe, W. Stroebe, & R. Hansson (Eds.), *Handbook of bereavement: Theory, research, intervention* (pp. 255–267). Cambridge, UK: Cambridge University Press.

Sanders, C. M., Mauger, P. A., & Strong, P. A. (1985). *A manual for the grief experience inventory*. Palo Alto, CA: Consulting Psychologists Press.

Schlenker, B. R. (1980). *Impression management: The self-concept, social identity, and interpersonal relations*. Monterey, CA: Brooks/Cole.

Schut, H., Stroebe, M., van den Bout, J., & deKeijser, J. (1997). Intervention for the bereaved: Gender differences in the efficacy of two counseling programs. *British Journal of Clinical Psychology, 36*, 63–72.

Schwab, R. (1990). Paternal and maternal coping with the death of a child. *Death Studies, 14*, 407–422.

Schwab, R. (1996). Gender differences in parental grief. *Death Studies, 20*, 103–113.

Schwab, R. (1998). A child's death and divorce: Dispelling the myth. *Death Studies, 22*, 445–468.

Schwartz, N. (1990). Feelings as information: Informational and motivational functions of affective states. In E. T. Higgins & E. M. Sorrentino (Eds.), *Handbook of motivation and cognition* (Vol. 2, pp. 527–561). New York: Guilford Press.

Seogin, F., Jamison, C., & Gochneaur, K. (1989). Comparative efficacy of cognitive and behavioral bibliotherapy for mildly and moderately depressed older adults. *Journal of Consulting and Clinical Psychology, 17*, 403–407.

Sharkin, B. S. (1993). Anger and gender: Theory, research and implications. *Journal of Counseling and Development, 71*, 386–389.

Sharpe, M. J., & Heppner, P. P. (1991). Gender role, gender role conflict, and psychological well-being in men. *Journal of Counseling Psychology, 38*, 323–330.

Shorter, B. (1996). *Susceptible to the sacred: The psychological experience of ritual*. New York: Routledge.

Shuchter, S., & Zisook, S. (1993). The course of normal grief. In M. Stroebe, W. Stroebe, & R. Hansson (Eds.), *Handbook of bereavement: Theory, research, intervention* (pp. 23–43). Cambridge, UK: Cambridge University Press.

Silverman, P. R. (1981). *Helping women cope with grief*. Newbury Park, CA: Sage.

Silverman, P. R. (1986). *Widow to widow*. New York: Springer.

Silverman, P. R. (1988). Research as process: Exploring the meaning of widowhood. In S. Reinharz & G. Rowles (Eds.), *Qualitative gerontology* (pp. 217–240). New York: Springer.

Silverman, S. (1997). Justice Joseph Story and death in early 19th century America. *Death Studies, 21*, 397–416.

Smith, J. P., Tran, G., & Thompson, R. (2008). Can the theory of planned behavior help explain men's psychological health-seeking? Evidence for a mediation effect and clinical implications. *Psychology of Men and Masculinity, 9*, 179–192.

Snyder, M. (1974). Self-monitoring of expressive behavior. *Journal of Personality and Social Psychology, 30*, 526–537.

Sorokin, P. (1937–1941). *Social and cultural dynamics* (Vols. 1–4). New York: American Book Company.

Spielberger, C. D. (1988). *State-trait anger expression inventory*. Orlando, FL: Psychological Assessment Presources.

Staudacher, C. (1991). *Men and grief*. Oakland, CA: New Harbinger.

Stillion, J. (1985). *Death and the sexes*. New York: Hemisphere.

Stillion, J., & McDowell, G. (1997, June). *Women's issues in grief.* Presentation to the Association for Death Education and Caring Annual Meeting, Washington, DC.

Stroebe, M. (1994). The broken heart phenomenon: An examination of the mortality of bereavement. *Journal of Community and Applied Social Psychology, 4,* 47–61.

Stroebe, M. (1997, June). *Coping with bereavement: The sense and nonsense of science.* Keynote address presented at Association for Death Education and Counseling, Washington, DC.

Stroebe, M., & Schut, H. (1995, June 29). *The dual process model of coping with loss.* Paper presented to International Work Group, Oxford, England.

Stroebe, M., & Schut, H. (1999). The dual process model of coping with bereavement: Rationale and description. *Death Studies, 23,* 197–224.

Stroebe, M., & Stroebe, W. (1983). Who suffers more: Sex differences in health risks of the widowed. *Psychological Bulletin, 93,* 279–301.

Stroebe, W., & Stroebe, M. (1993). Determinants of adjustment to bereavement in younger widows and widowers. In M. Stroebe, W. Stroebe, & R. Hansson (Eds.), *Handbook of bereavement: Theory, research, intervention* (pp. 208–226). Cambridge, UK: Cambridge University Press.

Sue, D. W., & Sue, D. (2008). *Counseling the culturally diverse: Theory and practice* (5th ed.). New York: Wiley.

Thomas, A., & Chess, S. (1977). *Temperament and development.* New York: Brunner/Mazel.

Thomas, A., & Chess, S. (1985). The behavioral study of temperament. In J. Strelau, F. Farley, & A. Gale (Eds.), *The biological basis of personality and behavior* (Vol. 1, pp. 213–226). Washington, DC: Hemisphere.

Thompson, N. (1995). Men and antisexism. *British Journal of Social Work, 25,* 459–475.

Thompson, N. (1997). Masculinity and loss. In D. Field, J. Hockey, & N. Small (Eds.), *Death, gender, and ethnicity* (pp. 76–88). London: Routledge.

Thompson, N. (2001). The ontology of masculinity – The roots of manhood. In D. Lund (Ed.), *Men coping with grief* (pp. 27–36). Amityville, NY: Baywood Publishing.

Thompson, R. A. (1994). Emotion regulation: A theme in search of a definition. In N. A. Fox (Ed.), The development of emotion regulation: Biological and behavioral considerations. *Monographs of the Society for Research in Child Development, 59*(2–3, Serial No. 240).

Tudiver, F., Hilditch, J., Permaul, J. A., & McKendree, D. J. (1992). Does mutual help facilitate newly bereaved widowers? Report of a randomized controlled trial. *Evaluation and the Health Professions, 15,* 147–162.

Vachon, M. (1987). *Occupational stress in the care of the critically ill, dying, and bereaved.* New York: Hemisphere.

Vail, E. (1982). *A personal guide to living with loss.* New York: Wiley.

Van der Hart, O. (1978). *Rituals in psychotherapy: Transition and continuity.* New York: Irvington Press.

Van der Hart, O. (1988). *Coping with loss: The therapeutic use of leave-taking rituals.* New York: Irvington Press.

Versalle, A., & McDowell, E. (2004). The attitudes of men and women concerning gender differences in grief. *Omega: The Journal of Death and Dying, 50,* 53–67.

Viney, L., Henry, R., Walker, B., & Crooks, C. (1992). The psychosocial impact of multiple deaths from AIDS. *Omega: The Journal of Death and Dying, 24,* 151–163.

Walden, T. A., & Smith, M. C. (1997). Emotion regulation. *Motivation and Emotion, 21,* 7–25.

Walter, T. (2008). The new public mourning. In M. Stroebe, R. Hansson, H. Schut, & W. Stroebe (Eds.), *Handbook of bereavement research and practice* (pp. 241–262). Washington, DC: American Psychological Association.

Webb, N. B. (1993). *Helping bereaved children.* New York: Guilford Press.

Weinberger, D. A., Schwartz, G. E., & Davidson, R. J. (1979). Low-anxious, high anxious, and repressive coping styles: Psychometric patterns and behavioral and physiological responses to stress. *Journal of Abnormal Psychology, 88,* 369–380.

Weisman, A. D. (1979). *Coping with cancer.* New York: McGraw-Hill.

Weisman, A. (1984). *The coping capacity: On the nature of being mortal.* New York: Human Science Press.

Weiss, R. (1998). Issues in the study of loss and grief. In J. Harvey (Ed.), *Perspectives on loss: A sourcebook* (pp. 343–352). Philadephia: Brunner/Mazel.

White, E. B. (1952). *Charlotte's web.* New York: Harper-Collins.

Wolfelt, A. (1990). Gender roles and grief: Why men's grief is naturally complicated. *Thanatos, 15*(3), 20–24.

Wolfenstein, M. (1966). How is mourning possible? *Psychoanalytic Study of the Child, 24,* 423–460.

Wong, Y. J., Pituch, K. A., & Rochlen, A. B. (2006). Men's restrictive emotionality: An investigation of associations with other emotion-related constructs, anxiety, and underlying dimensions. *Psychology of Men & Masculinity, 7,* 113–126.

Worden, J. W. (1996). *Children and grief: When a parent dies.* New York: Guilford.

Worden, J. W. (2008). Grieving children and adolescents: Lessons from the Harvard Bereavement Study. In K. J. Doka & A. Tucci (Eds.), *Living with grief: Children and adolescents* (pp. 125–137). Washington, DC: Hospice Foundation of America.

Worden, J. W. (2009). *Grief counseling and grief therapy: A handbook of the mental health practitioner* (4th ed.). New York: Springer.

Wortman, C., & Silver, R. (1989). The myths of coping with loss. *The Journal of Consulting and Clinical Psychology, 57,* 349–357.

INDEX